CHASING PHANTOMS

MICHAEL BARKUN

CHASING PHANTOMS

Reality, Imagination, & Homeland Security Since 9/11

The University of North Carolina Press   Chapel Hill

Library of Congress Cataloging-in-Publication Data
Barkun, Michael.
Chasing phantoms : reality, imagination, and homeland
security since 9/11 / by Michael Barkun.
p. cm.
Includes bibliographical references and index.
ISBN 978-0-8078-3470-1 (alk. paper)
1. Terrorism—United States—Prevention. 2. Civil defense—United States.
3. Emergency management—United States. 4. Imagery (Psychology)
I. Title.
HV6432.B365 2011
363.325′160973—dc22
2010041420

cloth   15 14 13 12 11   5 4 3 2 1

FOR JACKSON

CONTENTS

SEVEN

EIGHT

PREFACE

As I observed the extraordinary fear that gripped both the nation and its policymakers in the months after 9/11, it seemed to me that a significant aspect of terrorism and the response to it remained unexplored. For the fear that we can all still recall came not from an enemy whose forces and weapons we could see but from an adversary that was effectively invisible. The nineteen hijackers had lived among us undetected and unmolested, a fact that quickly aroused fear of sleeper cells and of terrorists indistinguishable from the innocent persons around them. When a month later the anthrax letters began to arrive, new anxieties came with them, evoked this time by minute disease-bearing agents that might be in the very air we breathed. The fear of terrorism thus resolved into fear of unseen dangers, and though much has been said about terrorism, its link with the unseen is a subject that has aroused curiously little interest.

The complexity in understanding the problem of unseen dangers lies in the fact that terrorism exists in two domains—in the world and in our minds. It can take one shape in the world outside and another in the imagined worlds that we fear await us. As the chapters that follow demonstrate, we often seek to understand these worlds by constructing narratives about them, broad and gripping stories about how evil is organized and why it occurs. In the case of terrorism, where full and reliable information is often difficult to come by for governments as well as citizens, these narratives help to fill in the blanks.

Within days of each other in the late fall of 2008, two events took place that vividly illuminate the gap between the reality of terrorism and the imagined threat of terrorism. They also suggest two kinds of stories. The first began the day before Thanksgiving when a handful of individuals—perhaps as few as ten—paralyzed the center of Mumbai, India's financial capital. Armed only with AK-47s, grenades, and explosives, they fought for two and a half days, during which they held two major hotels. To some, the Mumbai attack exemplified a larger narrative of terrorism as a phenomenon in which weak local or regional groups, using conventional weapons, lash out against their enemies.

The second event occurred four days after the last Mumbai attacker was killed—on December 2nd—when a report was issued in Washington by a panel created by Congress. The report, titled *World at Risk*, was produced by the Commission on the Prevention of Weapons of Mass Destruction, Proliferation and Terrorism, chaired by former senators Bob Graham of Florida and Jim Talent of Missouri. It concluded that "more likely than not" terrorists would use a weapon of mass destruction "by the end of 2013"—that is, within the next five years—and that it would probably be a biological weapon, although the commission did not wholly discount the possibility of nuclear terrorism.[1] The report played to a different narrative, a narrative that emphasized terrorism driven by increasingly empowered groups that might be able to bring states to their knees.

The juxtaposition of these events is striking, for at almost the moment that the commission was prophesying that terrorists would employ exotic, high-tech means of attack, a tiny group of terrorists was temporarily holding a major metropolis at bay with conventional weapons. Aside from the military-quality explosives, which they made relatively little use of, their armaments might easily be obtained legally or on the black market. Although the reality seemed dramatic, the means the attackers employed were banal, yet at the same time the commission was obsessed with an imagined world of apocalyptic super-weapons.

The commission's fixation on the imminent use of biological or nuclear weapons by terrorists was typical rather than exceptional for official and semi-official statements. If it appeared unusual, it was only in its timing, alongside the indisputably conventional character of the Mumbai attack. If we look to the reasons for the concern about weapons of mass destruction (WMD) in the hands of terrorists, it can hardly be as a result of their use, for no terrorist group has ever employed them. The only nonstate group to do so was the Japanese religious sect Aum Shinrikyo, which developed both biological and chemical weapons before deploying the nerve gas sarin in the Tokyo subway in 1995.

These two different pictures—the one emphasizing a small group using conventional weapons, the other concentrating on high-tech weapons of mass destruction—as we can see, support radically different narratives. The discussion that follows explores the search for a compelling narrative about terrorism, and in particular the attraction that the WMD storyline holds, even though terrorists (unless we include Aum Shinrikyo) have never employed such weapons. We tell stories to make sense of the world, and given the fragmentary intelligence we have about terrorist groups, the existence of a narrative provides a way of assembling the available and uncertain information into a pattern. That pattern often fills gaps where information is lacking and gives the information we have coherence.

The obsessive fear that terrorists might use WMD is rooted in the larger apprehension of unseen danger, which a terrorist attack epitomizes. The perpetrator is invisible until the moment he strikes. Through some form of concealment he gains access to a target. It seems of a piece with the perpetrator's invisibility that he should employ weapons that are also invisible, and none more so than biological agents that cannot be seen and that insidiously invade the body. Thus the terrorist wielding biological weapons provides a complete picture of unseen danger, where neither the weapon nor its wielder can be detected until it is too late.

Even as the WMD danger was advanced by the authors of *World at Risk*, other commentators insisted that it was the Mumbai attack that really held the clue to the direction of future terrorism. It was small cells using low-tech weapons, they argued, that indicated the shape of things to come. Thus two different scenarios were in play. There was, and continues to be, a search for a storyline, a master-narrative of terrorism. And how could there not be, where information is imperfect and fragmentary?

The chapters that follow seek the origins, nature, and implications of this fear. Chapter 1 asks what it means to be "unseen." In other words, how should we understand "invisibility" in the broadest sense? It turns out to be a more complex concept than might be supposed and overlaps upon the related issue of secrecy as well as the various modalities of concealment. Chapter 2 approaches terrorism itself through a somewhat indirect path, by examining it as a form of disaster. Since Americans in the post-9/11 era fear mass-casualty terrorist attacks, terrorism is in fact for us a species of disaster. However, as a form of humanly caused catastrophe, it requires an analysis that examines the differences between natural calamities and those caused by human action. Humanly caused disasters may be the result of accident or negligence, but they may also be intentional, as is surely the case with terrorism. Finally, catastrophes of all kinds demand analysis in terms of the interrelated ideas of hazard, risk, and vulnerability, which can pose acute problems in the case of humanly caused mass-casualty events that, unlike natural disasters, are less frequently routine and repetitive and more likely to be novel and unfamiliar.

Much of current homeland security policy is based on trying to force the invisible into visibility—unmasking the disguised malefactor or discovering the hidden weapon. As we shall see in Chapter 3, despite lengthy and costly efforts, it cannot be said that truly effective techniques are in place to reveal either. Existing methods may have some deterrent force, since they may discourage terrorists. But they have not sealed the United States at its borders in the manner that some homeland security advocates had hoped.

The Department of Homeland Security has had to deal with only a single real-world, large-scale emergency event. That was, of course, the flooding of New Orleans after Hurricane Katrina in 2005. The department's massive failure is commonly ascribed to the Federal Emergency Management Agency's feckless director, Michael Brown, and thus is regarded as insulated from the larger questions of terrorism response. However, as Chapter 4 makes clear, notwithstanding Michael Brown's failings, the Hurricane Katrina problems lay far deeper, with the "all-hazards" approach to emergency management mandated by presidential order, and the inability of the Department of Homeland Security to put it into practice. Consequently, far from being an aberration that can be ascribed to a single incompetent individual, the department's failings revealed flaws in fundamental policy decisions about how to handle emergency situations.

Both the general public and the members of the policymaking elite carry with them ideas that have been shaped by broad cultural forces that encode our ideas about evil and danger. Individuals, regardless of their official positions, do not, in other words, approach issues such as terrorism with minds that are blank slates. The cultural forces help configure what the geographer Yi-Fu Tuan has called "the landscape of fear," our inner mental landscape made up of that which creates anxiety and terror.[2] This interior mental landscape coexists with and helps to structure the incoming sense data about the external world. Chapter 5 examines some of the cultural forces that have produced the landscape of fear, particularly those expressed in popular culture and are thus the common property of both policymakers and the general public.

Unseen dangers not only trigger unusually intense fears; they also raise issues of defilement, for invisible evil threatens the purity and integrity of its targets. This has always been the case for disease and disease carriers, and, as Chapter 6 illustrates, a clear line may be drawn from nineteenth-century nativist fears of disease-bearing immigrants to twentieth- and twenty-first-century fears of bioweapons-bearing terrorists. Because of terrorists' penchants for concealment and because so many contemporary terrorists operate from religious motives alien to the mind-sets of most Americans, they also shake our rational-scientific belief system, which Max Weber famously said produced "the disenchantment of the world." By threatening to re-enchant the world, unseen religious terrorists introduce a threat beyond that of their weapons alone. It is religion, after all, more than sheer destruction that has given contemporary terrorism its special edge, the sense that its practitioners aim not for some concrete political goals but for an apocalyptic consummation.

Terrorism and homeland security policy, because it has been so strongly influenced by the fear of unseen danger, is thus governed both by non-rational as well as rational considerations. Most of the literature about terrorism emphasizes the rational considerations, such as the organizational structure of adversaries and the most efficient way of integrating national emergency management and counterterrorism forces with first-responders. While these practical issues are of undoubted importance, they do not exhaust the subject. The analysis presented here emphasizes the neglected nonrational considerations that coexist with matters of optimization and best practice. Many of those issues are laid out in the first six chapters. I bring them together in a more systematic form in Chapters 7 and 8.

Chapter 7 introduces a vocabulary of concepts that might be used as building blocks in a model of the nonrational processes in homeland security policy. I draw these concepts from the work of two scholars, the sociologist Stanley Cohen and the historian of religion David Frankfurter. Each of them, although working with different data, attacks the question of how and why communities respond in disproportionately intense ways to perceived enemies within. They both help to provide us with a language we can use to understand how a society responds to threats. Chapter 8 applies their concepts to counterterrorism and homeland security, utilizing narrative theory, since different views of the terrorist threat ultimately resolve into choices between different stories—different ways of "connecting the dots" so that whatever information is available can be assembled into a coherent narrative. These archetypal stories then become the bases from which policy prescriptions follow. The struggle between supporters of competing storylines, particularly about the evolution of al-Qaeda since September 11th, has often been bitter, so much so that one blogger compared it to the feud between the Hatfields and the McCoys.

The Epilogue summarizes the changes in terrorism and homeland security policy made during the Bush administration, together with those made during the early days of the Obama presidency, in order to establish a frame of reference to examine the vexing question of the domain of choice for policymakers following the 9/11 attacks. I make no attempt to deal with homeland security under Barack Obama in the same detail as the analysis of policies under George W. Bush. Finally, I lay out some general prescriptions for a rational homeland security policy.

This is not a history of homeland security. Not only do I concentrate on the aspect of it that deals with invisible dangers, but, with the exception of comments in the Epilogue, I confine myself to the portion of the Bush presidency between the 9/11 attacks and the inauguration of Barack Obama. The policies established during this period—September 11, 2001, to January 20, 2009—are policies with which we continue to live. This interval includes the reactions to the traumatic events of September 11th, as well as significant governmental reorganizations, most importantly, the creation of the Department of Homeland Security, the most sweeping alteration of the federal government since the early days of the Cold War. The present work, however, is in no sense a complete history of counterterrorism during the Bush administration. I have sought, rather, to concentrate on aspects of the period that speak most directly to the issue of unseen dangers. Chapters 3 through 8, where the bulk of this analysis appears, is intentionally written without attention to events that occurred after the conclusion of the Bush presidency. It was often said in the months after September 11th that "nothing will ever be the same." With the passage of time, the hyperbolic character of this statement has come to be recognized, but at the same time the sense remains of defending against a peculiarly elusive and mysterious enemy whose capacity to evoke fear is inextricably bound up with its invisibility. The United States, having so recently come out of the Cold War, knows what it is like to face external threats, but those threats were always in the form of tangible, visible enemies—other states with determinate, unchanging physical locations. Now the dangers are strange, shifting, and unseen. The halting and emotion-laden nature of our response suggests the difficulties involved in dealing with so shadowy an enemy.

ACKNOWLEDGMENTS

In the strange way that the present can sometimes grow out of the past, this book is the distant progeny of a volume I published more than thirty-five years ago, *Disaster and the Millennium*. Although the major thrust of that work was the influence of disasters on apocalyptic social movements, toward the end of the book I discussed the capacity of the great totalitarian movements of the twentieth century to manufacture disasters. It seemed to me that Hitler's Germany, Stalin's Soviet Union, and Mao's China were sinister laboratories where their respective dictators created mass catastrophes in the form of the Holocaust, the Terror, and the Cultural Revolution for their own bizarre personal and ideological reasons. But it did not occur to me then that in the following century, we might also fear the disaster-creating potential of organizations. Yet in the post-9/11 climate, that is precisely the focus of our anxieties.

Much of the impetus for this book came from an interdisciplinary graduate course at my institution, Syracuse University, that brought together students and faculty from the Maxwell School of Citizenship and Public Affairs, the College of Law, and, for a time, the Newhouse School of Public Communications. I am profoundly grateful for the intellectual stimulation provided by the Perspectives on Terrorism course and by the insights I gained from my faculty colleagues involved in this collaborative effort: David Bennett, David Crane, Melvin Levitsky, Joan Deppa, and William Banks.

I was first tempted to reflect on the implications of Hurricane Katrina by an invitation from David Frankfurter and Robin Sheriff to speak at the University of New Hampshire in 2005, only a few months after that calamity, as part of the Saul O. Sidore Memorial Lecture Series. While I eventually modified my views about Katrina, as expressed in Chapter 4, the New Hampshire lecture was an essential preliminary effort.

Chapter 5 began as a paper presented at the International Workshop on Global Terror and the Imagination, held at the University of Pittsburgh in 2005, and appears here in altered form. I am most appreciative of the participants for their comments and of the organizers, Pamela J. Stewart and Andrew Strathern, for creating an ambiance of unusual intellectual vitality.

A preliminary statement of my thoughts on the linkage between terrorism and fear of the invisible appeared in the article "Terrorism and the 'Invisible,'" published in 2007 in *Perspectives on Terrorism*.

David Rapoport generously agreed to read the entire manuscript despite his own heavy workload, and I have benefited greatly from his comments. David Ronfeldt was also generous with bibliographical and other suggestions. My thanks, too, to Tammy Hnat-Comstock of the Maxwell School's IT Group for patiently helping me to format the manuscript for publication. From the time this work was only an idea, my editor at the University of North Carolina Press, Elaine Maisner, has demonstrated her faith in the project and has been a continuing source of encouragement.

Finally, my greatest debt of gratitude is to my wife, Janet, who has always been my muse.

CHASING PHANTOMS

one

INVISIBLE DANGERS

This is a book about invisible dangers. But what do we really mean by "invisibility"? Its meaning is not self-evident. I employ the word "invisible" in a broader sense than is customary, to refer not merely to what cannot be seen but to anything that cannot be detected by the unaided senses. This extension to broader forms of concealment is necessary because the English language has no single word to gracefully describe that which escapes all of the senses, not merely the eyes. The dangers with which I will be concerned are those that are not merely *invisible*, but are also *produced intentionally* or *believed to be produced intentionally*. This excludes dangers that may be invisible but are undetected because of inefficiency, ineptitude, accident, or corruption. It also leaves out dangers that are invisible but clearly unintentional, such as radon gas that seeps into a home.

If, like Superman, we had X-ray vision and a host of other paranormal capacities, much that is now concealed would be visible. However, invisibility is inevitable because of the limitations of the human senses. Marvelous though they are, they are also profoundly limiting because of such obvious factors as distance, physical barriers, and darkness. We can neither hear nor see what is said and occurs on the other side of a wall. We cannot detect a colorless, odorless gas, and are unlikely to be suspicious of a colorless liquid that tastes like water. As a result, whatever exists that falls outside the capabilities of our senses of vision, hearing, touch, smell, and taste, is, in the broadest sense, invisible. These problems are compounded by the fact that even those whose senses are acute find that alertness flags with fatigue, so that even the most vigilant make mistakes and in the end must sleep.

Since these limitations have long been known, compensatory practices were developed. Communities built fortifications and employed watchmen and sentinels, particularly at night; food-tasters protected rulers from poisoning; and spies sought to overhear the deliberations of the enemy. More recently, attention to "body language" suggests that the truly observant might pick up subtle cues to evil intent by carefully observing posture, gesture, facial expression, and demeanor. Nevertheless, reliance upon the unaided human senses still leaves us feeling deeply vulnerable, particularly where evildoers are thought to operate by stealth.

The development of the state system, though it did not eliminate problems of invisibility, did reduce them. The size of state military formations made them difficult to hide, particularly when armies and fleets often took days or weeks to mobilize and deploy. The convention to employ uniforms and other distinctive markings for combatants furthered the visibility of state violence, a practice entrenched in international law. It is true that states have also engaged in surreptitious activities, such as espionage and the planting of so-called fifth columnists (a term not coined until the Spanish Civil War of the 1930s), but these always remained marginal to central national defense policies.

To the extent that states faced significant invisible dangers, these came from within rather than from without. The major form they took was criminality. The criminal was the archetypal invisible evildoer, acting by stealth and/or violence, often at night. Such activity produced major public order problems only when private violence took organized form, as in criminal gangs, or was politicized as separatist or insurgent movements. The size and sometimes the armaments of such groups represented a significant increase in scale beyond ordinary criminal behavior, yet these groups often employed tactics that involved invisibility. This has been notably true of the guerrilla, who appears indistinguishable from the nonfighting population among whom he or she lives. Beginning in the Cold War period, major powers often found it advantageous to covertly support such groups for their own policy ends as a substitute for or supplement to state-against-state violence. As a result, even before the current period of concern for terrorism, the overall level of visibility associated with large-scale violence dropped, as a result of the increasing number of intrastate conflicts associated with separatism, drug-trafficking, ethnic and tribal conflicts, and an array of other issues.

Intentional and Attributed Invisibility

For present purposes, invisibility may be divided into two main categories, intentional invisibility and attributed invisibility. Intentional invisibility occurs when an actor intends that his or her actions be unseen. The effort may or may not be successful, but the motivation for invisibility comes from the individual or organization. This is the domain of secrecy, a domain shared both by governments and by their invisible enemies. It depends upon either defeating techniques that have been developed to enhance the senses, and thus make invisibility more difficult, or "hiding in plain sight" and so making oneself indistinguishable from a harmless crowd. Attributed invisibility, on the other hand, involves some observer erroneously attributing invisibility to others. As we shall see, such attributions are mistaken unless there is also intentional invisibility practiced on the actor's part. These mistakes sometimes occur because of the observer's ignorance, confronting a strange culture, for example, and imputing to its members designs they do not have. Alternatively, errors occur because observers carry in their minds ideas about the secrets they believe others have and insist upon projecting these on them, even in the absence of evidence.

Intentional Invisibility

Intentional invisibility implies an individual's or group's desire to prevent others from knowing the existence of itself, its actions, its artifacts, or its plans. This is, therefore, the domain of secrecy, whose preeminent students, Georg Simmel[1] and Sisela Bok,[2] agree is deliberately produced for the purpose of concealment. The aim is to prevent others from gaining access. Sometimes the desire is to deny access to everyone else; sometimes it is to deny access only to those deemed unworthy or lacking the proper credentials.

Secrecy is often thought of as the restriction of information. This can take the form of restricted access to texts, but it may also involve the closure of physical areas, such as military bases or sacred sites. It may refer to hidden identities, as in the "secret agent," who has an innocuous "cover" but a second, more significant identity known only to a few. All of these examples traffic in forms of invisibility, for secrecy blocks visibility, whether of data, places, actions, or persons, making their content or true nature unavailable.

In all cases, such restricted access to information occurs by design rather than by inadvertence. The aim is to parcel out visibility only on those terms the secret-keeper wishes. In the most extreme case, a single individual may attempt to create invisibility. A common example is the diarist who keeps his or her daily ruminations hidden. But a person may seek more profound invisibility by adopting the life of a recluse, as did the Unabomber, Ted Kaczinski, physically withdrawing from social interactions. Where there is a political agenda, as is the case with terrorist organizations, the challenge of invisibility is particularly great, for in addition to the difficulty of establishing invisibility without physical withdrawal, there is the greater problem that the host society continually seeks to thwart invisibility and reveal the hidden malefactor.

Typically, there have been two devices for maintaining secrecy, *organizational forms* and *forms of communication*. Organizational secrecy creates invisibility through clandestine groups whose existence and purposes are known only to members. In some cases, especially organizations built on a cellular model, members often have only partial knowledge of who the other members are. Secret societies require elaborate modes of recruitment in order to filter out spies, informants, and agents provocateur, and to make sure that those admitted have the requisite degree of commitment. These may be solemnized by oaths or initiation ceremonies. Where members may not know one another's identity, mechanisms must exist to validate the authenticity of membership claims. Nineteenth-century groups developed elaborate systems of handshakes, passwords, and other recognition rituals.[3]

Privileged communication within secret groups has a long history. Much of it involves the use of forms of encryption, ranging from the primitive to the sophisticated. Clandestine organizations have sometimes kept secrets from their own members by creating an internal hierarchy associating rank with levels of knowledge, a practice found, for example, in Freemasonry. The same differential access to doctrine, albeit with a far simpler set of ranks, appears to have been the case in Aum Shinrikyo. Of the ten thousand Aum members in Japan, only eleven hundred were "renunciates" who broke with their families and adopted the lifestyles of Buddhist monks and nuns. Of these only about one hundred and fifty appear to have been involved in criminal activities.[4] In that sense, invisibility may be said to exist internally as well as externally, to the extent that the organization as a whole may attempt invisibility vis-à-vis the outside world, while creating degrees of invisibility within, depending upon what has been revealed to particular classes of members.

If the host society is only moderately curious about the beliefs and structure of a secret organization, the attention that must be paid to the maintenance of invisibility need not be great. However, where an actually or potentially hostile relationship exists, maintaining invisibility becomes particularly difficult. In such situations, in addition to the apparatus of organizational and communications secrecy already described, invisibility may be sought through two additional modalities, *technical invisibility* and *crowd invisibility*.

Technical invisibility refers to invisibility that defeats attempts to enhance the human senses. As indicated earlier, those senses have significant limitations that make invisibility possible. Especially since the postmedieval rise of science, devices and techniques have been developed that transcend sensory limitations. For example, the eye was extended by such optical innovations as the telescope and the magnifying glass, and the ear by a variety of surreptitious listening devices. As the ability to move people and messages increased, so too did the ability to detect and intercept such transactions, even when attempts were made to keep them secret. Such efforts are too numerous to catalog here, but they include the breaking of codes, aerial and later satellite reconnaissance, and the "bugging" of telecommunications traffic. X-ray machines at airports now routinely examine passengers' luggage. After September 11th, much attention has been given to developing technologies that can detect the presence of minute quantities of dangerous chemicals and biological agents. Large cities increasingly use closed-circuit television (CCTV) to monitor public spaces, a practice initially intended for crime control but later touted for its counterterrorism potential. CCTV essentially places electronic "eyes" both in open areas, such as city streets, and in enclosed spaces, such as elevators and parking garages, although it is not always clear how the many signals produced can be monitored. To a certain extent, the polygraph, too, can be thought of as an extension of the senses. The individual whose superficial appearance bespeaks innocence is said to proclaim guilt by physiological responses, evidence of which an ordinary questioner would presumably not have access.

However much the technology has advanced, it has not produced transparency. That is, neither governments nor the general public believe that the technology can detect all terrorists or reduce the threat of a major attack to something approaching zero. A recent demonstration was the September 2006 alert in Great Britain of a plot to blow up transatlantic airliners through explosives concocted on board by combining separate, relatively innocuous liquids. The liquids would not have been detected using existing technology, and the only protective measure, and the one adopted, was that of banning quantities of all liquids carried by passengers in their hand luggage. As in conventional warfare, with its struggle between offense and defense, there is a struggle between those who attempt to maintain invisibility and those who seek to make them visible by the technological extension of the senses. What is curious about the airliner plot, of course, is that the bomb components would have been visible but would have appeared harmless, not unlike the many other liquids passengers bring aboard. The components would then partake of another modality of invisibility, crowd invisibility.

Crowd invisibility is incorporated in the well-known phrase "hiding in plain sight." It is often said that individuals achieve anonymity as members of a crowd. They do so where the number of people in a class is large. Where the qualities that differentiate them can no longer be noticed, one person seems very much like another. The same is true, by extension, of members of any other class, even an inanimate one. In a collection, say, of hundreds of shipping containers in a port, one may seem very much like another, even if there are small differences in appearance. These cease to be noticeable in so large a grouping, just as the differences among members of a crowd in a stadium do not attract attention.

Whether the case is a person in an audience or a shipping container in a port, the issue is not literal invisibility. Rather, it is *functional invisibility*, for no member of the class can be readily distinguished from any other member. If, however, there is reason to believe that some members are in fact more dangerous than others, then their ability to melt into the whole becomes an acute problem. Much of the attention given to the technological extension of the senses is driven by this dilemma. How can a suitcase which contains a bomb be distinguished from other suitcases? How can a hijacker be distinguished from other passengers? If they cannot, the suitcase and/or the passenger achieve crowd invisibility. The same is true of the so-called sleeper cell, the group of individuals with hostile intent who live conformist and superficially blameless lives while awaiting instructions. It, too, melts into the environment and remains functionally invisible unless its members falter in their conformity to the mores of the larger society.

The problem of crowd invisibility was first posed in guerrilla warfare, for (to use Mao's famous metaphor) the guerrilla "swims in the sea of the people." Dressing like, and living among, noncombatants, the guerrilla cannot be readily distinguished from them. However, guerrilla warfare is generally an ongoing struggle, so that the guerrilla slips continually in and out of the civilian role. That is, he or she becomes alternately visible and invisible, the former while fighting, the latter seeking to escape. Terrorists, on the other hand, are assumed to undertake only occasional operations. Indeed, in the case of suicide bombers, they do so only once. Hence they will seek to be invisible far more often than they will be visible. The guerrilla is therefore less an invisible enemy than a frustratingly evasive one, whereas the terrorist seeks to be genuinely invisible.

Crowd invisibility evokes a special fear, for it makes normal life suddenly abnormal by endowing seemingly innocuous persons or objects with menace. A striking portrayal appeared in the 1956 science-fiction film, *The Invasion of the Body Snatchers*, in which mysterious extraterrestrial organisms landed in a small California town. They gradually took over the bodies of the citizens, who looked exactly as they did before but were now vessels to do the bidding of their malevolent alien masters. Commentators quickly pointed to the film as a metaphor for Cold War fears, when many Americans believed Soviet communism had infiltrated American institutions.[5] Thus, like the film's insidious "pod people," who looked harmless but were capable of great evil, Soviet agents were said to lead exemplary lives while boring away from within.

Profiling has been offered as the commonest solution to crowd invisibility, usually by identifying characteristics of those persons being sought. Unfortunately, this is almost always an inefficient technique due to its overinclusiveness, which produces large numbers of false positives. Profiling seeks to find some subtype within the crowd that can reveal what was previously invisible. If profiling were perfect, that subtype would include all the individuals sought and only those individuals. However, in practice such subtypes are almost always so large as to themselves constitute crowds—for example, all individuals with Arab surnames or swarthy complexions. Aside from issues of morality and legality, such efforts do little to penetrate crowd invisibility.

A second technique to penetrate crowd invisibility is to randomize searches in the hope of either deterring or detecting evildoers. Deterrence will obviously have no effect on a suicide bomber with no wish to live, although he or she might be deterred by the thought of not being able to accomplish a mission. In any case, if the goal is complete security, which public expectations may demand, randomization will almost certainly fail, particularly if the adversary has the capacity to flood the system with dangerous individuals or objects.

Attributed Invisibility

It is one thing when individuals or groups try to achieve invisibility, and quite another when outsiders merely ascribe invisibility. If their ascription of invisible danger matches actors' intentions, there is no problem. If, on the other hand, outsiders believe individuals or groups are acting clandestinely to achieve an evil purpose, without the actors in fact doing so, we have left the realm of intentional invisibility and entered that of erroneous attributions of invisible danger.

There is a special case that, while it does not fit clearly under unintentional invisibility, is close enough to it and important enough to warrant consideration. This occurs in situations of contact between radically dissimilar cultures or belief systems. In some cases, one group may be physically embedded within another, as a minority within a majority culture. In others, different societies may come into contact. In either situation, at least one side, and sometimes both, will be burdened by ignorance. This may be in the form of the inability to understand the other's language, failure to appreciate its customs, or lack of knowledge about its beliefs or sacred books. As a result, the observers lack the ability to correctly interpret behavior and intentions, and are likely to impute risk and danger where none exist.

In such a condition of ignorance, the entire observed group may appear "invisible," for its opaqueness in the eyes of outsiders makes it virtually disappear. As the frequent racial slur would have it, "They all look alike," or in the title of Ralph Ellison's novel, the individual members become "invisible men." By acts of outsiders' attribution, they unwillingly acquire crowd invisibility. This invisibility and particularly the associations of danger with this amorphous "other" are amplified by any practices that cannot be publicly viewed. Thus, in nineteenth-century America, nativists fearful of Roman Catholicism and its immigrant members fastened upon the closed precincts of convents as loci of danger and the centers of alleged Catholic immorality. A few decades later, anti-Mormons made similar claims about what went on behind the closed doors of polygamous households.[6] The effect of the observers' ignorance is to project danger onto the other based on their own fears rather than clear evidence. This tendency is compounded to the extent that the targeted group appears to close itself off from observation.

The core of unintentional invisibility, however, is what may be termed "the invisibility of the unreal." The threats that underlie intentional invisibility are real threats, although their seriousness may be a matter for dispute. But the threats that are purely a matter of attributed invisible dangers have no existence outside the minds of the attributors. They are, therefore, unreal, without external, empirical referents. That does not, of course, mean they are unimportant. If those making the attributions of dangerous invisibility are numerous or occupy important policymaking positions, the consequences may be both real and significant.

Many historical examples of such unfounded attributions exist. One of the most dramatic in Western history was the European witch persecutions of the sixteenth and seventeenth centuries, when large areas of Western and Central Europe were obsessed by fears of satanic conspirators in their midst. A second occurred immediately after the French Revolution, when some argued that the revolution had been brought about by the machinations of a secret quasi-Masonic society, the Illuminati, even though the Illuminati had been suppressed by European governments before the French monarchy fell. Subsequently, the Illuminati were blamed for many other upheavals, including the Russian Revolution. The history of anti-Semitism is replete with similar false attributions, often built around the notion of an international Jewish cabal bent on world domination, of the kind described in the Czarist forgery, *The Protocols of the Elders of Zion*.

These and other examples are said to be secrets about invisible evil, but they are imagined secrets that exist only in the minds of beholders. They develop in part because of a ready subterranean supply of raw material in the form of urban legends, stereotypes, and rumors about invisible evil that seems capable of surviving across generations despite the lack of confirming evidence. They claim to identify individuals and groups that engage in or are plotting secret evil. These robust traditions, maintained orally and in fringe literatures, are occasionally elaborated into conspiracy theories, the most complex intellectual manifestation of unintentional invisibility. The machinery of oral transmission has now, of course, been substantially augmented in both its global reach and its speed by the Internet. The Internet has resulted in two powerful changes: First, it has leveled the playing field, so that individuals and groups with very limited capital may produce websites as professional looking as those of mainstream organizations. Further, there are no gatekeepers preventing purveyors of fringe ideas from seeking an audience. Second, the speed and geographic reach of the Internet vastly exceed those of oral transmission. Ideas that might once have remained within subcultures or national groups now easily cross boundaries and do so before opposing views can overtake them.

Conspiracy theories offer a worldview built around imagined secrets. They do so because the conspiracist makes three cardinal assumptions: that nothing happens by accident; that everything is connected; and that nothing is as it seems. The result is a world stripped of accident, negligence, randomness, and incompetence, in which everything is meaningful if only it can be decoded. Thus the mere appearance of innocuousness is no guarantee that evildoing is not going on. Since conspiracists believe the workings of evil are invisible, the visible world, seen naively through the senses, is deemed misleading. It must be interpreted through the theoretical lens that a conspiracist worldview provides, which makes the nonvisible domain of evil, visible.

Even though these imagined evils have no genuine empirical correlates, those who make the mistaken attributions think otherwise. They do not do so as matters of faith but because they are convinced that the attributions are empirically supportable. This conviction is manifested in two ways: First, the drive for empirical demonstration often encourages the development of a pseudo-scholarship, replete with the superficial adornments of academic writing: copious footnotes, lengthy bibliographies, and technical jargon. Such ritualism is particularly likely to occur where the proponents of spurious invisible dangers encounter opposition from such mainstream institutions as universities and professional groups.

The second method involves changes in existing techniques or standards for gathering and evaluating evidence, in order to bring "evidence" into line with expectations. Where traditional methods cannot produce compatible data, there is a drive to make changes that will give the appearance of empirical verification. This may involve methods of procuring evidence that once would have been shunned or accepting as evidence reports that would once have been rejected. It may involve the systematic use of torture to extract confessions to nonexistent plots, as was done during the Soviet purges in the 1930s. Or it may involve the relaxation of rules of evidence, as occurred during the Salem witch trials, when so-called spectral evidence from witnesses' dreams was made admissible.

Conspiracy believers also tend to be preoccupied, often to the point of obsession, with certain unintentional invisible dangers. These are the dangers associated with invisible forms of pollution and defilement. Because conspiracists concentrate on locating some single source of danger external to themselves or their group, they emphasize the boundary between purity and impurity. Hence whatever violates that boundary—particularly poisons or other undetectable impurities—is a constant concern. Often impurities others would consider accidental, such as chemical residues in food, they regard as deliberate attempts by the evil power to attack their bodies. Not surprisingly, therefore, those concerned with intentional invisible dangers often have intense preoccupations with attributed dangers as well, since in both cases, their own sphere of purity is at risk.

Invisibility as a Weapon

The users of intentional invisibility employ it because it is prudent to do so. Invisibility confers three major benefits upon the user: First, and most obviously, it avoids detection. Like H. G. Wells's *Invisible Man*, the unrecognized terrorist, the guerrilla in civilian clothes, or other malefactor can move where he or she likes, confident that the enemy is unaware. In like manner, even the militaries of states recognized and legitimized the use of camouflage as a practical and acceptable means of avoiding detection.

Another major advantage of invisibility is that it causes others to misestimate one's true strength. A case in point comes from the early nineteenth century, when Western and Central Europe were especially rich in secret societies hostile to absolutist regimes. Archival sources have revealed two things about the secret society phenomenon: first, that many governments believed they were in imminent danger of being overthrown by these revolutionary conspirators; second, that in fact the clandestine organizations were small, inept, and utterly incapable of taking control of modern states. The misperception by authorities was wholly due to the invisibility of their adversaries, which led them to grossly overemphasize the magnitude of the threat. This was demonstrably the case during the heyday of secret societies in Europe from roughly the time of the French Revolution until the middle of the nineteenth century.[7]

A somewhat comparable situation now exists with regard to al-Qaeda. Students of terrorism argue, on the basis of fragmentary evidence, about its size, organizational structure, geographical location, capabilities, and intentions. Periodic audio and video recordings make clear that Osama bin Laden and Ayman al-Zawahiri survive but provide little more information. The result is a stream of conjecture, none of which can yet be confirmed. However, the dominant tendency of analysts is to consider al-Qaeda a still potent organization that remains a considerable danger despite the measures taken against it since September 11th.

Finally, the invisible world is a world we fear. In part, the fear is driven by the lack of information already mentioned, which makes it difficult to plan rationally for contingencies in the way one would against a visible enemy. Beyond that, however, is the less easily conceptualized issue of invisibility in a largely materialist culture. Even though Americans stand apart from the peoples of other industrialized nations by the importance they attach to religion, this remains a society deeply imbued with a materialistic and scientific ethos. Even for believers, everyday life remains dominated by what they can see, hear, and touch. While there is a realization that we do not live in a riskless world, unseen threats seem particularly disturbing.

A case in mind was the Washington-area sniper attacks in 2002. They seemed to come from nowhere and occurred in public spaces, such as shopping center parking lots and gas stations. The victims were chosen randomly, and there was no sign of the perpetrators. A significant proportion of the respondents in a survey taken near the end of the shootings pronounced themselves more frightened by these attacks than by the September 11th terrorist attacks, although it is difficult to separate the issue of the randomness of victims from the invisibility of perpetrators in evaluating this finding.[8] Nonetheless, it is almost certain that the fear would have been lessened (although, of course, it would still have been substantial) had the shooter been seen by witnesses.

The idea that a society in which technology exerts such firm control over nature is yet pervaded by invisible evil powers is difficult to accept. As Keith Thomas demonstrated in his magisterial work, *Religion and the Decline of Magic*, until about the mid-1600s, English society was suffused by belief in invisible forces.[9] Much of this belief was carried by organized religion, but a substantial portion was borne by nonreligious ideas in the form of magic, astrology, alchemy, witchcraft, belief in ghosts and fairies, and the like. By and large, the developed West in later periods segregated belief in the invisible to organized religion. There have, of course, been exceptions in such forms as popular superstition and occultism, but these never achieved the dominance they had before Thomas's watershed period. He points out that the shift, in fact, predated many of the technological and scientific solutions to problems that magical methods sought to address and in that sense represented a shift in cultural aspirations for understanding rather than a reflection of changed capabilities.

A World Disenchanted and Re-Enchanted

In his famous 1918 address at Munich University, "Science as a Vocation," Max Weber, borrowing a phrase from Friedrich Schiller, asserted that the rise of science and technology in the West had led to "the disenchantment of the world." By disenchantment, Weber meant that we live in a world that is comprehensible and controllable. Although we ourselves may not understand the underlying laws of nature that are involved, we know that someone else does and that therefore "one can, in principle, master all things by calculation."[10] In contrast, those who live in societies that are not dominated by the rationality of scientific inquiry (whom Weber termed "savages") are surrounded by mysterious, invisible powers that are beyond understanding. Instead, they must be either appeased or managed by means of magic.

Inevitably, Weber's discussion of disenchantment entangled him in a broader analysis of religion. He saw the intellectual life of science and that of theology as unbridgeable realms, with the latter resting on presuppositions about meaning that are valid only for the believer. At the same time, he saw about him a world in which, because science and technology had risen to such heights, disenchantment had become dominant. By implication, then, the sphere of the sacred had accordingly contracted: "The fate of our times is characterized by rationalization and intellectualization and above all, by the 'disenchantment of the world.' Precisely the ultimate and most sublime values have retreated from public life either into the transcendental realm of mystic life or into the brotherliness of direct and personal human relations."[11] This was surely a view of science and rationality tinged with regret for a lost world once permeated by sacred powers. It did not appear in Weber's time that this lost world could ever be reclaimed, that once disenchanted by science, the world could ever be re-enchanted. There is an unstated but implied unilinear conception of history here in which "magical elements of thought are displaced," and once displaced, do not return.[12]

Re-enchantment seems therefore to imply a reversal of secularization, and it was the seemingly implacable march of secularization that gave Weber's disenchantment thesis such persuasive force. Yet in the century since he delivered his address, much has changed. The major change, of course, is a level of religious activity in the world that he neither expected nor predicted. It has been uneven, more intense in some places, weaker in others. It has been significant in the United States, the Middle East, and South Asia, but not in Western and Northern Europe, for example. Yet if one includes less conventional forms of religious expression, the picture grows more ambiguous.

Christopher Partridge argues that the spread of what can broadly be termed "New Age" religious activity, even though it is rarely institutionalized, has accomplished nothing less than the re-enchantment of the West.[13] Partridge does not deny that disenchantment took place, broadly along the lines Max Weber described. However, he asserts that the process had been accompanied, at least since the 1960s, by a parallel growth in "alternative spiritualities": "Western re-enchantment may be characterized by new hybrid forms of religion which are the result of a dialectical process of the re-enchantment of the secular and the secularization of the sacred."[14] These alternative spiritualities, often linked to Eastern religions and mysticism, neo-paganism, alternative healing, and interest in the paranormal,[15] rarely look like conventional religion. With neither authority structures, dogma, nor (in many cases) regular forms of worship, the individual is left to make his or her own choices about belief and practice. Notwithstanding the absence of familiar forms of religious organization, believers still see themselves in an environment invested with power and divinity, in a manner not unlike what Weber identified with the enchanted world.[16]

That new forms of religious expression have developed seems clear. Their importance is more difficult to establish. Attempts to determine the numbers of New Age believers in the United States, for example, have produced extremely low figures, but then religious identification surveys generally prove unreliable in producing more than "guesstimates" even for groups as significant as Jews and Muslims. Partridge concedes that believers in alternative spiritualities tend to come from the "middle and educated classes,"[17] which would give their beliefs a cultural impact out of proportion to the number of adherents. Although some elements in the New Age milieu have been mainstream, such as techniques of alternative medicine, much still remains culturally and religiously alien to the general population.

Re-enchantment and Terrorism

Interestingly, most of those who have discussed Weber's disenchantment thesis in connection with terrorism have not done what Partridge sought to do, that is, examined the worldviews of those within Western societies. Instead of focusing on target societies, they have focused on the disenchantment thesis as it might apply to the terrorists themselves. Thus Maria Pia Lara suggests that Osama bin Laden had to re-enchant the world in order to stave off the "vertigo of secularization" created by the modernization process.[18] Arthur Saniotis provides a much more elaborate analysis, in which jihadists engage in rituals for the purpose of re-enchanting the world.[19] Their "violence becomes a means of achieving mystical mastery for restoring the power of the sacred cosmos in an otherwise 'disenchanted world.'"[20] The invisibility of jihadists leads Saniotis to suggests their similarity to jinn, the invisible creatures in Islam capable of doing harm to humans. Like them, jihadists can see their victims but not be seen by them, cannot be easily controlled, and can slip across boundaries.[21]

Saniotis's emphasis on terrorism-as-ritual resembles Mark Juergensmeyer's influential dramaturgical approach, in which religious terrorism is seen as a theatrical presentation with a cast (terrorists), a stage (the physical location of an attack), and one or more audiences.[22] However, Juergensmeyer notes that while attacks may be performances, they may also be *performative*, in the sense that the acts not only are meant to vividly symbolize some position, identity, or grievance but are also intended to enact some transformation.[23] Here one enters a domain where religion and magic cohabit, for the transformative character of a terrorist act may be lost on some of its audiences. This is evident in the absence of statements of responsibility, explicit demands made upon targets, and the lack of any clear strategic link between the act and a group's goals, at least so far as outsiders can perceive. It may be that the only audience terrorists care about is an audience of one, the deity. It may be that the transformation that matters to them is one that is invisible to others and can be seen only with the eye of faith. In their enchanted world, the means-ends linkages that others look for are less relevant than the invisible, supernatural forces that they regard as the determinants of history.

Curiously, the concept of re-enchantment has not been employed to explain the psychic challenges faced by the target society. Yet if one thinks for a moment about the 9/11 attacks, it is obvious that the intangible effects were at least as great as the tangible ones. There was, at the most general level, the sudden sense of vulnerability; but there was also the awareness that the perpetrators had long lived unmolested and effectively invisible as they prepared. It was assumed, too, that al-Qaeda had already secreted second-wave sleeper cells for post-9/11 attacks, a belief that only gradually dissipated. It in fact received pseudoconfirmation from the mysterious appearance of the envelopes containing anthrax spores in October, the origin of which was not determined until many years later. These circumstances led many Americans to believe quite suddenly that they were living in a very dangerous place.

The danger was also mysterious. Although the connection of the 9/11 attacks with al-Qaeda was quickly established, the organization was known only to specialists before September 11th, and the organization itself remained silent. The nineteen hijackers left no manifesto or list of demands. Mohamed Atta's "Last Night" document, found in his luggage, was clearly intended only for the hijackers themselves. The mystification was inadvertently enhanced by the absence of a quick public investigation. The National Commission on Terrorist Attacks on the United States, popularly known as the 9/11 Commission, was not created until late 2002, and did not release its report until July 2004. U.S. military action against Afghanistan, where al-Qaeda had been based, commenced in October 2001. By mid-November, Osama bin Laden and his close associates were believed to be cornered in fortified caves near the border with Pakistan, but they slipped away into the latter's uncontrolled tribal areas.

Thus by the end of 2001 the American public was left feeling scarcely more secure than it did in mid-September. An invisible, previously unknown religious organization was somehow capable of moving across borders, whether those of the United States or Afghanistan. It used bizarre but powerful means of destruction. Few were then willing to wholly discount its connection with the anthrax mailings, although such a link appeared unlikely. It might strike anywhere or at any time. Although at that moment it did not speak, journalists discovered the "Declaration of War" Osama bin Laden had issued five years earlier. Its vocabulary and the religious worldview it conveyed seemed to come from another, parallel universe. As al-Qaeda's shadow lay over post-9/11 America, the world suddenly became re-enchanted—filled with mysterious, malevolent powers that did not obey rational, calculable laws.

But there is, of course, a difference between this re-enchantment and the other varieties described earlier. Descriptions of enchantment, dis-enchantment, or re-enchantment invariably describe situations driven by forces within a society. The world appears enchanted, disenchanted, or re-enchanted because of internal developments. Weber, concentrating on disenchantment in the West, emphasized the role of science. Christopher Partridge suggests that this disenchantment has given way to a partial re-enchantment because of internal religious developments over the past forty years. In both cases, gradual internal processes have been at work. How-ever, the post-9/11 re-enchantment described here is of a different sort.

A strange world of invisible dangers was abruptly discovered by Ameri-cans in the fall of 2001. Unlike those in traditional societies inured to liv-ing in an enchanted world, we have long lived in a primarily disenchanted world. As a result, we lack the traditionalist's armory of magic, ritual, and placatory gestures with which to keep evil at bay. Some rituals have in fact been developed, part of what John Mueller calls "security theater." These include the presence of armed and uniformed soldiers in airports and ever more complex procedures at security checkpoints. Mueller suggests that even if such measures do nothing to increase actual levels of safety, they may still be useful if they make people less afraid.[24] The color-coded Homeland Security Advisory System, which has never been below yellow, suggests a government always on guard, constantly assuming risks and alert to danger. Yet given the invisible character of the danger, protective rituals have not always resulted in a secure public.

Part of the problem lies in the difficulties of tracking an elusive enemy, but part also lies in the gulf between terrorist and victim. For victim socie-ties in the West are overwhelmingly made up of individuals whose world is disenchanted. Notwithstanding the religious developments chronicled by Christopher Partridge, the description Max Weber gave ninety years ago is still broadly valid. But religious terrorists, such as al-Qaeda, live in a differ-ent ideological universe. Their world is enchanted, and explicitly so in its re-jection of modernity. Their use of violence without demands, their disdain for claims of responsibility, their seeming lack of interest in obvious tactical considerations all place them outside the rational/scientific domain of the disenchanted world, and they are all the more frightening for that reason. Potential victims thus face not merely violence and the threat of violence but the incursion of an enchanted worldview that threatens to re-enchant their own world long after they cast enchantment off. Religious terrorism is thus an attempt at coercive re-enchantment; beyond all of its other effects, it pushes victim societies back into a world they forsook centuries earlier. The secularized societies that find themselves threatened by religious terrorism are frightened not only because of the damage they believe terrorists can do to them, but because religious terrorism seems to have emerged from some primordial age, when religion suffused everything.

two

DISASTER AND TERRORISM

The fear of terrorist attack—particularly by invisible perpetrators employing invisible weapons—must be read against the backdrop of the larger class of human disasters. For they constitute merely one example, albeit a particularly terrifying example, of a mass-casualty event. Disasters themselves make up a broad swath of disturbances capable of destabilizing and even destroying human communities, sometimes through natural forces against which there are no adequate defenses, sometimes because human actions have set destructive forces loose. Although terrorism is commonly viewed through the lenses of politics or military tactics, we view it here under the aspect of disaster. An additional reason for doing so, beyond the sheer mayhem such attacks may cause, is the special anxiety we feel in the presence of unseen dangers. The hidden malefactor, the death that comes without shape or warning—these give to disaster a special edge.

Social groups—whether they are communities, nations, or entire regions—fear events that may plunge their populations into conditions of peril, poverty, or disabling anxiety that their institutional framework cannot control. This fear of collective stress[1] outlines the domain of disasters, the wars, epidemics, earthquakes, hurricanes, and, more recently, terrorist attacks that threaten the continued stability of ordered social life. The later chapters of this book focus upon a special manifestation of this fear—the fear of dangers that are unseen. But before we can understand the nature of that fear we must understand the character of disaster itself, for while the term is used loosely in everyday speech, the actual nature of disaster is complex. It has changed over time as a result of the changing behavior and capacities of human societies, and the way in which individuals and groups react to actual and potential disasters depends upon other concepts—hazard, risk, and vulnerability

Types of Disasters

The most basic distinction between types of disasters is between natural disasters and humanly caused disasters, which will be referred to here as *anthropogenic*. Natural disasters arise out of forces in the natural world. Examples come easily to mind: floods, storms, earthquakes, volcanic eruptions, tsunamis, and the like. They may be described as *homeostatic*.[2] That is, insofar as they reflect the rhythms and limits of nature, it can be assumed that the environment will return to the equilibrium that existed before the disaster struck. "There is," Kenneth Hewitt and Ian Burton point out, "an underlying pattern of magnitudes and frequencies . . . nature remains fairly constant over decades and even centuries."[3] Anthropogenic, humanly caused disasters are clearly different for a number of reasons. The most obvious is causation. Events such as major wars, economic depressions, genocides, and mass-casualty terrorist attacks occur because of human actions. Such events do not necessarily result in homeostasis. Unlike natural calamities that often have relatively clear boundaries and rhythms, anthropogenic catastrophes can have such unclear spatial and temporal boundaries that they threaten and often do spread in unpredictable ways that make a return to equilibrium problematic. They may take on a *metastatic* quality.[4] Where disasters occur because of human errors, the results of those errors may not fall into clear patterns; and where disasters result from the application of technology, the magnitude of disasters can increase in unforeseeable ways.[5]

Before about the middle of the eighteenth century, homeostatic events were the predominant form disaster took. There were anthropogenic disasters from time to time—fires in cities largely constructed of wood, for example, such as the great London fire of 1666; or protracted wars with immense civilian casualties, such as the Thirty Years' War in the early seventeenth century. But by and large, disaster events were predominantly those that resulted from natural forces that could not be predicted, understood, or defended against. By around 1750, however, the relationship between natural and anthropogenic disaster began to change. The rise of centrally administered states in the West resulted in political entities capable of directing enormous and growing military power at their adversaries as well as having a much greater capacity to impose their will on their subjects. Western Europe was on the threshold of the Industrial Revolution, which would lead not only to immense economic expansion but also to deteriorating conditions of employment, unpredictable economic fluctuations, and sudden shifts in status hierarchies.

At the same time, disasters were being differently understood. A pivotal event was the Great Lisbon Earthquake of 1755, used by Voltaire as a central feature for the plot of *Candide*, and no wonder, for the earthquake resulted in a lively debate between those who read the event theologically as a divine warning to the wicked and those who postulated impersonal underground forces that might eventually be fitted into a fully functioning scientific theory. In the traditional religious view, earthquakes were God's means of communicating his displeasure to an errant humanity, a view expressed not only after Lisbon but after two minor tremors in London five years earlier.[6] The seventeenth and early eighteenth centuries marked the end of that long period in which natural disasters were clearly the dominant form of mass misfortune. This period, however, overlapped upon the seedtime of modern science and technology, forces that favored the view that such misfortunes were not the outcome of divine wrath but rather the workings of processes that in principle could be understood, predicted, and controlled. The belief in scientific mastery clearly preceded evidence that mastery could in fact be achieved, but the belief in mastery became the way in which increasing numbers of people perceived disasters, a view at once less religious and more optimistic.

Ironically, the optimism that flowed from science and technology did not take into account the fact that that same science and technology could also produce disasters, namely, anthropogenic disasters. The same power that might afford mastery over nature might also allow some human beings to impose enormous suffering upon other human beings. The double-edged character of science and technology—its capacity to mitigate some disaster suffering while increasing other kinds—was not immediately clear but became so later, particularly in the twentieth century.

To this point, I have treated natural and anthropogenic disasters as completely separate categories. Yet that is an oversimplification. The two are often interrelated in complex ways, and these links must be taken into account. For example, people may become disproportionately victimized by natural disasters as a result of human decisions about residential patterns. Decisions to live in flood plains, above fault zones, or adjacent to forests makes one more likely to be a victim of a flood, earthquake, or forest fire. The relative obviousness of this observation has not prevented the continued settlement of vulnerable areas, a point made with particular starkness by the fate of New Orleans after Hurricane Katrina in 2005, since much of the city was built below sea level; or the likely fate of populated parts of southern California should a major earthquake occur there. Within communities, differential power relationships may consign some groups to more risky locations than others.[7] Given the repetitious character of homeostatic natural disasters, which occur over and over again, generation after generation, the likely consequences of these locational decisions are known, although perhaps dealt with by denial.

In other cases, human actions may do more than alter patterns of potential victimization. They may actually modify natural processes. The best-known case, of course, is the current widely discussed global climate change. It almost certainly would not have occurred, or at least would not have occurred at anything like its present pace, had not human energy consumption occurred in the manner that it has. While the issue of global warming lies far outside the reach of this discussion, it is enough to say that situations like it suggest the care that must be taken in drawing a line between disasters that are naturally caused and those that are humanly caused. The same is true of analyses of Hurricane Katrina. On the one hand, the flooding of New Orleans would not have occurred absent a hurricane or in a location significantly above sea level. On the other, the flooding occurred because of levee breaks, and subsequent investigations revealed that the levees failed not because of the storm's ferocity but because the levees had been improperly designed and constructed. Here, too, the interweaving of natural and human factors is so complex that distinguishing between natural and anthropogenic disasters becomes virtually impossible.

Regardless of the intricacies of causation, one trend is clear: There has been an immense rise in the number of disaster victims. Between 1992 and 2001, they doubled, from 78,292,000 to 170,478,000.[8] The vast majority of these victims lived outside Europe and North America, in the developing world.[9] Whether through greater exposure to natural forces, less access to mitigation and recovery resources, or both, these populations have borne the brunt of contemporary disasters. Yet we should not think the developed world is invulnerable. For the very basis of its strength contains the seeds of vulnerability.

The prosperity and power of the developed world depend in large part on economies of scale and on the ability to draw upon and concentrate resources. These may be seen in characteristics as diverse as the administrative state, national militaries, industrial economies, power grids, national and international trade, highway and railway networks, civil aviation, and other features woven into the texture of everyday life. The effect of such developments is twofold: First, it necessarily reduces local self-sufficiency. Areas that might once have supplied most of the goods and services needed by their populations now require at least some necessities to be acquired from outside, by either public or private suppliers. Thus, the ability of a town and its rural environs to "go it alone" should something happen elsewhere is severely reduced. This reduction in redundancy—for that is what the decline in self-sufficiency means—leads to the second effect: The expansion in the size of units and the complexity of their interrelations create communities of shared fate. On the one hand, that means that benefits spread over ever-larger areas, an argument often used for loosening restrictions on trade. On the other hand, the interactions that bind distant people and communities together can also transmit negative consequences. Damage in one place may produce injury in a distant part of the network. This can be seen vividly in the cascading effects of a degraded electric power grid, but the same principle also holds true for disturbances in financial markets, disruptions in oil supplies, major terrorist attacks, and other threats to highly integrated systems. The capacity of developed societies to protect themselves against disasters, particularly natural disasters, may thus be offset by some of the very factors that contribute to their power, for the degree of cohesiveness that is a major constituent of that power also makes it more likely that damage will be communicated from the point of impact to distant places that lack the capacity to function independently.

Hazard, Vulnerability, and Risk

The analysis of mass-casualty events inevitably comes back to three concepts: hazard, vulnerability, and risk. What analysts cannot agree upon, however, is whether it is possible to define each independently, or whether each is in fact a function of one or both of the others. If it is the former, the concepts may be examined separately and each applied to situations of actual or potential disaster. But if they are intertwined, they need to be regarded as the coexisting aspects of disaster contexts, inseparable elements each of which depends upon the others. An even more vexing problem arises over the relationship between objective and subjective elements. To what extent, for example, is risk a property of the "real world" that can be objectively calculated, as opposed to an attribute determined by subjective perceptions? If it is the latter, it will almost certainly vary from group to group, perhaps even from person to person; and these multiple, subjective perceptions of disaster's likelihood may themselves class with the determinations made by those who claim some special expertise, such as scientists.

To the extent that hazard can be conceptually disentangled from vulnerability and risk, it tends to be understood as a disaster that has yet to happen, "a latent danger."[10] It implies "the probability of a damaging event occurring" as the result of some external force that cannot be controlled.[11] A hazardous event would be characterized by the "continuous or sudden (accidental) releases of energy, matter or information or [would] involve perturbations in social and value structures."[12] Alternatively, a hazard might be understood not through some abstract definition but rather as a combination of dimensions that differentiate its severity from other unpleasant events. Such dimensions might include magnitude, extent, frequency, and duration.[13] On the other hand, perhaps the threat does not actually have to exist in order to constitute a hazard. Perhaps it need only be necessary that large numbers of people believe it to exist.[14] Thus, hazards exist as much in the minds of potential victims as in the environments in which they live. But while the hazard appears to be the disaster itself or at least the belief in it, these definitions themselves suggest how difficult it is to separate hazard from the cognate notions of vulnerability and risk. For if one is invulnerable, an external event can hardly constitute a hazard, much less a disaster. And if a hazard is a potential or probable disaster, it is scarcely surprising that discussions of hazards quickly draw in concepts of risk.

Risk has sometimes been defined independently of other concepts but often in combination with them. One reason is that there is simply no consensus among analysts about what risk actually is.[15] As an independent idea, risk has been taken to mean an uncertain future event that might or might not happen[16] or, more concretely, "the probability of future loss and damage."[17] More often, risk appears closely linked to both hazard and vulnerability. Thus, risk becomes the probability that harm will result from a particular hazard.[18] This is implied in the notion that risk is "a situation

. . . where something of human value . . . is at stake and where the outcome is uncertain."[19] But risk might be seen as embedded in a far more complex relationship among risk, hazard, and vulnerability: hazard becomes a risk factor external to the potential affected social system, while vulnerability becomes an internal risk factor. Risk therefore emerges from the manner in which hazard and vulnerability condition one another: "one cannot be vulnerable if one is not threatened, and one cannot be threatened if one is not exposed and vulnerable."[20]

Having examined hazard and risk, a separate discussion of the concept of vulnerability seems almost superfluous. It is, to be sure, the "the propensity to suffer loss"[21] and "the predisposition to be affected" by some damaging force.[22] But that predisposition cannot be separated from the strength of the force—that is, the hazard—as well as the likelihood of its occurrence—that is, the risk. "Vulnerability is . . . a function of exposure to risk, resistance to risk, and resilience in the face of disaster."[23]

The contemporary understanding of risk—and by extension, hazard and vulnerability—has been powerfully altered by the work of the German sociologist Ulrich Beck. Beck speaks of our living in a "risk society," more dangerous than that which confronted earlier generations. His reasoning is that powerful and poorly understood new technologies can create disastrous effects that are impossible to anticipate, cannot be controlled, and spread across national boundaries.[24] These are anthropogenic disasters, turning consumer products into hidden poisons, degrading the environment, and seeding the world with insidious sources of radiation. Beck makes clear that such dire consequences are unintended; indeed, they result from science and technology run amok. What is more interesting for our purposes is his emphasis upon the *invisibility* of the causes. Contrasting the nineteenth-century and the present, Beck notes that "hazards in those days assaulted the nose or the eyes and were thus perceptible to the senses, while the risks of civilization today typically *escape perception*."[25] "The focus," he continues, "is more and more on hazards which are neither visible or perceptible to the victims; hazards that in some cases may not even take effect within the life spans of those affected, but instead during those of their children; hazards in any case that require the 'sensory organs' of science—*theories, experiments, measuring instruments—in order to become visible or interpretable as hazards at all.*"[26]

The significance of Beck's approach is threefold: It lies first in the centrality of technology for risk, and the concomitant assertion that natural disasters have been displaced as the principal source of mass death and destruction. Second, he employs risk and hazard interchangeably, despite the attempts of others to maintain conceptual separation. Third, he implies, although he does not draw out, a conception of invisibility and its relationship to the sensory organs. Thus there is one form of the visibility-invisibility distinction that can be made based upon the capacities and limitations of ordinary human sensory organs and a second distinction based upon what he terms "the 'sensory organs' of science." This second distinction allows the limitations of the human senses to be transcended, for example, through such devices as X-rays or radar. We shall explore these distinctions at greater length below.

As a result, hazard, risk, and vulnerability seem inextricably bound together. The dangers that confront groups are balanced against the strength and resilience of individuals and institutions. The disasters may occur, in which case the actual degree of vulnerability will be tested. Risk is a dicier matter. For most homeostatic, natural disasters calculations of risk can be made with a fair degree of accuracy, quite well for hurricanes, very poorly if at all for major earthquakes. In the case of metastatic, anthropogenic disasters—especially those likely to cause massive casualties, such as large-scale terrorist attacks—calculation of probabilities is impossible. That is, in fact, true for virtually all events that are uncommon. Attempts to assign probabilities to extremely uncommon events are based on guesswork, often disguised by quantification that produces the spurious impression of precision. Yet where risk is concerned, our minds abhor a vacuum, and in the absence of reliable calculations of risk, we operate on the basis of what are in fact notions of subjective risk. This is akin to the distinction Richard Posner makes between risk and uncertainty: the probability of the former can be estimated while that of the latter cannot.[27] This occurs not only in situations such as terrorist attacks where objective risk calculation is impossible but also in situations of everyday life where we either do not have access to expert knowledge about actual risk or we wish to reject such knowledge so as not to deny ourselves the pleasure of what some might consider high-risk behavior. Thus subjective risk might come into play when deciding whether to walk at night in an unfamiliar neighborhood or whether to continue smoking, as well as whether to take precautions against an earthquake, an accident at a nearby nuclear power plant, or some other relatively remote possibility. Given the nexus of hazard, vulnerability, and risk, when risk becomes subjective, so too do perceptions of hazard and vulnerability.

The mind may magnify not only the likelihood of potential dangers but also their severity and the weakness of one's own situation.

These considerations suggest that disaster lives as much in our minds as in the collective experience of communities that have undergone traumatic events. On one level, therefore, disasters are facts. That is, they are events experienced by individuals and groups who have been assailed by hazards that reveal vulnerabilities. They are risks that have become actualized. But on another level, one may look at the world under the aspect of disaster, with an attitude of foreboding, seeing it always in the wings, as it were. What might at other times seem to be relatively innocuous events become premonitory signs of onrushing cataclysms. There is, in other words, an apocalyptic sensibility, a tendency that can be seen in certain times and places to imagine disaster as a constant presence, regardless of its actual occurrence. External data about hazard, risk, and vulnerability are interpreted by cultural frameworks—derived from religion, politics, or popular culture—that may give to the data a strongly subjective, indeed a distorted, character.

As the preceding suggests, risk and the concepts associated with it are bound up with more than merely data about the actual occurrence of damaging events. Once we begin to unpack them, we are confronted with a complex set of psychological issues as well. For what people understand to constitute risk is a function of how they and those they listen to see the world. It is, in other words, a matter of perception. That makes it subject to a wide range of factors: the information available, the credibility of the sources, the behavior of those around us, our past experiences, social status and the feelings of power or powerlessness that go with it, and so on.

Risk and Its Amplification

In the 1980s, a number of social scientists interested in risk began to notice that the general public often holds ideas about risk that vary significantly from those of experts. Often the public views some specific hazard, such as nuclear power plants, as much more dangerous than those whose professional qualifications give them some authority to speak on the question. This led to the development of models of *risk amplification* to try to understand the gap between public and expert views.[28] In the subsequent decades, many examples of such gaps have appeared, usually, although not always, concerning anthropogenic as opposed to natural hazards. Thus, they have involved such events as pollution, but sometimes disease outbreaks as well. Most of the time, laypersons who have been studied believed risk was greater than what scientific experts or other authorities believed it was. But occasionally the public had lower risk expectations, a phenomenon that has come to be called "risk attenuation".

Despite the many individual studies devoted to risk amplification, the issue of terrorism has rarely come up. Rather, the subjects studied have tended to be limited events, often the kind that lend themselves to analysis by scientific or medical specialists, such as the BSE ("mad cow") outbreak in Great Britain. Risk amplification means not only that people feel more endangered but also that this sense of increased jeopardy can spread outward. The initial conception of the social amplification of risk hypothesized that part of the amplification process involved so-called ripple effects, the spread of consequences beyond the directly affected persons. These ripple effects might ramify from the local community all the way to the entire society in which the affected persons are embedded.[29] Immediately after the September 11th attacks, one of the central figures in risk amplification research, Paul Slovic, wrote a very brief essay on terrorism, calling it "a new species of trouble." He made two points: First, he suggested that risk analysis was no longer sufficient. It needed to be supplemented by vulnerability analysis as well, in order to reduce risk. Given the relationship between the two concepts that we have already seen, this seems clear and straightforward. Second, 9/11 led him to view ripple effects in a new light: "In the aftermath of September 11, we are witnessing not just ripple effects but cascading waves of impacts, likely to batter us for much of this new century. In bringing risk analysis to bear on decision making, we should make a determined effort to take the social amplification of risk into account."[30]

What, then, does the social amplification of risk mean? It means, at a minimum, that people in different social positions often perceive risk differently, even when they have access to the same information. It also means that the availability of information does not by itself determine risk. What matters is both the trust consumers place in sources of information and what those consumers do with the information.

People will adjust their risk estimates up or down in keeping with what the information provides, as long as it comes from trusted sources.[31] The media, obviously a major information source, often "frame" stories so that specific events become "episodes in continuing narratives built around particular master themes and central motifs."[32] If these accounts come from

what is considered a credible source, both the individual event description and the overarching frame narrative may be accepted. However, most
risk amplification studies deal only with conventional media that are easily available for study, such as newspapers. Little attention is given to the
increasingly wide range of information now available from such sources as
the Internet, with its proliferation of everything from primary source documents to urban legends, and whose reports spread more rapidly than those
of old-style media.

Wherever the information comes from, it does not land on readers' or
listeners' tabulae rasae. None of us is a blank slate, and incoming information will be sifted and modified by a variety of filters: culture, class, peer-
group influences, past experiences, and so forth. It might be argued that
experts, too, have filters, and that they, too, are in some sense prisoners of
culture, class, and peer group. This is no doubt true, except that there is a
presumption of countervailing pressure in the form of professional disci-
pline, especially for those grounded in science and medicine.

Not only do media themselves place news stories in narrative frames.
Members of the public, the consumers of information, do so as well. Research on risk amplification reveals that laypersons often themselves as-
semble information into "risk stories," narratives with villains, intention,
dramatizations, and morals that create a compelling tale.[33] While these folk
interpretations may incorporate elements of media's framing narratives,
they represent an independent source of risk amplification. As we discuss
later, risk stories are important not only to the general public but also to
policymakers, for they, too, need them to make sense of the world.

The result of this research underscores that there are multiple conceptions of risk. In some cases, risk may be calculable in probabilistic terms.
In other instances, danger may only be roughly estimated through some
methodology. Whether in the one instance or the other, we are in the domain of professional expertise. Yet, as we have seen, the lay public has its
own views of risk, which may diverge sharply from those of professionals,
even when they have the latter's information and conclusions before them.

Disaster Obsessions

The most extreme manifestation of such distortions occur in eras characterized by what may be termed "disaster obsessions," where large numbers of people become convinced that they live in an insecure world on

the verge of cataclysmic events. There have been two such periods in the recent American past. The first occurred in the 1970s. The second began in the mid-1990s and is still in progress. In both periods, disaster obsessions were conditioned by both religious and secular factors. On the religious side, the rise of evangelicalism carried a strong millenarian current. This apocalyptic view of the end of history assigned special significance to both natural calamities and wars, especially those in the Middle East, as markers of the "last days."[34]

The decade of the seventies was an era marked by fears of both religious and secular apocalypses. And little wonder. It was preceded by the unprecedented political tumult and civil disorder of the late 1960s. It began with the Vietnam War still unresolved. The presidency of Richard Nixon ended in 1973 with a cascade of scandals. The Arab oil boycott of 1973 in response to the Yom Kippur War threatened the very survival of industrial economies, as drivers engaged in fistfights struggling for places in gas station waiting lines. The same scenario was played out on a slightly smaller scale in 1979 after the Islamic revolution in Iran. In response, America was saturated with not one but two apocalyptic literatures.[35]

In 1970 Hal Lindsey and C. C. Carlson published their millenarian tract, *The Late Great Planet Earth*, which became the largest-selling paperback book of the decade, but it was only one of a swelling religious genre.[36] Far more unexpected was the appearance of secular counterparts. They were written by academics and intellectuals, were very widely discussed and reviewed, and prophesied imminent calamity, and possibly the extinction of all human life. The means described varied, but they included nuclear war, environmental pollution, overpopulation, and energy shortages. Most influential among many such volumes were Barry Commoner's *The Closing Circle* (1971), Donella H. Meadows et al.'s *The Limits to Growth* (1972), and Robert Heilbroner's *An Inquiry into the Human Prospect* (1974).[37] Straddling the religious-secular divide was Aleksandr Solzhenitsyn's 1978 Harvard commencement address, "A World Split Apart," with its implied pronouncement of doom on the post-Renaissance West.[38] In short, America was saturated in doom-laden visions, the future seen under the aspect of disaster.

The disaster obsession of the 1970s was not without some basis in reality, since as the brief historical summary above suggests, it arose out of the troubling events of the late 1960s and early 1970s. Yet with the distance that hindsight affords, it is safe to say that the mordant pronouncements of that decade were far more pessimistic than circumstances warranted. There was no nuclear war. Growth did not slow down or stop. In fact, it accelerated. The disasters that were to preoccupy a later decade (and to which we shall shortly turn) were altogether absent from the apocalyptic scenarios described in the 1970s, which have a character all their own. The writers mention neither terrorism, climate change, nor global pandemics. This is not to say that their analyses were superficial or undeserving of serious consideration, only that they were rooted in the special concerns of their times. However, the most striking aspect of this literature is its concentration upon anthropogenic disasters. The pervasive disaster consciousness that emerged had virtually no concern for the homeostatic natural disasters that had preoccupied earlier periods, doubtless in the belief that the powers of science and technology now held these dangers at bay. Indeed, it was these very powers, the authors argued, that constituted the sources from which future disasters would come. This assertion seemed partially validated by a series of accidents in the 1980s that triggered highly publicized disasters. Although none was of the apocalyptic scale prophesied in 1970s literature, all were humanly caused and all emerged out of technological processes or devices. They included the oil spill from the *Exxon Valdez*, the chemical release from the Union Carbide plant in Bhopal, India, and the accident at the Chernobyl nuclear reactor.[39]

The disaster obsessions that began to reappear in the mid-1990s both resembled and diverged from the nightmare visions of the 1970s. While anthropogenic disasters formed a part of this new constellation, natural calamities made a surprising reappearance. In part, this came from the return to public consciousness of the fear of epidemic disease. This motif, which stretched back to such events as the Black Death in the fourteenth century, had been muted by triumphs in medicine and public health. The first mass inoculation with the Salk vaccine occurred in 1954 and led to the eradication of polio. The World Health Organization's smallpox eradication program began in 1967, and the last naturally occurring case in the world was recorded in Somalia in 1977. It was little wonder, therefore, that fear of the spread of disease receded from consciousness. Yet the sense of personal safety was short-lived. There was the sudden, although small-scale, emergence of Legionnaires' disease in 1976. But it was HIV/AIDS that signaled the beginning of a new era of disease fear. The first warning by the Centers for Disease Control came in 1981, and by the late 1980s, HIV/AIDS was a subject of national concern, with increasing discrimination against sufferers. West Nile virus appeared in 1999 and, although rarely fatal, caused significant anxiety in the New York City area. Around the same time—1996–97—the first cases of avian influenza, the H5N1 strain, began to appear in Asia and spread toward Europe. Although human cases were relatively few and seemingly limited to those who had direct contact with contaminated fowl, fear increased that a mutated form of "bird flu" could produce a global pandemic the mortality from which might exceed even the great influenza epidemic of 1918. Finally, SARS (Severe Acute Respiratory Syndrome) emerged seemingly out of nowhere in 2002, and while, like West Nile, it claimed relatively few lives, its appearance too suggested that new diseases could manifest themselves unpredictably in developed countries. This was to feed the subsequent concern about biological weapons.

Disease was not the only natural catastrophe of the period. The Asian tsunami of 2004 was striking not only because of its scope and intensity but because, unlike many natural disaster touching less developed areas, the tsunami struck many resort areas frequented by Western tourists whose amateur videos were played and replayed all over the developed world. Then there were the catastrophes that straddled the natural/human line in the manner discussed earlier, such as the flooding of New Orleans in 2005, where natural forces functioned as enablers whose effects were amplified by human ineptitude and negligence. The issue of global climate change gestated longer, as claims of global warming and its effects met with resistance. However, by about 2005, even most skeptics had come to accept that climate change was occurring and that human actions were the main cause. Controversy remained about how quickly its effects would appear in such forms as rising sea levels and changes in rainfall patterns, as well as what might be done to slow its onset.

If there was a single wholly anthropogenic disaster fear that emerged in the period after about 1995, it was fear of terrorist attacks using weapons of mass destruction. The catalytic event was, of course, the attacks on September 11, 2001. Despite the fact that they were low-tech, inasmuch as the hijackers used box cutters to take control of the aircraft and carried no weapons of mass destruction (WMD), the level of casualties and the imagery of the World Trade Center collapse made it seem as though nuclear, biological, chemical, or radiological weapons were a natural next step. This conclusion seemed plausible because of two background events. One was the mysterious anthrax letters sent to media and political targets a month after the 9/11 attacks. Although there were only twelve fatalities and the distribution of anthrax by letter was a highly inefficient method, the resulting anxiety was extremely high, no doubt because the attacks occurred so soon after 9/11. The other event took place much earlier: the 1995 sarin gas attack in the Tokyo subway by the Japanese religious sect Aum Shinrikyo. This attack, too, killed only a dozen people, although many more were sickened. Yet, although the deaths were few, the repercussions were global, for Aum had apocalyptic beliefs, substantial funds, well-trained scientists, and a long-standing chemical weapons program. While some might have argued that despite all of these factors it had very little success, the predominant view was quite the opposite: that the incident demonstrated the ability of a nonstate actor to enter an arena previously monopolized by states.

A final factor played into the disaster obsessions of the late 1990s and early 2000s, and that was the end of the Cold War. The East-West conflict imposed on the world both a geopolitical order and a psychic order. The geopolitical order forced a significant number of states to fall into the orbit of either the United States or the Soviet Union and, if neither, then to band together as "non-aligned." By the psychic order, I refer to the tendency of many, particularly in the United States, to conceive of the world in Manichean terms, to utilize, as President Reagan did, the polarity of "free world" and "evil empire." The effect of both the geopolitical and the psychic conceptions was to simplify and organize an otherwise complex reality. When, however, the Soviet Union broke up in the early 1990s and the Cold War ended, these conceptions suddenly became meaningless. The world that emerged was immediately more complicated, more difficult to understand, and more frightening, even though the possibility of a U.S.-Soviet nuclear exchange had been removed. Now there were no overarching organizing concepts, no clear notions of good and evil, only conflicts in strange places few knew anything about, such as Bosnia and Herzegovina and Somalia. The locus of evil could no longer be clearly identified, as it had been from the late 1940s until the collapse of the USSR. The rise of the terrorist to a premier position in both public and official imagination was a response not only to the attacks that had been perpetrated but to the need to fill the "enemy vacuum" that the end of the Cold War had created.

Disaster as Event and Construct

What does the foregoing tell us? It suggests that "disaster" exists as both a phenomenon in the world, in which uncontrollable stresses wreak death and destruction on human populations, and as a mental construct through which members of those populations view the world. The slipperiness and malleability of key ideas such as hazard, risk, and vulnerability reflects the degree to which an understanding of disaster emerges out of an interaction between external events and internal mental categories. Disaster is not something that is simply "out there," clearly and unambiguously labeled. Instead, it emerges out of human interpretation. That interpretation may then be imposed on an unclear world to try to understand the likelihood that disaster is about to take place or will emerge in the near future. Thus the interpretive framework with which disaster-related ideas are connected both interpret the past, seeking to draw meaning from past suffering, and look forward into an indistinct future to see whether the shape of coming disaster may be discovered.

When disaster exists as a construct, "[a]ll that is necessary is the public perception that either a hazard exists or an impact has taken place for a disaster to have occurred."[40] The operative word here is "perception," since the perception of disaster creates a social reality, irrespective of any measures of damage. The belief itself may then call forth collective responses that can significantly modify or even extinguish normal patterns of behavior as a community responds to what it believes to be an emergency situation. Depending upon how disruptive these responses are, perception of a disaster becomes, as it were, a self-fulfilling prophecy, in which belief in a disaster creates behavior that may itself have disastrous consequences for the society involved, where actions intended to protect in fact erode the very normalcy believed to be at risk. For example, such protective measures as evacuation, quarantine, and intrusive searches may create disruptions of nearly as great a magnitude as the events they were seeking to prevent.

As the brief description of what I have termed "disaster obsessions" shows, even eras close in time may differ substantially in the calamities they fear. To some extent, of course, that is simply an artifact of their different historical experiences. Had not the 1970s begun with the Arab oil boycott, the fear that industrial economies would run out of energy would almost certainly not have achieved the salience it did. Nonetheless, when comparing the differences between the 1970s and the current period, one can only be struck by the dissimilarities in what (in a quite different context) Susan Sontag once called "the imagination of disaster."[41] Are such differences driven only by immediate experiences? If so, then attempts at long-range prognostications may be irredeemably flawed. If other factors condition them, what might they be—ideology, religion, popular culture?

These questions are of special significance given the current preoccupation with terrorism. For a mass-casualty terrorist attack would be, as was 9/11, an anthropogenic, metastatic disaster, especially so if, unlike September 11th, it involved chemical, biological, radiological, or nuclear weapons. The potential unboundedness of such disasters lies in the capacity of terrorists to deliberately construct any attack to make it unlike any previous attack.[42] As we have seen, whether such an attack actually takes place, belief that it might or will places it at the center of contemporary consciousness alongside other calamities of the moment, such as climate change, a flu pandemic, or a category 5 hurricane. Its perceived importance is in part a function of events, including not only 9/11 but subsequent attacks in Madrid and London, as well as those that were alleged to have been blocked. But its importance is also a function of assumptions, both examined and unexamined, about bad things that may happen to us and about what frightens us. The chapters that follow look at some, although certainly not all, of those assumptions. I have chosen to concentrate on those beliefs we have about dangers that are unseen.

Unseen dangers seem particularly close to our current fears because those fears are centered on malefactors and weaponry that in large measure are unseen. Unlike enemy nations that have a tangible home ultimately identifiable with some territory, nonstate groups have a geographical insubstantiality. That is compounded to the extent that such groups may use means that make them even harder to identify, such as sleeper cells, or weapons that by their nature are largely or wholly invisible. An even greater measure of invisibility appears when terrorist acts are committed not by large, well-administered organizations, but by small, ad hoc groups, or by individual freelancers, wannabes with idiosyncratic visions answerable to no one. In such circumstances, we seem surrounded by unseen enemies.

The significance of this issue of unseen dangers lies in part in its effects on the public and in part on those it has on policymakers. For the public, it becomes a major source of fear that cannot be assuaged, because, short of bringing the unseen to a condition of visibility, the fear will still be thought to be somewhere, "out there," with government powerless to protect us. For that government and its policymakers, the issue is more subtle. Policymakers are presumed to have at their command information of the highest available quality, as well as whatever defensive resources the society has available to protect itself. With these, they must make reasoned and prudent choices. Yet, it will be argued here, they are no more able than their fellow citizens to disentangle themselves from ideas about intangible dangers, for they, too, are implanted in the same cultural milieu. They may be able to articulate unseen dangers in the more elegant languages of bureaucratic argumentation, but they, like the less articulate public for whom they speak, look out upon the same "landscape of fear."[43]

However, the imperatives of government and the demands of the public are that the invisible be made visible. Unseen dangers must be made manifest so that they may be detected before damage is done and in order that the special fears that attach to invisibility might be neutralized. Considerable efforts have consequently been made both on identifying terrorists who might otherwise melt into the population and on locating secreted WMD. Yet, as we shall see in the next chapter, despite these efforts, much of the domain of unseen dangers is likely to remain beyond our ken, at least for the immediate future.

three

MAKING THE INVISIBLE VISIBLE

REVERSE TRANSPARENCY AND PRIVACY

For reasons of both national security and political survival, decision-makers can scarcely remain passive in the face of a landscape of fear. As the strategic theorist Colin Gray observed shortly after September 11th, they must be seen to be acting even if what they do does not constitute an intelligent response.[1] If the adversary is invisible, then a key element in the response is to bring the unseen to a condition of visibility. The enemy must be forced to reveal himself, an enterprise that requires that the means used to achieve invisibility be neutralized or penetrated. While this applies primarily to terrorists themselves, it may also apply to weapons smuggled into the country, particularly those that act in invisible ways, such as biological, chemical, and radiological devices.

The frustration states face when they believe they confront unseen dangers results in strenuous efforts to make these dangers clearly apparent. Since what concerns us here are dangers that are caused or believed to be caused intentionally, the drive to make them visible can become an overriding policy objective, as the events after September 11th have shown. The attempt to force the invisible to manifest itself generally occurs in three ways: by extending the senses, usually through technological means, often for the purpose of detecting otherwise invisible weapons; by extending the senses in order to distinguish invisible malefactors who would otherwise melt into the general population; and by modifying legal procedures in the belief that traditional procedures are incapable of dealing with unseen dangers. The first two seek to penetrate what I earlier called technical and crowd invisibility. The third results from the fact that penetration of invisible evil and attempts to give it substance often fail to meet the canons of proof traditionally required by legal systems.

These efforts have significant implications for two related concepts: transparency and privacy. As we shall see, the former, which is usually applied to government, is placed under great strain in situations of unseen danger, when the state is likely to become less transparent and more opaque. But there is a second, less obvious result, discussed at the end of the chapter, which I term "reverse transparency," in which requirements of openness once incumbent upon government now devolve upon individuals, with significant reductions in personal privacy.

Extending the Senses: Making Invisible Perpetrators and Their Weapons Visible

Terrorists themselves benefit from "crowd invisibility," the ability to make themselves indistinguishable from the mass of the innocuous general public, as discussed in Chapter 1. Various attempts have been made to bring them to a level of visibility. This might be done either by identifying terrorists themselves, assuming that individuals could be matched against names on a list of terrorists, or by identifying and excluding all nonterrorists, leaving a residual group. One technique, profiling, will be discussed at a later point. We begin here with biometrics, the method that most closely approximates an extension of the senses. Biometrics is the use of unique physical and behavioral traits for purposes of identification. For example, fingerprints are required for all individuals entering the United States. Initially, only two prints were required, but eventually visitors were required to provide all ten fingerprints. While these were once taken at foreign visa-issuing consular offices, by 2008 they were taken at all points of entry.[2] They will eventually also be required upon departure from the United States.[3] However, their utility in rendering the unseen visible depends upon the ability to compare fingerprints taken with an available but necessarily incomplete repository of prints of either all harmless individuals or all known terrorists. The terrorism watch list, already in use at border crossing points, has been relatively unproductive. In 2006, it resulted in nearly 20,000 encounters involving both American citizens and foreign nationals. Of these, more than half were logged by Customs and Border Protection personnel. Out of the 10,000 or so, 550 people were detained, but only a small number were arrested, most apparently for nonterrorism-related offenses.[4]

Biometric identifiers, including but not limited to fingerprints, would logically generate very large databases. Concern for the identification of terrorists and their separation from the general population has significantly accelerated the development of enormous collections of information that might be unique to specific individuals. Thus in February 2008, the FBI awarded a $1 billion contract to Lockheed Martin to develop "what is expected to be the world's largest crime-fighting database of biometric information." This project, called the Next Generation Identification System, is being executed in coordination with the Departments of Homeland Security, State, and Defense.[5] At almost the same time, the British press reported an FBI initiative called "Server in the Sky," which would permit the instant transmission of biometric data among law enforcement agencies in the United States, the United Kingdom, Canada, and other allied countries.[6]

Such data would presumably provide conclusive identification of individuals passing through controlled spaces such as airport checkpoints or border crossings. However, the search has also been on for noninvasive techniques that might pick terrorists out of groups in public places or "recognize" them in situations where their forms of identification, whether documentary or biometric, raised no suspicions. These methods fall under the rubric of "behavioral surveillance" and encompass the collection of data about a host of both voluntary and involuntary physical actions and processes. These include facial expressions, vocalization, motor activity, organ activity controlled by the autonomic nervous system, and activity within the brain itself.[7] However, a recent review of relevant research by the National Research Council cast doubt on the success of efforts to utilize such information for purposes of counterterrorism.

In principle, behavioral surveillance raises the same questions as those posed by the "lie detector," which also secures physical data in order to make inferences about an individual's psychological state, possible deception, and likely behavior. The primary difference is that techniques of behavioral surveillance would need to operate in such a way that the individual would not know that he or she was being observed. The National Research Council's review concluded that in principle the acquisition of physical data could provide information about psychological states. However, the presently available methods are unable to distinguish between terrorists and others, with resulting large numbers of false positives. In addition, as with poly-graphs, behavioral techniques may be open to effective countermeasures by those they seek to identify. At best, therefore, behavioral surveillance might be employed as a means to stimulate further screening.[8]

The principal contemporary area in which sense-extension has been employed in order to counter unseen dangers is connected to weapons ter-rorists might use, especially so-called weapons of mass destruction. This despite the fact that virtually all terrorist attacks have employed visible, con-ventional weapons, usually bombs. Notwithstanding the banal character of terrorists' weapons, however, the fear that they will someday employ weap-ons of mass destruction, many of which deliver lethality by invisible means, remains intense. In 2005, Sen. Richard Lugar (R-Ind.) surveyed eigthy-five experts on national security and nonproliferation about their expecta-tions concerning future use of chemical, biological, nuclear, or radiological weapons by terrorists. Fifty percent thought such a weapon would be em-ployed within the next five years, and 70 percent thought it likely within the next ten, with radiological weapons viewed as most probable.[9]

None of these weapons are detectable by the senses alone, absent un-usual luck or remarkably accurate intelligence. In some cases, the weapons themselves might be hidden before use. In other cases, even after use, the weapon might not be detectable by the unaided senses, which might be unable to recognize the presence of radiation, certain toxic chemicals, or microbes. After detonation or dispersal, all but a nuclear device require some additional form of detection. The result has been the development of sensor technologies, accelerated after 9/11. The requirements for such tech-nologies are daunting. Notwithstanding the effort and resources put into the acquisition of these capabilities, at present the technologies leave much to be desired. As the Government Accountability Office concluded, "More than 6 years after the events of September 11, 2001, local first responders do not have tools that can accurately and quickly identify the release of CBRN [chemical, biological, radiological, and nuclear] material in an urban environment."[10]

Sensors must be practical to operate and provide usable information quickly. They must be sensitive, especially given the likelihood that weap-ons may be concealed or shielded. Ideally, they should generate neither false negatives—weapons that are missed, with potentially catastrophic results—nor false positives—false alarms, with all the inconvenience and subsequent public complacency that follows.[11] They must be able to detect weapons in environments filled with background "clutter."[12] Authorities in New York City have deployed biological sensors to detect disease-causing agents but have also complained that the federal government has given less than full support to the acquisition of the expensive devices. Such disagreements become entangled both in competition over conflicting budgetary demands and in philosophical differences over the best way to monitor potential bioterrorism: for example, is it better to develop such sensors or instead to work toward more refined diagnostic tests and more integrated medical record keeping?[13] This is a significant issue, since a disease outbreak caused by an attack will initially present in a manner indistinguishable from a naturally occurring disease. As a result, the Department of Homeland Security (DHS) has given priority to the development of a National Biosurveillance Integration Center to look for patterns and anomalies in disease outbreaks.[14] In addition, the Department of Homeland Security's BioWatch program, under which the monitoring programs were placed, has exhibited serious systemic problems in its handling of laboratory samples, according to the department's inspector general.[15] BioWatch involves aerosol collectors that, as of 2008, were "operative in over 30 of the Nation's largest metropolitan areas." However, their filters must be taken each day and subjected to laboratory analysis, a cumbersome and time-consuming process to be superseded by a so-called Generation 3 system of automated detectors. Under the present system, therefore, "identification and confirmation of biological warfare agents does not occur until several hours to more than 1 day after release of the agent, and the quantity of the agent released cannot be determined."[16]

The problem of nuclear and radiological weapons is even more challenging, since their use would be far more damaging. It therefore has been a top priority of the DHS, largely through its Domestic Nuclear Detection Office (DNDO). The basic thrust of the DNDO has been in detecting such weapons at foreign ports, at U.S. ports of entry, or elsewhere along U.S. borders principally through the monitoring of cargo.[17] While the DHS inspector general provided a positive evaluation of the DNDO, his report is couched in exceedingly general terms, such as the office has "made progress."[18] By the end of 2008, almost all cargo entering the United States was scanned for radioactivity.[19] However, the ability to detect radioactive sources is effective only if the source is not well shielded. If it is shielded, existing instruments may not be sufficiently sensitive. In the hope that nuclear or radiological weapons would be discovered prior to reaching American territory, therefore, relatively little attention has been given to technological capabilities for actually discovering such weapons on U.S. soil.

Finally, in March 2006, the DNDO initiated a pilot program called Securing the Cities, principally focused on New York, which has involved trucks and helicopters armed with detection devices that sweep urban areas seeking sources of radioactivity.[20] In 2008, the numerous jurisdictions within the New York metropolitan area received $29 million in grants to help create a radiation detection system.[21]

There have been neither actual nor attempted attacks using chemical, biological, or radiological weapons. At the same time, the sensors desired are to have a zero failure rate, or as close to it as is possible, bearing in mind that pre-attack detection of a biological weapon is unlikely.[22] Thus the senses are being extended in an environment in which practical testing is difficult, and, indeed, the circumstances requiring their use may not arise.

Profiling

Secretary of Homeland Security Michael Chertoff announced as one of his 2008 goals "determining who the unknown terrorist is, the terrorist whose name we haven't yet identified but who is nevertheless a real threat and someone that we ought to keep out."[23] His suggestions for ferreting out such invisible evildoers, however, did not rise above such devices as the ten-finger print and the watch list, both discussed above, neither of which appear tailored to the problem. While Secretary Chertoff did not mention profiling, it can scarcely have been far from his awareness.

In a general sense, profiling seeks to identify malefactors through some set of background characteristics, ties to associates, or behaviors. In its crudest form, it leads to the unproductive and ethically questionable phenomenon of overinclusive classes, such as all Muslims or all Arabs. Well before 9/11 the issue had become highly charged because of allegations that some police profile all African Americans as potential criminal suspects. The application of profiling to terrorists clearly requires a finer-grain methodology, which, like sensors, would need to be relatively free of both false positives and false negatives. There are clearly some techniques in use that are not in the public domain, such as those employed to screen airline passengers. Given their secret and proprietary character, there is no way to know the variables upon which they are based or their level of success. However, there are numerous open exercises in profiling by scholars. These occur after the fact, based on data about or derived from known terrorists. These studies fall into two groups: those that deal with suicide terrorists, and those that deal with terrorists not recruited for or primarily committed to suicide missions.

Although this is not the place to exhaustively summarize this literature, the overall impression it gives is this: there is an array of patterns in both demographic characteristics and behaviors rather than some single master template to which the vast majority of jihadi terrorists correspond. Students of suicide terrorism cannot agree on motivations.[24] Studies of European jihadi terrorists suggest the difficulty of constructing a profile based on demographic characteristics. As a Dutch counterterrorism official put it, "To have a profile that you can recognize, so that you can predict, 'This guy is going to be radical, perhaps he will cross the line into terrorism'— that, I think, is impossible."[25] Characteristics can change over time, so that a profile valid at one time may cease to be valid a year or two later. This appears to have been the case with jihadi terrorists between, say, 2000 and 2008. What the research does converge on is a point made by Marc Sageman in his influential monograph, *Understanding Terror Networks*, namely, that individuals affiliate with terrorist organizations through preexisting social networks, particularly those that involve their peers.[26] This is, of course, a proposition long established in the study of social movements. It makes the terrorist potentially visible, but only to the extent that one can identify some node in a network.

The REAL ID Program

In 2005 Congress passed the REAL ID Act, giving effect to a recommendation by the 9/11 Commission that identification documents be made more difficult for terrorists to obtain. While this act did not establish a national identification card, it did, as will be seen, create the framework for a de facto card. It would be possible to move about the country without it but effectively impossible to do so by air. The substance of the act was a requirement that the Department of Homeland Security develop a way of securing the integrity of driver's licenses and similar forms of identification on a national basis. After considerable effort, including consultation with states, the governmental units that actually issue driver's licenses and identification cards, the DHS finally promulgated a regulation in January 2008. The aim of the program is to create licenses that include security features that are based on proof of identity and citizenship or legal status, whose underlying source documents have been verified, and that have been issued by offices that themselves meet security standards. The assumption is that everyone under fifty holding state licenses or cards will have those that meet the new standards by December 2014, and that those over fifty will have them by December 2017.[27]

The DHS somewhat disingenuously asserted that "REAL ID is not a national identification card," since "each State will issue its own unique license."[28] This is technically true. There is no requirement for all individuals to secure state-issued cards, nor is there a requirement for all states to participate in the program. However, individuals without cards that meet REAL ID standards would face significant delays in boarding commercial airplanes or entering a federal facility unless they have a comparable form of identification, such as a passport. It seems unlikely that a state would refuse to participate, since doing so would significantly disadvantage its citizens. Since the emergence of strict security regimes at airports, driver's licenses and comparable state-issued IDs for nondrivers have become in function, if not in name, identification cards. Secretary Chertoff acknowledged as much when he conceded that "as long as people use driver's licenses to identify themselves for whatever reason, there's no reason for these licenses to be easily counterfeited or tampered with, and there's every reason to have the confidence that the license is secure and reflects a person's true identity and their legal presence in the United States."[29] That identification function would be increased by REAL ID, since the reliability of state-issued documents would be significantly enhanced. As Secretary Chertoff himself pointed out, to the extent that employers use the cards to avoid hiring illegal immigrants, market forces will "make them attractive to people who are using identification for other purposes."[30]

In one respect, REAL ID will not maximize available technology. Unlike future passports, the cards will not include biometric identifiers. However, they will include, in addition to the holder's signature, a digital photograph. Americans have been resistant to the concept of a national identification card on the grounds that it would lodge excessive control in the federal government. However, there appears to be no concerted opposition to REAL ID.

The Observation of Public Spaces

By definition, in public spaces—streets, parks, plazas, lobbies, museums, commercial establishments, and so forth—individuals can be observed. That is what makes such spaces public. By the same token, the ubiquity of such spaces in modern cities and the numbers of people who move through them affords individuals anonymity, the ability to melt into a mass of strangers. This offers the crowd invisibility discussed in Chapter 1. However, the ability to move unnoticed through public spaces has been increasingly challenged by new technologies of observation, principally closed-circuit television systems. These systems, originally designed to deter crime, have been adapted to other missions, from traffic control to counterterrorism.

CCTV cameras have reached their fullest development in Great Britain, which "has more public CCTV cameras than any other post-industrialized nation," with an astonishing 1.5 million in the country as a whole.[31] Within the United Kingdom, no area is more filled with cameras than London, where the average resident is viewed approximately 300 times a day.[32] Within London, the center of the financial district at the heart of the City of London alone is monitored by over fifteen hundred cameras.[33] The diffusion of CCTV in Britain began as a crime-control measure in order to provide security in public spaces. The linkage with terrorism began after the Provisional IRA bombed economic targets in the City of London in the early 1990s. Over the past fifteen years, crime-control and counterterrorism missions for CCTV have been simultaneously separate and overlapping.[34]

Although London is by far the most camera-saturated city in the world, its example has been quickly taken up in the United States. Washington, D.C., had 19 city-owned cameras downtown and a total of 73 in operation as of fall 2007.[35] But by the fall of 2008, 5,600 cameras were in place with the expectation that they would eventually feed into the District's Homeland Security and Emergency Management Agency. Chicago's Office of Emergency Management and Communications oversees 200 cameras.[36] The most ambitious American system, however, is in New York City. A survey by the New York Civil Liberties Union found 4,468 cameras in Manhattan in 2005, covering nearly every block of such neighborhoods as the financial district, Tribeca, SoHo, and Greenwich Village.[37] This did not include large-scale CCTV plans for the subway system, unveiled after the July 2005 bombings on the London Underground. New York expects to install thousands of cameras and motion sensors. However, the network planned for the New York subway system has been significantly delayed by the need to replace aging fiber-optic cable.[38]

The addition of new capabilities has increased the reach of CCTV. The first of these was Automatic Number Plate Recording (ANPR). Beginning in the late 1990s in the United Kingdom, it became possible for cameras to read automobile license plate numbers with roughly 90 percent accuracy. These readings were automatically fed to a police database and matched numbers fed to the camera operator.[39] The next major development—already implemented in some U.S. airports—is facial recognition technology. In principle, such a system would produce a mathematical face-print, which would then be compared to face-prints in a database. Ideally, in such a system, "even in a large group, an individual cannot hide." However, the accuracy and reliability of existing systems is unsatisfactory.[40] This is quite apart from such issues as the accuracy and completeness of the database against which facial scans are compared and the intrusive character of camera placements.[41]

Not surprisingly, Great Britain has moved ahead of the United States in attempting to exploit the potential of visual identification technology. Beginning in the summer of 2008, British airports began to compare facial recognition technology against the data contained on the computer chips within biometric passports.[42] At about the same time, some CCTV systems were programmed to "recognize" behavior likely to precede the commission of a crime and alert operators, although whether such behavioral "cues" might be identified for terrorists is an open question.[43]

The presence of such cameras in virtually every urban space, from streets to elevators and corridors, means that short of being in a domicile or some other unambiguously secluded area, the individual is always at risk of being observed. The more sophisticated such systems become, the more information can be gleaned from the observations. If technology alone is the determinant, the day when the individual can be assured of anonymity in the city's crowds is swiftly coming to an end.

Unseen Danger and the Legal Process

During the proceedings at Salem in 1692, the judges hearing witch accusations quickly realized that there would be no convictions unless they loosened the rules of evidence. As a result, where before two eyewitnesses were needed to convict for a capital crime, it now became sufficient that there be two witnesses, even if each testified to a different offense. The court also agreed to accept so-called spectral evidence, testimony that a specter resembling a defendant had been seen, and since Satan was said to be incapable of taking on the appearance of an innocent person, the defendant, in league with Satan, must have put the specter in play.[44] Until cooler heads prevailed, this "dumbing down" of evidentiary standards appeared to be the only way in which the insidious but invisible powers might be held to account in court.

As Lee Loevinger has written, "the rules [of evidence] are basically principles of exclusion, the purpose and effect of which is to put various classes of evidence beyond the consideration of the fact-finding tribunal."[45] The Salem court chose to admit what would ordinarily have been excluded. The same is sometimes true where contemporary terrorism is concerned.

On November 13, 2003, President George W. Bush issued an executive order establishing military commissions to try detainees held at Guantanamo Bay. On the matter of evidence, the order held that it was to be admitted if, in the opinion of the presiding officer, it would "have probative value to a reasonable person."[46] This had the effect of granting virtually unfettered discretion to the presiding officer, virtually eliminating rules of evidence, and allowing material to be included or excluded by fiat. As of this writing, no proceedings have yet been held, since legal controversies concerning the detainees continue to work their way through the federal courts.

If one response to the unseen dangers of terrorism was to suspend conventional rules of evidence, the other was recourse to torture in order to secure confessions or statements revealing evidence. This occurred in two ways, one more visible than the other. The more visible way, as the result of the release of documents from the executive branch, took the form of a reconceptualization of torture. This was necessitated by the fact that the United States is a party to the Convention against Torture and Other Cruel, Inhuman or Degrading Treatment or Punishment. As a condition of ratification, torture was criminalized under U.S. law. However, in an influential memorandum of August 1, 2002, Jay S. Bybee of the Department of Justice's Office of Legal Counsel interpreted "torture" so narrowly that most acts that would intuitively strike a reasonable person as torture were effectively excluded.[47] This memorandum was sent to Alberto Gonzales, then White House counsel. Large sections of it reappear in a Defense Department document as well.

The less visible recourse to torture occurred in facilities operated by the CIA. At the time of this writing, documents concerning these facilities have not been released. However, in late 2007 it became known that the CIA practiced the simulated drowning technique known as "waterboarding," along with other methods under the euphemistic category of "enhanced interrogation techniques" (EIT). These events apparently occurred mainly in 2002 and 2003. EITs were first employed in August 2002.[48] Although videotapes of interrogations were destroyed in 2005, the practices employed were reported to a small number of members of Congress of both parties: Nancy Pelosi (D-Calif.), Jane Harmon (D-Calif.), Bob Graham (D-Fla.), John D. Rockefeller IV (D-W.Va.), Porter J. Goss (R-Fla.), and Pat Roberts (R-Kans.). None apparently opposed the activities at the time they were briefed.[49]

Evidence also began to emerge about the origin of the techniques utilized by interrogators. They had not been developed by accident. Instead, many of them came from psychologists who had been affiliated with the Armed Forces' Survival Evasion Resistance and Escape training program (SERE). They were acting in a significant consulting role both at Guantanamo and at CIA sites by 2002.[50] SERE was a byproduct of the Korean War, during which American military personnel captured by the Chinese made false public confessions of war crimes. In an effort to prepare service members for the harsh treatment they might receive from their captors, all of the service branches initiated programs that simulated prison conditions in Communist countries. The programs varied in length and severity. The longest ran three weeks and included waterboarding, although that technique was not used on American prisoners in the Korean War.[51] The other techniques were hooding, sleep deprivation, forced nudity, and exposure to extremes of temperature and sound, among others.

With the exception of waterboarding, the forms of coercion employed in the SERE exercises were a potpourri of techniques used not only by the Chinese but by the Soviet KGB and its predecessor, the NKVD. Although Chinese and Soviet systems were somewhat different, both systematically degraded inmates, deprived them of sleep, and forced them to remain for prolonged periods in fixed positions.[52] The object in both cases was to coerce confessions from prisoners. In view of the use to which the techniques were put at Guantanamo and the CIA "black sites," it is ironic that Soviet and Chinese interrogators knew that they were obtaining false confessions. During the Soviet purges in the 1930s, there was no clear way of distinguishing between the guilty and the innocent, since the criteria for establishing guilt kept expanding.[53] The situation with terrorism detainees is quite different, since both interrogators and those who direct them are certain that they possess actual information, if only it can be ferreted out. Failure to confess is thus seen not as a sign that the prisoner has no information to give but rather as an indication that he is uncooperative and must be subjected to yet more coercion. The information is, as it were, invisible, locked in the detainees head, and must be made manifest. Only that explains why one suspect was waterboarded an astonishing 183 times.[54] The presumed need for these kinds of interrogation techniques was reinforced by the fact that, at the time, CIA analysts knew very little about al-Qaeda. Consequently, they could only imagine what the detainees themselves knew, and as a result they were led "to speculate about what a detainee 'should know'," which led interrogators to deploy torture or near-torture "heavily based . . . on presumptions of what the individual might or should know."[55] Invisible information needed to be made visible by whatever means necessary.

The recourse of the United States to military tribunals and torture is not unique in the annals of terrorism. As Richard Bach Jensen has pointed out, the same techniques were utilized by Spain against anarchist terrorists at the turn of the twentieth century.[56] In that case, the principal consequence was to unintentionally transform those in custody into martyrs to the cause.

Transparency and Its Reversal

Many of the developments just described are linked in some way to the concept of transparent government. That implies that the workings of government—particularly the activities of executives and bureaucracies—should be publicly visible through the free availability of information. The acts of decision-makers should not be shrouded in secrecy; rather, their records should be available so that they might be held accountable.[57] The movement toward more government transparency gained speed in the 1990s, as dictatorships collapsed and new democracies sought to enhance their legitimacy by embracing freedom of information regimes. In 1986, only a dozen states had freedom of information statutes, but by 2004, the number had risen to fifty-nine.[58] In seeking to set boundaries to the concept of transparency, the 1996 Johannesburg Principles of National Security, Freedom of Expression and Access to Information cautioned that while information might be restricted on national security grounds, such restrictions were not legitimate "to protect a government from embarrassment or exposure of wrongdoing, or to conceal information about the functioning of its public institutions, or to entrench a particular ideology, or to suppress industrial unrest."[59]

Inevitably, however, the heady days of the 1990s, alive with promise about full disclosure, met with a certain amount of disillusionment. Officials anxious to manipulate open government rules in ways that preserved their autonomy, exchanges of information across borders, and the use of large databases all reduced the effective force of transparency reforms.[60] In addition, when the Bush administration took office in early 2001, it demonstrated an unusual concern for secrecy—in effect, reduced transparency—in the executive branch well before September 11th.[61] The effect of September 11th was to further extend the domain of secrecy in at least two ways: by removing from public view information, such as maps, that might be thought useful to terrorists and by creating systems of detention for suspected terrorists outside of both public view and routine judicial notice.

As traditional governmental transparency was shrinking, however, another form of transparency was expanding: individual transparency. It was now not government, but the individual, who was supposed to demonstrate transparency; most vividly at airport security checkpoints, where he or she needed to demonstrate identity, passenger status, and absence of the ability to harm. This is *reverse transparency*. Where once individuals, in their capacities as members of the electorate, demanded of the government that it show how decisions were reached; it was government that now demanded of individuals that they prove who they were and that they posed no threat. In different ways, other techniques described here had the same effect, whether CCTV cameras, sensing devices, or profiling techniques.

Reverse transparency has immediate implications for personal privacy. When government denies transparency to citizens—that is, when it is opaque—information it possesses becomes secrets. These secrets often fall into well-known categories, such as "internal agency memoranda, tax records, crime control, diplomacy, and national defense."[62] In democracies at least, governments generally are expected to provide some justification for withholding information from the public, since as a rule there is an obligation of accountability. When individuals are keepers of secrets, however, when they choose to be opaque, the situation is different. As Sisela Bok points out, at the individual level secrecy and privacy are not identical, but they may substantially overlap. "They do so most immediately in the private lives of individuals, where secrecy guards against unwanted access by others–against their coming too near, learning too much, observing too closely. Secrecy guards, then, the central aspects of identity, and if necessary, also plans and property."[63] The conundrum of reverse transparency is: Does it so diminish the individual's ability to maintain secrets that it breaches the domain of privacy?

A related aspect of reverse transparency is the increasing separation of what was once the equation of privacy and anonymity. Historically, one way of protecting one's privacy was by being in situations where one could not be readily identified. In large cities, with masses of people and large public spaces, one could move with the reasonable assurance that one was a stranger among strangers. This conveyed a sense of privacy even though the individual was not in the protected space of a home. This aspect of privacy largely eluded DHS secretary Michael Chertoff, for in defending the REAL ID program he asked,

> Is it somehow an invasion of privacy to require that when people present identification to come into a building or to get on an airplane that that identification be genuine and valid? Now I guess you could make the argument . . . but I guess you could make the argument that you should have the right to get on an airplane without telling anybody who you are, and that it's wrong for us to be able to check a watch list to see whether Mohammed Atta . . . is getting on an airplane. [W]hat is the privacy argument for making it easy to forge . . . identification, or to impersonate somebody, or to lie about who you really are?[64]

What Chertoff missed was the price in anonymity that must be paid for the added security achieved by measures such as those that accompany commercial air travel. The traditional assurance of anonymity is eroding, in part because of these kinds of security measures, but also because of broader technological and social changes.

Computers and their offspring, such as credit card purchasing and Google searches, have placed large amounts of information about individuals in the hands of others. In 2007, Donald Kerr, the director of the National Reconnaissance Office and a former assistant director of the FBI, argued that the penetration of this technology had effectively eradicated anonymity. "Protecting anonymity," he said, "isn't a fight that can be won." He urged in its place that privacy be redefined without the inclusion of anonymity and that its protection be assigned to "a system of laws, rules, and customs," presumably for the purpose of keeping the users of technology in check.[65] Whether one agrees with his views or not, the fact that a person in his position articulated them gives them something of the character of a self-fulfilling prophecy. Such a prophecy is reinforced by a generational shift in privacy thresholds, a point to which Kerr himself alluded.

The same technology that enables surveillance and databases also makes possible YouTube, Facebook, webcams, and the sundry other paraphernalia of contemporary narcissism. This narcissism, especially of the young, is evident in their desire to be connected to and to perform for others. The result has been twofold: First, there has been a generational shift, in which those who came of age before a computer-saturated society generally have a higher privacy threshold than those born after; and second, those born after as a result are less likely to see reverse transparency as an invasion of privacy, since they themselves already individually practice reverse transparency in their relations with others.

Privacy may be achieved in two ways: One is through positive measures, such as physical barriers to intrusion by others (doors, curtains, etc.), as well as forbearances on others' parts—in effect, their promise not to act in intrusive ways. This is in line with the classic 1890 formulation by Samuel D. Warren and Louis D. Brandeis that privacy is the "right of the individual to be let alone."[66] Although they had interference by newspapers in mind, the same notion might be applied to government as well. The other way to achieve privacy is through inefficiency. This may appear initially perverse, but if one reflects, it becomes clear that the anonymity enjoyed historically by city-dwellers as opposed to, say, inhabitants of a small village, was due to the fact that few if any people knew where others were or what they were doing at any particular time. They could, in effect, get lost. If there was information about their whereabouts, it was so scattered as to be useless. The fact that information about one's activities and location were difficult if not impossible to obtain in large urban areas conferred on the individual an effective invisibility, whereas the village-dweller, who was known to all the other inhabitants, could be continually observed by them.

The historic urban invisibility was, of course, a variant of crowd invisibility. It was a function of large numbers of people living in densely populated cities, moving rapidly in the conduct of multiple activities related to work, family life, leisure, and so forth, all taking place in different locations. This form of invisibility was also a form of privacy, for though an individual might be seen, little could be known of him or her at any given time or outside of some specific, limited encounter, after which he or she moved off to something quite different. We might see many people but would know little about them.

Reverse transparency is particularly corrosive of this form of privacy. It impinges on the individual in precisely those settings where anonymity was in the past most likely: public spaces. These are now apt to be monitored by CCTV and/or subject to security checkpoints. In addition, the separate encounters that might make up an individual's day and would in the past be known to nobody but him- or herself can now be put together through databases and their analysis by data-mining. Credit card transactions, telecommunications records, and similar pieces of information can be brought together with a speed and completeness unthinkable in earlier periods. Inefficiency—the inability to put disparate pieces of information together quickly—no longer protects personal privacy. It may be argued, of course, that this same inefficiency also benefited lawbreakers, who could commit crimes in different jurisdictions in the knowledge that authorities in different places might never be able to connect the crimes and trace them to a single perpetrator. However, the implication for privacy is far-reaching and extends beyond simply what becomes known about the individual, for it breaks down the barrier between the private realm and the public realm, a division understood in the Western world since the end of the seventeenth century.[67]

Intrusive technologies vary considerably in the degree to which they are accepted by the public. Video surveillance seems to be broadly accepted, not only in the United Kingdom, where it first reached saturation levels in urban areas, but more recently in the United States, where its growth has been exponential. A Harris poll revealed that 63 percent of Americans surveyed approving CCTV monitoring in September 2001—hardly a surprising finding. However, the level rose to 70 percent in July 2006, by which time the number of cameras was much greater. A CBS News poll found that one-third of respondents to a 2002 survey considered such surveillance to be an infringement of their privacy. However, when in 2007 the "threat of terrorism" was added to the question, the number criticizing CCTV dropped to 23 percent.[68] This ready acquiescence in ubiquitous observation perfectly tracks a media-saturated culture of constant self-presentation.

Public views about technology regarding the human body elicit quite different reactions. Fingerprint scans seem to gain high levels of public support, but facial scans are viewed as significantly "less valuable."[69] What remains unclear is the reason for the discrepancy: Is it because the public knows more about fingerprints than it does about facial recognition technology? Is it because facial recognition technology is considered less reliable? Or is it because facial recognition technology is deemed to somehow violate bodily integrity in a way that fingerprints do not?

Reverse transparency has appeared partly as a result of technological factors but has been greatly accelerated by the pressures of an environment dominated by fear of unseen terrorists. It is difficult to know how the concept of privacy might have developed had terrorism never been an issue of public policy. But now that it is an issue, it exerts a distorting effect, further reducing the individual's sphere of unobserved and untrammeled autonomy at precisely the time when that sphere is already contracting.

four

HURRICANE KATRINA, UNSEEN DANGERS, AND THE ALL-HAZARDS POLICY

It may seem perverse to connect the flooding of New Orleans after Hurricane Katrina in 2005 with unseen dangers. The hurricane was all too visible, shown on millions of television sets in the garish colors of weather radar while it was well out to sea. The events in New Orleans itself seem remote from the domain of unseen dangers. The proximate cause of the devastation was less the hurricane itself than the failure of the levees that protected those portions of the city below sea level. The human suffering came to be seen as a consequence less of the levee breaks than of the ineptitude of those charged with aiding victims. Only later did it become clear that in addition to the failures of rescuers, the levees themselves broke because they had been improperly designed and constructed. Had they been correctly built, they would easily have withstood Katrina. Whether one focuses upon the failings of rescuers or engineers, however, the New Orleans calamity looks less like a natural and more like an anthropogenic disaster, and an unintentional one at that. Hence it would seem to fall clearly outside the confines of this book. However, if we look at the failures of those charged with aiding actual and potential victims and track those failures back through national policy decisions made years before Katrina, it turns out that what happened in New Orleans flowed from assumptions about unseen dangers.

Those assumptions were woven into the fabric of New Orleans decision-making in complex ways, easily overlooked in a superficial narrative of events. Such a narrative might more easily emphasize the role of Michael

Brown, then director of the Federal Emergency Management Agency (FEMA). Without wishing to exculpate Brown, whose failures were numerous, there is merit to his claim that he was made a scapegoat.[1] For the failures were less individual failures than they were systemic failures. To grasp the manner in which systemic failures grew out of earlier policy choices, we must move backward through the following stages: from the role of Secretary of Homeland Security Michael Chertoff, to the National Response Plan (NRP) put in place by his predecessor, to the presidential directive that called the National Response Plan into being, and, finally, to the "all-hazards" policy to which the presidential directive sought to give effect.

The Role of Secretary Chertoff and the National Response Plan

We know a good deal about Secretary of Homeland Security Michael Chertoff's actions during the period of Hurricane Katrina, not only because of subsequent Senate and House hearings but because transcripts are available of video conferences held on the critical days of August 28 and 29, 2005. These conferences linked all relevant federal, state, and local officials. The hurricane passed into the Gulf of Mexico on the 26th. By the 27th, Mayor Ray Nagin had declared a state of emergency in New Orleans and issued a voluntary evacuation order. The order became mandatory the following day. By that time, lines had begun to form at the Superdome where there were already 10,000 people inside. The levees broke on the 29th, the day Katrina made landfall, although the hurricane came ashore east of the city. By August 30th, much of New Orleans was under water, and there was widespread looting. Any regular CNN viewer would have had a clearer picture of developments on the ground than someone listening to the reports of the conferees. With the exception of the weather briefing given by Max Mayfield, then director of the National Hurricane Center, the conferences consisted largely of descriptions of developments within the reporting bureaucracies, not all of them accurate. The conferences were dominated by Michael Brown of FEMA. In both video conferences, Secretary Chertoff appeared only briefly, near the end, when he delivered perfunctory remarks, in which he thanked the participants and asked whether there was anything further that he could do.[2] These comments might be dismissed as the platitudes expected of a senior official speaking to line officers were it not for the matter of the NRP.

The National Response Plan was a creation of Chertoff's predecessor as secretary, Tom Ridge, issued in December 2004. Although the drafters envisioned phased implementation over periods of 60–120 days—that is, extending into the spring of 2005—implementation could be accelerated at the discretion of the DHS secretary. The declared purpose of the plan was to "[establish] a single, comprehensive framework for the management of domestic incidents."[3] Secretary Ridge described its approach as "unique and far reaching," in that it sought to bring together all federal resources that "for the first time, eliminates critical seams and ties together a complete spectrum of incident management activities to include the prevention of, preparation for, response to, and recovery from terrorism, major natural disasters, and other major emergencies."[4] To that end, the NRP included a letter of agreement signed by fifteen cabinet secretaries, numerous other high administration officials, and executives of major voluntary organizations.[5]

The voluminous plan, which runs over two hundred pages, has the character of what Lee Clarke calls a "fantasy document." That is, we can see that in retrospect its primary function was to assert that an organization was in control of a dangerous situation.[6] The picture it paints is of a federal government whose manifold agencies are seamlessly coordinated and a country whose federal system permits each level of government to perform its appointed functions, while each meshes effortlessly with the others according to agreed-upon protocols.

Insofar as Hurricane Katrina is concerned, the nub of the National Response Plan lay less in its basic text than in an appendix, the Catastrophic Incident Annex. The purpose of the Catastrophic Incident Annex was to provide for "an accelerated, proactive national response to a catastrophic incident."[7] A catastrophic incident was defined as causing "extraordinary levels of mass casualties, damage, or disruption severely affecting the population, infrastructure, environment, economy, national morale, and/or government functions." It "could" result in "national impacts" over a "prolonged period of time," and the ability to respond to the incident would "almost immediately" be beyond the resources available to the locality in which the incident occurred, so that organizations based in states and cities could not handle it. By significantly disrupting government operations and emergency services, such incidents could threaten national security. By definition, the annex's "catastrophic incidents" become, in the language of the National Response Plan, "Incidents of National Significance," for which accelerated federal action is required.[8]

The purpose of the Catastrophic Incident Annex was to provide a means for short-circuiting the regular procedures for supplying federal assistance, in order to allow those resources to flow to impacted areas more rapidly. As the annex somewhat delicately puts it, "This may require mobilizing and deploying assets before they are requested via normal NRP proto-cols."[9] The issue of requested aid became a contested matter later, when the Senate Committee on Homeland Security and Governmental Affairs concluded that one of the factors in the laggard federal response was the failure of Louisiana governor Kathleen Blanco to correctly state her needs to Washington.[10] Under the Catastrophic Incident Annex, such aid is to be provided on an expedited basis, through notification of and coordina-tion with states if possible, but without such coordination if it would cause delay. Not only does the secretary of homeland security have the power to declare an Incident of National Significance and marshal and deploy re-sources without waiting for a state's requests, he may do so even before the president has issued a disaster declaration.[11] In all events covered by the National Response Plan, including those considered catastrophic, the prin-cipal coordinating responsibilities fall to the principal federal official (PFO), someone so designated by the secretary of homeland security to represent him, integrate the federal government's role with the activities of states and localities, mediate conflicts among agencies, manage the flow of informa-tion to the public, and in general take on comprehensive oversight.[12]

In fact, Secretary Chertoff did activate the Catastrophic Incident Annex and appoint a principal federal official, but he did so in such a peculiar manner as to drain these provisions of any usefulness. Both came at aston-ishingly late points in the trajectory of the New Orleans disaster. Both the designation of the event as an Incident of National Significance and the designation of Michael Brown of FEMA as the PFO took place on the same day, Tuesday, August 30, by which time most of New Orleans was under water, 12,000 people were in the Superdome, and 3,800 National Guard troops were on active duty in Louisiana. When Secretary Chertoff appeared before the House Select Committee on Hurricane Katrina Preparation and Response on October 19, 2005, he sought to explain the timing of the deci-sions in response to questions from Representative Bob Shuster.[13] He was asked why he had not named a PFO earlier, perhaps two or three days be-fore the storm hit. He dismissed the designation as a mere technicality, that

Brown was already "the battlefield commander," although in fact Brown had not gone down to Louisiana until August 28, by which time the situation was already dire. Chertoff clearly saw the PFO title as simply formalizing a role Brown was occupying de facto, something that conferred no new powers or responsibilities.[14]

Secretary Chertoff had somewhat more difficulty responding to questions about his late designation of an Incident of National Significance, although in the end his response was much the same: the designation was merely a technicality. He argued that calling an Incident on August 30 had no legal importance, given that President Bush had declared a state of emergency the preceding Saturday, August 27; and indeed by then it probably made no difference. Chertoff correctly pointed out that "the main thing that an Incident does is that if there had not been an emergency or a disaster declaration, there would have been some legal limit on our ability to reach out and bring aid into the area."[15] But surely this is to beg the question. The whole point of the Catastrophic Incident Annex was to provide a mechanism to engage events that moved so quickly one could not wait for the usual machinery of presidential declarations or, for that matter, state requests. Its purpose was to expedite federal actions, not to ratify actions already taken. The time for the secretary to have made designations under the annex would have been, at the latest, August 26, the day Max Mayfield made his famous call to Mayor Nagin warning that Katrina might well be a storm with enormous destructive force. While one might explain Secretary Chertoff's recourse to legalism in terms of his judicial background, surely other factors must have been in play. Millions of Americans could see what was happening on the streets of New Orleans, yet in the bitterest of ironies, those centrally charged with alleviating the suffering seemed paralyzed even though they had the means to act. In order to gain some sense of why individuals of good will might have been so strangely obtuse, we must move yet another step backward, to the presidential decisions that set the National Response Plan in motion.

Homeland Security Presidential Directives and the "All-Hazards" Policy

The National Response Plan originated from a presidential order, Homeland Security Presidential Directive 5 (HSPD-5), issued February 28, 2003. One of its provisions directed the secretary of homeland security to "develop, submit for review to the Homeland Security Council, and administer a National Response Plan." The plan was to be unclassified, with the possible exception of classified annexes and was to draw together the federal government's multiple efforts into a "domestic prevention, preparedness, response and recovery" plan. Most important for our purposes, that plan was to be "all-discipline, all-hazards."[16] The "all-discipline and all-hazards" mantra was repeated in Secretary Ridge's preface to the plan itself.[17] HSPD-5 was the first homeland security presidential directive in which "all-hazards" appeared. However, the term was not explicitly defined. The closest HSPD-5 came to offering an implied definition was in its statement that the policy of "the United State Government [is to] establish a single, comprehensive approach to domestic incident management" that would cover "terrorist attacks, major disasters, and other emergencies."[18] A more formal definition appeared several months later when the president issued Homeland Security Presidential Directive 8 (HSPD-8) on December 17, which stated that "the term 'all-hazards preparedness' refers to preparedness for domestic terrorist attacks, major disaster, and other emergencies."[19] However, neither document indicated what those "other emergencies" might be. They could involve any of a number of "technological disasters," such as nuclear reactor accidents, hazardous materials spills, and massive power outages.

The logic supporting an "all-hazards" approach seemed clear. Regardless of an incident's cause, first-responders were likely to come from the impacted locality or nearby areas. Often they were the same organizations, regardless of whether the incident was a natural disaster, industrial accident, or terrorist attack. Those involved were likely to be law enforcement agencies, fire departments, rescue squads, hospitals and their emergency departments, hazardous materials teams, and the like. From victims' perspectives, causes might not matter much. What mattered were the deaths, injuries, psychological trauma, and disruption of daily life. Disaster planners also argued that producing a generic plan was a way of achieving economy by recognizing that actions such as warning and evacuation might be needed in many different kinds of emergencies and that recognizing such commonalities was a way of avoiding constant and unnecessary reinventions.[20] This kind of plan was the more necessary in a political system as complex as that of the United States, with its layer cake of overlapping federal, state, county, and municipal jurisdictions. Indeed, one of the goals of the National Response Plan was to make coordination "seamless" among organizations that not only performed different but related functions but also were affiliated with different units of government.

The United States was not the only country moving in this direction. A few years before, in 2002, Sweden established the Swedish Emergency Management Agency (SEMA) in order to coordinate crisis management across all levels of government and across crises ranging from war and terrorism to epidemics and infrastructure disruptions.[21] Although the SEMA rhetoric did not utilize the term "all-hazards," in every other respect the agency appeared to anticipate HSPD-5 and the National Response Plan. However, examined more closely, the Swedish case exhibits features that set it apart. First, Sweden is much smaller, more politically centralized, with a far more concentrated population. Thus from a practical standpoint, the task of coordinating local and national resources, for example, is far less daunting. Second, and more significant, although SEMA was established in 2002, it was not a response to the September 11th attacks. Rather, the discussions that led up to it had begun long before 9/11. SEMA was in fact a response not to terrorism but to the end of the Cold War, which left Sweden's large civil defense organization without a clear mission and its armed forces with no likelihood of a combat role in the foreseeable future. Hence Sweden's adoption of what in fact was an all-hazards approach occurred within the context of a reconceptualization of national security.[22] This contextual factor stands in sharp contrast to the circumstances in which the all-hazards approach came to form the basis of the U.S. National Response Plan.

All-hazards emergency planning in the United States long predated HSPD-5. It was, in fact, a product of the Cold War, when it was referred to as "dual-use" or, occasionally, as "full spectrum preparedness." The Cold War context was dominated by the fear of nuclear attack, and that, in turn, raised issues of civil defense. The available modalities of civil defense in a nuclear age--primarily fallout shelters and, especially, mass evacuation-- were favored by the federal government but received little support from states and localities. In order to provide incentives for states and localities, the Defense Civil Preparedness Agency and its successor, FEMA, repackaged civil defense measures as generic techniques that could be applied to a wide range of natural disasters, such as earthquakes and tornadoes. On this basis, resources began to flow to local agencies under the "dual-use" rubric, eventually to be replaced by the now-familiar "all-hazards" one.[23]

Secretary Chertoff was bound by the all-hazards National Response Plan, as applicable to hurricane and flood, as to terrorist attack or to industrial accident. It contained, as we have seen, a Catastrophic Incident Annex that gave the secretary the authority to move more rapidly than either the president or state authorities should circumstances require it. The failure in New Orleans was not merely the failure of a few people, whether of Michael Brown or Michael Chertoff. Nor was it simply the failure of the National Response Plan, tested for the first time in a major disaster situation. Beyond those failures, New Orleans was a failure of the all-hazards policy, first enunciated in HSPD-5. Yet one must ask why. For there is no obvious answer. This was not an exotic disaster, nor was it unexpected. Indeed, there were two to three days warning, although forecasters were slightly off in estimating the hurricane's track.

When all-hazards emergency planning was introduced in the 1970s as a way of drawing states and localities into civil defense programs, so-called dual-use procedures were said to apply to both natural calamities and nuclear war. However, in the one case--natural calamities--there was ample practical experience, while in the case of the other--nuclear war--one could only speculate. The situation with regard to all-hazards planning as exemplified by HSPD-5 and the National Response Plan was quite different. Here, too, there were said to be two types of catastrophes--the commonplace ones, such as natural disasters and industrial accidents--and terrorism. However, in the case of terrorism, there had, of course, already been a mass-casualty attack on American soil only a few years earlier. There was an experiential basis, consisting of a single, albeit an exceptionally, powerful case. The issue was therefore not one of seducing reluctant local governments but of mobilizing organizations anxious to assume a meaningful role. Thus the "second coming" of all-hazards planning in 2001 differed from its introduction three decades earlier and has to its terrorism component a particularly powerful thrust.

The problem lay in a fundamental contradiction between, the Department of Homeland Security's commitment to an all-hazards approach and the department's own mission. On the one hand, it could be said that the department's mission was to make sure that the National Response Plan could be implemented. But of course that would only be a partially correct statement, for, on the other hand, the DHS's mission statement was quite clear: "We will lead the unified national effort to secure America. We will prevent and deter terrorist attacks and protect against and defend and respond to threats and hazards to the nation. We will ensure safe and secure borders, welcome lawful immigrants and visitors, and promote the free flow of commerce."[24] The thrust of that statement is protection against terrorist attack. The emphasis is on security, especially of borders, and defense. The all-hazards approach appears in only the most indirect and allusive way, through the ambiguous phrase "threats and hazards to the nation," which might be read as including events such as Hurricane Katrina or might be read as applying solely to threats such as al-Qaeda. The statement suggests, therefore, that whatever might have been promised in the National Response Plan, the DHS was caught in a double-bind, committed to acting against a range of hazards but really committed to giving priority to only one—terrorist attack. And that double-bind had existed even before the department had been established, so that we must move back yet another step, to the National Strategy for Homeland Security issued before the DHS came into existence.

The National Strategy for Homeland Security

On July 16, 2002, President George W. Bush issued the National Strategy for Homeland Security, a seventy-one-page document that, according to the president's accompanying letter, had been eight months in preparation.[25] The National Strategy was a product of the Office of Homeland Security, lodged in the White House and headed by Tom Ridge. The Department of Homeland Security, which Ridge would eventually lead, was then stuck in Congress. The president would sign the legislation in November 2002. The National Strategy document was not revised until 2007, two years after Hurricane Katrina.

The original National Strategy for Homeland Security, which laid out national policy at the time the DHS was established and at the time Katrina struck, was not an all-hazards document. Drafted in the immediate aftermath of the 9/11 attacks, it was narrowly focused on protecting the United States against terrorism: "The purpose of the *Strategy* is to mobilize and organize our Nation to secure the U.S. homeland from terrorist attacks."[26] The objectives of homeland security were to prevent attacks, reduce vulnerability to attacks, minimize damage if attacks occurred, and speed recovery.[27] To the extent that it was concerned at all with catastrophic incidents other than terrorist attacks, it was for incidental reasons.

To the drafters of the National Strategy, such events as natural disasters and industrial accidents only had relevance for one of two reasons: Either capabilities created for homeland security were dual-use in the sense that they might be applied to other catastrophic incidents, or existing resources created to deal with catastrophic incidents might be useful in achieving the objectives of homeland security. Thus, the National Strategy suggested: "We will build . . . a national incident management system that is better able to manage not just terrorism but other hazards such as natural disasters and industrial accidents."[28] In that case, homeland security measures might have an added value in nonterrorist situations. On the other hand, they pointed out that emergency response to both natural disasters and terrorist incidents involve "the same basic elements," arguing against separate first-responder organizations for each. Better "to create a fully integrated national emergency response system that is adaptable enough to deal with any terrorist attack, no matter how unlikely or catastrophic, as well as all manner of natural disasters."[29] Yet the emphasis is always on homeland security against terrorism as the first priority. If there is a payoff for other kinds of emergency response, so much the better. But this is not a holistic, all-hazards approach.

Beyond its single-minded focus on terrorism to the exclusion of other crisis situations, the National Strategy document concentrated on potential attacks far different from those that had occurred on September 11th, when nineteen primitively armed individuals had successfully commandeered four aircraft with catastrophic results. The National Strategy spent far more time discussing exotic weaponry such as chemical, biological, and nuclear devices than it did the conventional explosives terrorists in fact used in incidents that followed 9/11, for example, in Madrid and London. Instead, the authors seemed obsessed with weapons of mass destruction to the virtual exclusion of other possibilities. This fear was amplified by the knowledge that, especially in the case of biological and chemical weapons, the agents were likely to be unseen, which would mean that the federal government must "development sensitive and highly selective systems that detect the release of biological or chemical agents."[30] Not only were the weapons themselves unseen; so were those that employed them: "Our enemies seek to remain invisible, lurking in the shadows . . . often we will not know who our enemy is by name until after they have attempted to attack us."[31] Unlike Katrina, whose existence might be verified simply by looking out a window, this was a destructive force whose insidiousness was magnified by its insubstantiality.

This, then, was the orthodoxy in place when the Department of Homeland Security came into being, and it remained in place until a new document superseded the 2002 version. It remained the national strategy even as HSPD-5 promulgated an all-hazards approach and as the National Response Plan implemented the generalizations in HSPD-5. This, then, was the origin of the double-bind in which the DHS found itself, for it was charged with executing two quite dissimilar mandates. One gave primacy to protection from terrorist attacks; the other called upon the department to give equal attention to a broad range of harms, natural and anthropogenic, intentional and accidental. We may say that in the Katrina case, the rhetoric was all-hazards, but the reality was homeland security.

The National Strategy Revisited

It was probably inevitable, in both bureaucratic and political terms, that the National Strategy for Homeland Security in the form just described would be one of Katrina's more obscure casualties. A new version of the document emerged from the Homeland Security Council in October 2007. In an accompanying letter, a chastened president announced, "We have applied the lessons of Katrina to this *Strategy* to make sure that America is safer, stronger, and better prepared."[32] He might also have observed (although he did not) that, unlike its predecessor, the 2007 iteration finally brought homeland security strategy into at least rhetorical conformity with the all-hazards policy of HSPD-5. The drafters did so somewhat reluctantly, however, conceding that "while we must continue to focus on the persistent and evolving terrorist threat, we also must address the full range of potential catastrophic events, including man-made and natural disasters."[33]

Interestingly, the inclusion of disasters was not justified in typical all-hazards terms, that is, that all crises have certain common features or that all engage the efforts of similar response organizations. Instead, the new National Strategy rationalized the inclusion of natural and anthropogenic disasters in terms of their relevance to the fight against terrorism. The argument made was that severe disasters might create "possible cascading effects" that would expose societal vulnerabilities that terrorists might exploit. Such calamities might also reduce the confidence citizens had in their government—seemingly a clear reflection of the Katrina experience—and thereby make the country somehow more vulnerable. The conclusion was that "effective preparation for catastrophic natural disasters and man-made disasters, while not homeland security per se, can nevertheless, increase the security of the Homeland."[34] Although the document went on to invoke the mantra of "the all-hazards approach to homeland security,"[35] one could not help but feel that the drafters hearts were not really in it. The schizoid approach so evident in New Orleans in 2005 thus survived in the tangled language of 2007. Policy was all-hazards policy, with natural disasters to be given treatment equivalent to terrorist attacks. And yet that was not really so, for no matter what presidential policy had established, it was understood that not all crises were really equal.

A preeminent position was still to be given to the terrorist threat, and once that happened, invisible threats were bound to trump visible ones. For it was in the nature of fear of terrorism that that danger lay in the unseen— in outwardly innocuous individuals with inwardly malevolent designs, in sleeper cells awaiting the signal to activate, in high-tech weapons whose power to harm lay in invisible toxins, pathogens, and radiation. It was clear, even six years after 9/11, that at least at the governmental level, these fears were unabated. In 2005, they effectively subverted the all-hazards mandate during Hurricane Katrina, and there is no reason to think they will not do so in the future.

After the Flood

Given the public scandal occasioned by FEMA's conduct during and immediately after Hurricane Katrina, it was perhaps inevitable that the 2002 National Response Plan would be overhauled. A new model was unveiled in January 2008. Unlike the terrorism strategy, the newly christened National Response Framework (NRF) was fully consistent with the all-hazards mandate of Homeland Security Presidential Directive 5. The plan's drafters sought to describe "specific authorities and best practices for managing incidents that range from the serious but purely local, to large-scale terrorist attacks or catastrophic natural disasters." The plan was to be "a guide to how the Nation conducts all-hazards response."[36]

The post-Katrina changes were for the most part fairly modest. Past failures were at least tacitly acknowledged: "Nine months after Katrina's landfall, a notice of change to the NRP was released, incorporating preliminary lessons learned from the 2005 hurricane season."[37] The FEMA administrator was given enhanced status, at least rhetorically, to the extent that he or she is now designated as "the principal advisor to the President, the Secretary, and the Homeland Security Council on all matters regarding emergency management."[38] But this scarcely returns FEMA's head to the cabinet status enjoyed before the agency's immersion in the DHS. The NRF also contains an unambiguous statement that the federal government could act without either a presidential declaration of emergency or a state request for assistance, although precisely the same point could be found, perhaps not quite as directly stated, in the previous version.[39] As before, there was provision for appointment of a PFO to coordinate the response, but perhaps with an eye on the floundering Michael Brown, the PFO was now described as someone with "proven management experience and strong leadership capabilities."[40]

In one respect, the National Response Plan was not changed. The Incident Annexes, including the crucial Catastrophic Incident Annex that had been prepared in 2002, remained in effect.[41] And it was, of course, in part the failure to correctly apply the Catastrophic Incident Annex that led to the problems in New Orleans.

In the end, then, we have document upon document, in a rising stack of paper. Since as of this writing no additional test of national emergency management has taken place since the 2005 hurricane season, the significance of this sequence of plans cannot be determined. However, there seems no reason to think that the tension between the conflicting demands of terrorism response and disaster response is any less now than it was in previous years. The stack of paper, the seemingly unending sequence of plans, continues the illusion of control, notwithstanding the events in New Orleans.

The illusion of control is intimately related to the Department of Homeland Security's commitment to maintaining the absolute integrity of borders and with it a commitment to keeping invisible evil at bay. In this conception, the border functions less as a tripwire for defensive measures--its traditional function--than as a dividing line between realms of purity and impurity, and it is to that fundamental distinction that we now turn.

five

THE IMAGERY OF THE LANDSCAPE OF FEAR

The landscape of fear is an inner mental landscape, constructed of sense perceptions, memories, and the images our culture provides.[1] As a result, the interpretation we give to new data can be skewed by the imagery and predispositions we already possess. For example, on October 31, 1938, *The War of the Worlds* radio broadcast terrified millions. It was supremely a work of the imagination, the channeling of one Wells—the author, H. G.— by another Welles—the director and actor, Orson. The bizarre aspect of the phenomenon was that many who believed that the broadcast dealt with an actual event did not believe that it was about an invasion from Mars. Instead, over a quarter of those frightened by Welles's Mercury Theatre production and subsequently surveyed believed that it was really a report of an invasion by a foreign power, Germany or perhaps Japan.[2] Why either country would have disguised itself as extraterrestrials was secondary to the general anxiety that accompanied the war scare that gripped the world in the fall of 1938.

This strange episode suggests that when we think about terror, our minds are no more a blank slate than when we think about any other subject. We situate novel events within the mental frameworks already at our disposal. Not surprisingly, therefore, a film version of the H. G. Wells novel premiered three and a half years after the September 11th attacks. As its director, Stephen Spielberg, noted: "Every iteration of *War of the Worlds* has occurred in times of uncertainty. We live under a veil of fear that we didn't live under before 9/11."[3] In Orson Welles's adaptation, the Martians landed not in London, as H. G. Wells had it, but in New Jersey, from which they marched on and destroyed New York City. When Spielberg made his film in 2005, however, he did not directly show the destruction of New York.[4] That was presumably part of what he meant by the "veil of fear."

It would be reassuring to think that judgments made under stressful circumstances are simply the result of reasoned analysis. But that is not necessarily the case. Instead, reasoned analysis is often intertwined with the exercise of imagination. The landscape of fear is consequently constructed both from the products of reasoned analysis and from the exercise of imagination, although we are often not fully conscious of the results of the latter. Those involved in the policy domain, either as analysts or as decision-makers, cannot acknowledge, even to themselves, that their picture of the world is at least partially influenced by imaginative motifs.

Those motifs fall into three broad categories. The first, which I call the *subcultural*, takes the form of imagination already present in well-defined subcultures and applies it to cases of terrorism. These applications are rarely found outside the milieus in which they originated, but when they do come to the attention of outsiders, they often trigger intense opposition. This is usually due to the fact that those outside the subculture where the construct originated have no appreciation of the context that gave it meaning and thus tend to misinterpret it. The second category is what I refer to as the *diffusionist*. It consists of motifs that may have originated in relatively insular subcultures but have over time begun to seep into, and been accepted by, the larger society. While such themes and ideas may not colonize elite policymaking circles, they can achieve substantial currency in the general population, and to the extent that policymakers are embedded in that population, they may yet exercise an indirect influence. Finally, there are those motifs I term the *ambient*, in that they are imaginative products that are neither limited to small coteries nor imported from them into the cultural "mainstream." Rather, they take the form of ideas already widely known in the dominant culture but that have not been explicitly tied to actual cases of terrorism. Indeed, they may have been so profoundly absorbed that their influence lies below the threshold of conscious awareness. They maintain a pervasive and, as it were, free-floating existence, whether in forms of high cultural, intellectual, and artistic endeavor, or in popular culture and entertainment. Their application to terrorism is an unintended result of their having been internalized by a broad cross-section of the population, including policymakers and (sometimes) the terrorists themselves.

The Subcultural Imagination

The following three cases are all instances of the subcultural imagination, and are all responses to the September 11th attacks. They can be quickly identified, because in each case the imaginative structure chosen was quickly rejected as inappropriate by the general public. The first two come from Protestant evangelicalism, where pastors with strong end-time beliefs sought to fit the events into their theological frameworks. John Hagee, a prominent San Antonio evangelist who was later briefly associated with John McCain's 2008 presidential campaign, tells us that as he watched the television coverage of the World Trade Center attacks, he knew immediately what they meant: "Without question, I recognized that the Third World War had begun and that it would escalate from this day until the Battle of Armageddon."[5] He had quickly inserted 9/11 into the theological framework of dispensational premillennialism with its traditional commitment to identifying the "signs of the times," that is, the portents that signal the approach of the final days preceding the Second Coming. Although this mode of thinking has tens of millions of adherents in the United States who consider it a valid way of judging important international events, Hagee's claim for the apocalyptic significance of the attacks was not widely shared, even by conservative evangelicals. Hagee's attempt to fold the attacks into an apocalyptic framework seems to have failed largely because even committed millenarians shrank from accepting the World Trade Center and Pentagon attacks as a necessary part of God's plan, an obstacle even more evident in the next case.

The second example is a conversation between Pat Robertson and Jerry Falwell on Robertson's television program, *The 700 Club*, two days after the attacks. Robertson suggested that "it's happening [because] God Almighty is lifting his protection from us." Falwell agreed: "What we saw of Tuesday, as terrible as it is, could be miniscule, if in fact . . . God continues to lift the curtain and allow the enemies of America to give us probably what we deserve." He spelled the reasons out in detail: removing religion from schools, abortion, feminism, and homosexuality, among other sins.[6] Robertson and Falwell were utilizing what had once been a staple of American Protestantism, the jeremiad, a rhetorical exercise in which the speaker, like the prophet Jeremiah, links communal suffering to communal sins, where disasters become God's chastening instruments. The jeremiad flourished from the days of the Puritans well into the twentieth century. Indeed, during the early days of the Cold War, evangelists declared that the sinfulness of New York made it an obvious target for a Soviet nuclear attack.[7] Yet both Robertson and Falwell became targets of intense public hostility, even from their own followers, who accused them of "blaming the victims." Clearly, the reality of the 9/11 attacks made the jeremiad seem tasteless even to believers.

The third example is secular, and came from two eminent European creative figures, the German avant-garde composer Karlheinz Stockhausen and the British "bad boy" artist Damien Hirst. Media accounts of a press conference Stockhausen gave in Hamburg on September 16, 2001, reported that he had called the New York attacks "the biggest work of art," a phrase for which he would apologize many times in subsequent days. The phrase, however, was embedded in a dialogue in which Stockhausen stated that the person responsible for the work was in fact Lucifer, a point which went unmentioned in the press dispatches.[8] Hirst spoke almost exactly a year later, on the first anniversary of the attacks. He told a BBC interviewer that the World Trade Center attack was "kind of like an artwork in its own right. It was wicked, but it was devised in this way for this kind of impact. It was devised visually." He quickly issued a profuse apology.[9]

Both Stockhausen and Hirst were, in somewhat different ways, reflecting on what art historians have termed the "apocalyptic sublime," which combines arresting visual images with images of destruction capable of arousing feelings of terror. For the most part, these images have been associated with images from nature, whose forces evoke awe but dwarf and sometimes threaten human beings, for example, during earthquakes or volcanic eruptions. However, the apocalyptic sublime could also include reference to non-natural calamities, such as the sacking of Rome or the world destruction described in the Book of Revelation.[10] The sublime as a subject of aesthetic theorizing was a product of the eighteenth and nineteenth centuries and by 2001 was largely a concern of specialists in the arts, art history, and aesthetic theory.

However, one secular subculture generated responses to terrorism that were vigorously pursued within the subculture yet hardly known outside it. This was the world of conspiracy theorists, those who see the world under the aspect of plots, for whom nothing is as it seems, nothing happens by accident, and everything is connected. Their aim is to identify and describe the secret organization they are convinced is bent on global domination. Those associated with such theorists, who can legitimately be termed professional conspiracy theorists—figures such as David Icke in Britain and Milton William Cooper in the United States—professed no surprise at the September 11th attacks. They regarded the official explanation for the attacks as camouflage concealing the machinations of the "New World Order," the malevolent cabal whose plans for world conquest have long been a central feature of contemporary conspiracy thinking.[11]

None of these subcultural examples "traveled" well outside the subcultures that gave rise to them. The two religious cases did not secure much support even among coreligionists, who might have been expected to follow preachers' arguments better than outsiders. The implications seem clear, that where a mass-casualty event traumatizes an entire society, the separate understandings of the event that develop within subcultures—both religious and secular—rarely become accepted outside and may well be rejected inside, particularly if they appear to cast blame upon or denigrate the victims.

The Diffusionist Imagination

The diffusionist, the second type of imaginative exercise, is best represented by the growth of a cottage industry of so-called 9/11 studies. Unlike the 9/11 conspiracy theories mentioned earlier, this material did not emerge out of an already extant subculture; nor was it necessarily predicated on a conspiracist view of the world as plot-driven, although its internal logic often pushed it in that direction. Instead, it sprang from two sources, one European and the other American.

Widespread, publicly available skeptical views of the received accounts of 9/11 appeared in Europe at a time when most Americans accepted the official explanation of the attacks. Not until a year or so after the attacks did such skepticism gain traction in the United States. It did so partially because of the model provided by the 1963 Kennedy assassination and the reaction to the Warren Commission's report. That report engendered a lengthy, quasi-scholarly attempt to disprove the commission's findings and/or to prove alternative accounts. That model has come to be applied to the September 11th attacks through the creation of organizations, conferences, and publications built upon academic models that seek to invalidate the received account and/or to present evidence for a different version of events. This has led to the creation of Scholars for 9/11 Truth, Scholars for 9/11 Truth and Justice, and the latter's publication, the *Journal of 9/11*

Studies.[12] The alternative versions generally posited some potent organization considerably more formidable than nineteen men armed with box cutters and consequently representing a cause proportionate to the destructive effects.

This occurred at a time when conspiracy beliefs were achieving wide currency, manifested in such popular culture phenomena as the extraordinary successes of Dan Brown's novels, *The Da Vinci Code* and *Angels and Demons*. This fascination with conspiracies has been reinforced by the spread of urban legends associated with the attacks, such as the alleged presence of a UFO near the World Trade Center, or claims that the attacks had been predicted by Nostradamus, whose name became the fastest growing search term on Google in 2001. These queries peaked at noon on September 11th and continued at a rate of one hundred a minute for the rest of the day.[13]

These are examples of conscious, interpretive choices, in which elements of the imagination were used in order to make sense of highly disturbing and otherwise incomprehensible events. However, imaginative elements also appear at a lower level of conscious awareness to subtly change understanding, and it is to this ambient level that we now turn.

The Ambient Imagination

After the attacks, the filmmaker Robert Altman remarked, "Nobody would have thought to commit an atrocity like this unless they'd seen it in a movie."[14] Altman's observation hinted at a larger set of influences emanating from popular culture. Whether films had any influence on those who planned and carried out the hijackings is unknown, but they certainly influenced public understanding of the attacks. To raise this possibility is to risk being accused of trivializing horrible events and devaluing the victims. I hope it is clear that I intend neither. But I do want to suggest that images and motifs from both high and popular culture can become so embedded in our consciousness that they contribute to the way in which we understand the sources and nature of terror. This influence has manifested itself in two ways: the way we think about worst-case events, and the way in which we think about the architects of terrorist attacks against the United States. Both ways are clearly related to a fascination with disasters, and particularly with the possibility that disaster might overwhelm and destroy great urban centers.

As Max Page observes in his encyclopedic examination of fictional representations of the destruction of New York City, "September 11 was its own form of New York disaster movie, played out live on every screen in the world . . . the ultimate, encompassing disaster movie."[15] Less than two weeks after 9/11, the *New Yorker*'s film critic, Anthony Lane, noted "the degree to which people saw—literally saw, and are continuing to see . . .—that day as a movie."[16] The disaster movie template could be so readily imposed upon the events because New York had been focus of disaster representations ever since it had emerged as the preeminent American metropolis in the decades after the Civil War.[17] The early versions took the form of literature and art. Radio, film, and television came in the twentieth century. But whatever the medium, New York was always destroyed, over and over, by every conceivable means—hostile armies, extraterrestrials, mysterious diseases, novel weapons, and natural calamities.

More than forty years ago, Susan Sontag published an essay, "The Imagination of Disaster," that was ostensibly an analysis of the 1954 Japanese Godzilla film and its numerous sequels. However, the essay addressed larger issues of how destruction is thought about and represented. Sontag particularly noted that in world-destroying science-fiction films there was always "an obligatory scene . . . of panicked crowds, stampeding along a highway or a big bridge."[18] Her description eerily anticipates the televised scenes of screaming crowds running toward the camera in an effort to escape the onrushing cloud of dust created by the collapse of the World Trade Center towers. It was as if the crowd were reenacting a scene from a film, reversing the crowd scenes in Eisenstein's fictionalized depiction of the Russian Revolution, *October*, where he employed extras who had actually participated in the storming of the Winter Palace.

The resonance of the scenes near Ground Zero came not merely from the similarity to cinematic representations but from a much longer history of anxiety about the death of great cities. Images of urban ruin were stimulated for centuries by reflection on the ruins of the great cities of the ancient world. Thus Thomas Cole's famous series of paintings, *The Course of Empire*, painted between 1834 and 1836, has as its penultimate canvas *Destruction*. The huge painting shows a Greco-Roman city in flames, overrun by barbarian hordes, but it was almost certainly also influenced by the great Wall Street fire that swept Lower Manhattan in December 1835.[19] The 1836 exhibition of Cole's monumental canvases was a major event in its day, called by a contemporary "the most successful exhibition of the works of a single American artist ever held in this city."[20]

A much more recent and powerful image of a destroyed New York came from the great Mexican muralist Jose Clemente Orozco, who was there at the beginning of the Great Depression and, in 1931, produced a strange oil painting titled *The Dead*. It shows a grotesque scene of twisted buildings, some still standing but most in varying stages of disintegration, "skyscrapers bending and falling and cracking like breadsticks."[21] (Osama bin Laden, it will be recalled, appears to have wished one World Trade Center tower to have fallen into the other.) Although Orozco chose not to show human figures in the painting, his recollections of the crash record "speculators [who] had thrown themselves from their windows," prefiguring the bodies that fell from the World Trade Center.[22] A few years later, in 1937, Stephen Vincent Benet's much-anthologized short story, originally titled "The Place of the Gods" and later retitled "By the Waters of Babylon," was first published in the mass-circulation *Saturday Evening Post*. It depicts an awestruck youth from some remote future time wandering through the deserted ruins of New York, which has been destroyed by an unidentified calamity.

Creative figures such as Hirst and Stockhausen might be expected to be familiar with historic links between art and images of destruction. Those without such familiarity have, as already noted, ample reasons to regard the city as a fragile organism that may appear powerful but that can in fact be overcome and reduced to rubble. The capitals of great empires eventually collapsed. Thomas Cole was inspired to begin his series of paintings while sitting among Roman ruins. The theme of urban destruction runs through the historic and artistic record, from Thucydides's description of the plague in Athens during the Peloponnesian War to a comment made in the 1850s that a day would come "when Tartar horses slake their long thirst in the ruined fountains of the Tuileries."[23]

But it was popular culture that made the theme of urban destruction common property. From the dazzling, futuristic city in Fritz Lang's 1927 silent film *Metropolis* that teeters on the edge of implosion, to contemporary disaster movies, the vulnerability of cities has become a motion picture cliché. And no city has been destroyed on film more often than New York. These ubiquitous images become internalized, so that actual events are "read" in terms of their fictional antecedents: "Our popular culture has been in dress rehearsal for the city's destruction for decades: in books, at the movies, in computer games."[24]

The Mad Scientist

One reason that powerful urban centers can be made to appear so fragile in popular culture is because of the nature of the fictional villains arrayed against them. Many such personifications of evil are linked to the stereotype of the "mad scientist," the brilliant but untrustworthy genius who usually works in isolation, and is hence invisible, but holds the instruments of potential urban destruction. No other villain is so powerful a symbolic figure in the ambient imagination of anthropogenic disaster.

This stock figure can be traced from medieval alchemists, through Mary Shelley's Dr. Victor Frankenstein in 1818, to its apotheosis in the James Bond novels and films. Early exemplars, such as Dr. Frankenstein, were not intentionally evil. Instead, through accidents or character flaws, they unleashed forces they could not control, with predictably unfortunate consequences. They were almost always represented as social isolates, like the reclusive Rotwang in *Metropolis*. As Susan Sontag has observed about those who populate science-fiction films, "the scientist is one who releases forces which, if not controlled for good, could destroy man himself." "Science is magic," she writes, black magic as well as white.[25] Scientists' representation in films has been conspicuous. In British horror films between the early 1930s and the mid-1980s, they made up nearly a third of the villains. For films in general, the heyday of the mad scientist fell into a few periods: the mid-1930s, the years of the Second World War, and the period from the late 1970s through the early 1980s.[26] It is this latter period, of course, that has imprinted the figure of the evil genius on the contemporary consciousness.

By the time of scientists' appearance in the James Bond stories, therefore, the evil consequences associated with them were hardly accidental. These scientists are genuinely evil or are in the pay of men who have no scruples and mobilize science only for their own aggrandizement—Auric Goldfinger, who wants to use nuclear weapons against Ft. Knox; Ernst Stavro Blofeld, who has a virus that can make everyone sterile; and Hugo Drax, who has enough nerve gas to kill every person in the world. These sociopaths have in common vast scientific resources, goals of world domination, and access to weapons of mass destruction. They are in every respect save ideology identical to the terrorists of contemporary imagination. The fictional characters are only a few steps away from such real-life figures as the Pakistani nuclear scientist A. Q. Khan, who, although employed by a state, functioned as a kind of WMD freebooter, potentially feeding the appetites of anyone willing to meet his price. Such mythic evil geniuses work in isolated laboratories where their world-destroying technologies can be perfected in secret.

It was just such imagery of hidden lairs that came to be projected onto the speculation about Osama bin Laden's Tora Bora cave complex in the final days of the U.S. attack on the Taliban and al-Qaeda in Afghanistan. The myth of bin Laden's subterranean fortress began with a story in the London *Independent* newspaper on November 27, 2001, which described a mountain honeycombed with tunnels, behind iron doors, with "its own ventilation system and its own power, created by a hydro-electric generator," capable of housing 2,000 people "like a hotel." This story was quickly picked up and embellished by American media. The result was that on November 29th the *Times* (London) published a cut-away drawing titled "Bin Laden's Mountain Fortress," showing thermal sensing equipment and tunnels wide enough for a car to drive through. The *Times* claimed Tora Bora dwarfed Hitler's "Eagle's Nest." When "Meet the Press" was broadcast on December 2nd, Tim Russert showed the drawing to Defense Secretary Donald Rumsfeld, who suggested there might be many such sophisticated redoubts, and not only in Afghanistan.[27] *Asia Times* imagined the eventual assault on the Tora Bora cave in overtly cinematic terms: "Thrill-seekers will revel in imagining a bunch of ninjas . . . slouching toward the roof of the world on a mission to rid said world from evil incarnate. Next step is the showdown. If and when it happens, it will be fought with ultra high-tech weapons—from penetrating bombs . . . to 2 megawatt lasers. . . . The ninjas will be talking to each other through voice message devices embedded in their helmets or through messages written on a keyboard attached to their wrists. No big deal. Hollywood's been there, done that."[28]

The caves, of course, turned out to be, for the most part, just caves: "The troglodyte lair of Bin Laden turned out to be mythic."[29] But the true mythic element was the stereotype of the evil genius sequestered in an impenetrable sanctuary with all the advantages of science and technology at his command.

This nexus of scientific know-how and terrorism had, of course, already been revealed in 1995 with Aum Shinrikyo's sarin gas attack in the Tokyo subway. Aum had its hidden laboratories and scientific cadres. But there was also in Aum a sense of life imitating art, since many of its scientifically trained members had been steeped in Japanese science fiction before joining the sect. From the 1970s on, Japanese youth culture was pervaded by science fiction, especially in the form of looming global calamity.[30] The imminent disasters were often associated with some form of pollution or impurity that had to be cleansed in order to defeat the forces of evil. This may even have been true for Aum's leader, Shoko Asahara.[31] There is also circumstantial evidence that members of Aum's scientifically trained inner circle may have seen themselves as the realization of the guild of scientists in Isaac Asimov's Foundation Series of science-fiction novels.[32] Fiction may exert a particularly distorting influence on groups with apocalyptic goals, since it may not only reinforce their sense of themselves as a world-destroying force but may also lead them to seriously overestimate their capabilities. One of the paradoxes in Aum's case, for example, is that although the requisite scientific capacity seems to have existed, Asahara and his disciples appeared convinced that they also knew how to override scientific laws when necessary.

New York Targeted

Although New York destruction fantasies have a history that goes back to the nineteenth century, the advent of nuclear weapons raised such scenarios to an entirely new level, for now a single bomb could obliterate Manhattan and much of the rest of the city. This realization led to proposals that people and institutions now concentrated be dispersed into outlying areas where their chances of survival would be improved, essentially deconstructing Manhattan.[33] Whatever the underlying logic of such programs, the result was quite the opposite, for the Cold War years saw an unprecedented boom in the construction of high-rise buildings on the island, not least the World Trade Center itself.[34]

Prior to the September 11th attacks, the continuing stream of popular culture New York fantasies involved a number in which the World Trade Center was completely or partly destroyed. These appeared in conventional and animated films, as well as comic books, graphic novels, and computer games. As a conspicuous part of the city skyline, the World Trade Center was scarcely immune from depredations of various destructive forces let loose in disaster narratives.[35]

Consequently, by the time the Twin Towers were actually destroyed, on

September 11, 2001, not only had they been destroyed in works of the imagination but, regardless of whether those fantasies had actually been read or seen by anyone, the idea of the towers' destruction had been firmly implanted. That is what Max Page means when he suggests that even though the attacks were frequently said to be "unimaginable," "our culture has been imagining and even rehearsing these events for decades."[36] Popular culture has become so saturated with disaster motifs, and the destruction of New York has been so common a focus in these stories, that a massive attack on a New York landmark can seem simultaneously inevitable and profoundly shocking.

Policymakers and the Imagination

The imagination is powerful because it offers alternative ways of understanding disaster and risk. Of the three forms of imagination discussed here—the subcultural, the diffusionist, and the ambient—the subcultural is likely to have the least effect upon policymakers. This is because it is the most insular and idiosyncratic. Unless the vagaries of recruitment happen to have resulted in individuals being drawn from subcultures that hold unique ideas about disaster and risk, these views will remain within their respective coteries. There are, of course, exceptions, as when Republican administrations deliberately selected appointees with evangelical backgrounds, such as Secretary of the Interior James Watt and Attorney General John Ashcroft. However, policymakers generally reflect mainstream as opposed to subcultural values. For somewhat the same reason, the diffusionist imagination is unlikely to gain much traction in the policymaking community. While it represents subcultural ideas that have been picked up by a larger audience, those ideas still carry some taint, in the sense of representing deviant views of the world, as has been the case with conspiracy theories of the Kennedy assassination and the 9/11 attacks. Despite their success in breaking out of the isolation of their respective subcultures and gaining a hearing among others, these ideas challenge the received view of events, and that alone would make them unacceptable among policymakers. The ambient imagination, however, is another matter, for it is by definition neither insular nor deviant. It pervades the culture, and its ideas of disaster and risk, however fanciful, become the template that helps define reality.

It would be comforting to believe that policymakers stood outside the detritus of popular culture, the mass of images and stories made for and consumed by mass audiences. Most of it has little artistic merit and provides little social uplift. Most is forgotten as quickly as it is produced and consumed. The seriousness of the issues with which policymakers must deal argues for insulation from the trivial and transitory. Yet the very pervasiveness of popular culture suggests that such insulation is very likely impossible and that policymakers are immersed in the same sea of images and stories as their fellow citizens. The readiness with which Defense Secretary Rumsfeld acquiesced in the fanciful tales of bin Laden's cave suggests that he was as likely as those outside policy circles to have internalized the imagery of the high-tech villain's lair, more appropriate to James Bond than to the mountains of Afghanistan.

The larger issue, of course, concerns the construction of the landscape of fear. While policymakers have at their disposal information their fellow citizens do not, their inner world may contain many of the same furnishings, imagery and ideas drawn from the ambient imagination and expressed in popular culture. Because this material is so pervasive, its content may not be the subject of conscious awareness. Rather, it structures our expectations and perceptions. We expect the most sinister of evildoers to behave like their motion-picture counterparts—to appear and disappear as if by magic, to hide in remote, technologically sophisticated redoubts, to possess the most fearsome weapons science can devise. This nexus of invisibility and power underlies contemporary thrillers whose villains have the means to destroy great cities and even place the planet itself at risk.

In a media-rich environment where such stories proliferate, is it any wonder that we lose the capacity to distinguish between fiction and fact, between the disaster movie and real calamities? In the end, the motifs of popular culture come to be projected onto real-world events, not only because those motifs come easily to hand, but also because the events themselves are often so chaotic and troubling that they cry out for something that will give them structure and make them comprehensible. That is, after all, a prime reason why we tell stories, in order to make sense of the world.

This propensity to appropriate components of popular culture because elements of its stories help us make sense of the world is not confined only to the general population. It is also a temptation from which policymakers themselves cannot escape. For they, too, both are immersed in the same mass of imaginative ideas and struggle to make sense of the world. And they, like their fellow citizens, can easily lose sight of the boundary between the conceits of fiction and the characteristics of reality.

One consequence is to give to the terrorist the features of the stereo-typical fictional villain: functional invisibility, allowing him to move across borders undetected and disappear at will; a sophisticated hiding place that is undetectable and/or impenetrable; and access to weapons of mass destruction concocted by the rogue scientists at his disposal. These become the preeminent unseen dangers.

The categories and motifs of the surrounding culture constitute the inescapable "background noise" of the policymakers' world. Within that world, the explicit direction of policy comes from a line of directives and pronouncements from authoritative sources that will supposedly provide instruction where rapid choice is necessary.

six

UNSEEN DANGERS AS DEFILEMENTS

One cannot think for very long about unseen dangers without confronting ideas about pollution and defilement. In the first place, biological weapons, which occupy so large a place in current thinking about terrorism, make a direct connection between unseen dangers and pathogens, which have so significantly affected Western ideas about harm caused by invisible agents. Second, much of the thrust of homeland security policy has been on enhancing the security of borders and preventing anything harmful from crossing them. Two of the five goals DHS secretary Michael Chertoff set were "keeping bad people out of the country and keeping bad stuff out of the country."[1] As Chapter 3 indicated, much of his department's work has been directed at trying to make the discriminations that would allow these goals to be realized.

The 9/11 attacks and the subsequent anthrax letters occurred in an environment that had already been preoccupied with issues of contamination by two earlier developments, a preoccupation with new diseases and increasing controversy about illegal immigration. Nancy Tomes calls the period since 1985 a time of "germ panic," although she notes that "the current wave of anxiety might better be described as a viral panic."[2] Led by HIV/ AIDS but encompassing afflictions like Ebola as well, the post-1985 period erased previous levels of confidence about public health. At roughly the same time, America was undergoing a demographic shift under the pressure of mass immigration on a scale not seen since the period prior to the imposition of immigration restriction in 1924. A consequence of mass immigration has been the rise of what some have termed "the new nativism" in the form of organizations devoted to repatriating or blocking illegal immigrants, preventing the use of languages other than English, and similar causes.

The coinciding of terrorist attacks on America with these trends introduces a theme that is rarely directly addressed in discussions of terrorism: the theme of pollution and defilement. The presence of terrorists and/or their weapons constitutes the introduction of impurities, the violation of American territory in more than the technical legal sense. Homeland security is therefore an effort to prevent such contamination. Contemporary preoccupation with illegal immigration and infectious or contagious disease has made issues of purity particularly salient, even in contexts where they are not strictly speaking applicable.

The Immigrant as a Defiler

American hostility toward immigrants has a history that goes well back into the nineteenth century, when nativists identified immigrants with criminality, ignorance, disease, and "un-American" ideas. First the Irish, then southern and eastern Europeans, faced such charges, often interwoven with hostility to their Catholic or Jewish religion. Mass organizations and political parties, such as the "Know Nothings," both fed off of and stimulated anti-immigrant sentiment, which continued until restrictive legislation was passed in 1924.[3] However, these restrictions were eliminated by the Immigration and Nationality Act of 1965, which became effective in 1968. With the act coming into effect, a so-called new immigration began, much of it from Latin America, Asia, and Africa. It, in turn, has begotten its own form of nativism.

That nativism has taken two forms: organizations for the purpose of lobbying and supporting political candidates and paramilitary groups that promised to guard borders. In 1979, a Michigan ophthalmologist, John Tanton, founded the Federation for American Immigration Reform (FAIR). In succeeding years, Tanton and his associates created spinoff groups, turning FAIR and its associates into a network of purportedly grassroots organizations with the goal of cutting off immigration.[4] Despite their claims of mass memberships, they remained relatively small into the early 2000s.[5] By the middle of the decade, however, the organized anti-immigration movement had expanded massively.[6] This was due not only to increasing numbers of immigrants but to their distribution, for large pockets had appeared in small and medium-sized communities in the heartland that had never in the recent past experienced concentrations of non-English speakers. They were often drawn by the prospect of jobs others would not take, for example, in slaughterhouses. No matter what drew them, culture clashes were inevitable.

Beginning in about 2000, vigilante groups began to appear on the U.S. side of the American border with Mexico, seeking to forcibly bar the movement of illegal immigrants. In many cases, individuals and organizations on the extreme Right joined these efforts, piggybacking on the immigration issue.[7] It was inevitable that the September 11th attacks would resonate with those attracted to such paramilitary activities. In 2002, Chris Simcox, reacting to the 9/11 attacks, founded the paramilitary Civil Homeland Defense to patrol the Mexican border. In 2004, in collaboration with Jim Gilchrist, he founded the better-known Minuteman Project with the same objective.[8] Other, similar organizations followed, and soon the objective of blocking illegal immigration merged with homeland security and protection from terrorists.

These private efforts clearly conflict with the official activities of the Border Patrol. However, little was done to suppress them, in part perhaps because Congress, through the Department of Homeland Security, authorized the construction of a barrier to physically block access across the border with Mexico. This project, in California, Arizona, New Mexico, and Texas, was planned to consist of "pedestrian and vehicle fencing, roads, and virtual detection technology," together with barriers, lighting, and cameras. As an indication of the priority Congress attached to completion of the project, the secretary of homeland security was given extraordinary discretion to waive any legal requirements, such as environmental regulations, that might stand in the way of its completion.[9] The apparent goal was, as it were, to hermetically seal off the United States at its land border with Central America, allowing passage only through authorized entry points. While the justification for the barrier included disruption of "drug smuggling, human smuggling, and gang activity," the primary purpose clearly was to block easy passage across the border because that "imperils our ability to fight terrorism by stopping the illegal entry of terrorists."[10]

In the post-9/11 environment, it has become increasingly difficult to separate opposition to immigration from national security claims. The latter are sometimes used to disguise or rationalize the former. Sometimes, as in the barrier project, a project whose primary aim was homeland security facilitated opposition to immigration as a secondary and often unstated goal. Despite the security argument offered for the barrier across the 700-mile-long Mexican border, no comparably ambitious project has been implemented for the much longer and more porous boundary with Canada, where, of course, illegal immigration is a much smaller problem.

The Fear of Disease

If one touchstone of contemporary anxiety is the fear of immigrants, another is the fear of disease. Like fear of strangers from other lands, disease fears are not new. Indeed, the further back one goes, the more likely one is to find them, since the state of medicine and public health before the late nineteenth century was primitive. Louis Pasteur and his colleagues' linkage of disease with microorganisms beginning in the 1880s not only opened the way for disease control; it also made clear that contagious diseases were caused by unseen agents, invisible harm doers that might be in the very air we breathe. A collateral effect of these scientific discoveries was to elevate the status of bacteriologists, for these were the experts who made the invisible agents visible.[11]

It was not long before the fear of disease and the fear of immigrants intersected. The result was what has been called "medicalized nativism," the stigmatization of an immigrant group based on the belief that its members carry contagious diseases. These claims often rationalize preexisting hostility by giving it an apparently scientific justification. It also links the presence of outsiders with the fear of contamination.[12] Outsiders are not simply dangerous; they are potential defilers who bring impurities into what was a previously unsullied community.

While the heyday of disease fears coincided with the rise of scientific medicine, it is scarcely a subject of merely historical interest. Indeed, Nancy Tomes identifies not one but two "germ panics." The first, from 1900 to 1940, closely tracks the triumphs of scientific medicine that followed the work of Pasteur and Robert Koch. The result at the popular level was an obsessive concern about minimizing germs in daily life. The eventual development of antibiotics and vaccines created a new level of confidence and brought the panic to a close. However, a second panic began in 1985, driven by the appearance of HIV/AIDS, Ebola, and antibiotic-resistant bacterial illnesses, among other diseases. Tomes suggests that these panics resemble moral panics, in the high degree of societal concern and in the lack of proportion between the response and the cause.[13] During this period, the germ panic and fear of immigrants joined when in 1985 the Centers for Disease Control (CDC) for some months placed Haitians in an HIV high-risk category. In 1992 a group of Haitians was placed in detention in, of all places, Guantanamo for a year and a half based on HIV status.[14]

The "germ panic" that began in 1985 took in not only HIV/AIDS and Ebola but also "flesh-eating streptococcus and the West Nile virus," as well as SARS, and blended them with "what once seemed implausible scenarios involving bioterrorists and international conspiracies."[15] The "apocalyptic disease narratives" were quickly packaged in best sellers like Richard Preston's *The Hot Zone* (1994) and Dustin Hoffman's film *Outbreak* (1995).[16] These were, in fact, less part of a "germ panic" than a "viral panic," since viruses tended to be the pathogens of choice.[17]

Long before the 2001 anthrax letter scare, the media had amplified contemporary fears of disease. Rumors and news reports fed on each other, with every rumor about disease increasing the appetite for information, fed by 24/7 cable news networks and Internet sites.[18] Given the ease with which these reports melded with the products of popular culture, panic about new diseases quickly became joined to fears of terrorism, so that "the concept of 'nature strikes back' has been embroidered with conspiratorial plots involving corporate skullduggery, international espionage, and bioterrorist attacks."[19] It was scarcely surprising, therefore, that the American public readily accepted tales of Saddam Hussein's biological weapons, as well as the likelihood of a bioterrorist attack after September 11th.[20]

Nineteenth- and early-twentieth-century immigrants who were believed to bring with them pathologies—dread diseases and strange, un-American religions—entered the country legally. However, many in the late-twentieth- and early twenty-first-centuries have presumably entered illegally, but also are said to bring pathologies, whether in the form of disease or the capacity to erode the culture. Thus a continuing strain of xenophobia, stretching back well over a hundred years, has constructed a story of border-crossing cultural aliens who bring with them invisible poisons, sometimes in the form of beliefs that undercut uniquely American values, and sometimes in the form of disease-causing microbes. It has been an easy matter for this long-running story to morph into the tale of the toxin-bearing Islamic radical who, by dint of talents for disguise, dissimulation, and deception, could disappear into the general population.

Terrorism and Impurity

The bioterrorist has been said to resemble "Typhoid Mary" or the supposed "patient zero" who was said to have brought HIV/AIDS to North America.[21] Linking the bioterrorist with disease vectors converts the terrorist into a carrier of microorganisms. In that sense, the bioterrorist is *doubly* invisible: as part of a crowd, melting into the general population, and as someone ready to disperse an invisible agent of death. In an era already in the throes of a germ or virus panic, there could hardly be a more frightening image, made all the more sinister by the fact that the bioterrorist is assumed to be an outsider, someone from a different ethnic, national, or religious group—that is, an immigrant. But where earlier immigrants were thought to be merely inadvertent carriers of disease, they may now be carrying it purposely.

Thus the obsession with bioterrorism is not simply an artifact of the anthrax letters episode. That merely reinforced a predisposition that was already present. Rather, behind the fear of terrorists lay two other, earlier fears, the fear of immigrants and the fear of disease. Both, as we have seen, had roots going back into the nineteenth century, and both for separate reasons flared up again in the 1980s and 1990s, in time to reinforce the anxieties that emerged so powerfully after the September 11th attacks.

The same extreme fear associated with pathogens is also associated with poisons. This was evident in the reaction to poison gas during and immediately after the First World War. In fact, gas was an inefficient weapon during World War I,[22] far less lethal than, for example, the machine gun, yet its use occasioned extreme revulsion for years afterward. Kai Erikson speculates that the strength of the emotional response to the poison gas was common to reactions to toxins. They invade the body and do so in peculiarly insidious ways. Poison gas, he writes, "is furtive, invisible [although most used during World War I could generally be seen], unnatural. In most of its forms it moves for the interior, turning the process of assault inside out." More broadly, it is in the nature of poisons that "[t]hey slink in without warning, do not immediately damage so far as one can tell, and then begin their deadly work from within—the very embodiment of stealth and treachery."[23] Thus chemical weapons share with biological weapons not only the property of being unseen but also the ability to trigger a primordial source of fear in their potential victims.

Immigrant and disease fears, together with fear of poisons, posed issues similar to those raised by homeland security. Uppermost for all three is the issue of boundaries. For immigration policy, it is boundary control, so that no individual crosses the boundary without authorization. In our earlier discussion of the Department of Homeland Security's REAL ID program, we noted that one of the program's stated objectives was to provide a credential for individuals in the country legally. Margaret Humphreys observes of disease panic: "The crossing of boundaries is essential to the creation of panic. When the edge of safety cannot be defined, people react in ways that are not necessarily rational—cordoning off suspect populations; creating artificial boundaries that create the illusion of safety; fleeing somewhere, anywhere."[24] This linkage of panic and boundaries is not merely reflective of practical expedients, such as quarantine. It also raises fundamental questions about a community's conceptions of purity and defilement.

Mary Douglas, in her famous book on purity and impurity, defines dirt as "matter out of place," in the sense that something is regarded as defiling because it lies outside of a system of classification.[25] This is true of pathogens. It is also true of immigrants—in the eyes of opponents of immigration, even if immigrants are legal; in the law's and the community's eyes, if they are illegal. And, of course, it is true of terrorists, whether counterterrorism is construed as a law-enforcement effort or as a war. There is a sense in which all constitute instances of pollution. This is the most literally true for pathogens, where avoidance of germs often involves elaborate rituals of cleanliness.[26] But it has been true for immigrants as well, where opponents of immigration have alleged that their presence would produce racial or cultural dilution[27] and take pains to avoid contact with them. The terrorist, regarded as the greatest danger of all, is considered the greatest defiler, particularly the Islamic radical who might not only engage in acts of violence but also spread a fundamentalist ideology among previously non-violent coreligionists. Gustave LeBon and other late-nineteenth-century crowd theorists, writing under the influence of Pasteur's work, treated ideas as though they were microbial agents—a metaphor that linked microbes and ideas on the levels of both their invisibility and their capacity to cause harm.

Contemporary state boundaries, of course, have become increasingly permeable as people, goods, and ideas move in increasing volume across them, the process encompassed by the hackneyed term "globalization." Yet at precisely the time when borders are hardest to police, fear of terrorism has made their protection a matter of the highest priority. The danger is that even a small number of individuals may introduce fatal impurities. Yet eighty million persons come to the United States each year by air, and four hundred million cross the land borders. The difficulties of detecting terrorists and their weapons were addressed in Chapter 3. The former DHS secretary Michael Chertoff conceded that the medical condition of these travelers cannot be known with any certainty, absent prior intelligence.[28] Any attempt to seal borders from disease is therefore illusory.

It is worth noting that with a very small number of exceptions, no significant terrorists captured by the United States have been incarcerated in this country. A few, it is true, have been kept in military brigs on American soil or imprisoned after trial, such as Zacharias Moussaoui, Jose Padilla, and the 1993 World Trade Center bombers. But the great bulk have been sequestered at Guantanamo Bay or in secret facilities maintained in other countries by the Central Intelligence Agency. These locational decisions were made primarily in order to minimize the likelihood that the federal courts would intervene on behalf of detainees, although in the end a number of cases have been brought; or in order to maximize the ability of the detainees' custodians to have freedom of action in their interrogation. But beyond these self-interested considerations, keeping captured terrorists segregated outside the United States has the unintended function of boundary maintenance. That is, keeping them out maintains the purity of those within, as though their presence on unambiguously American territory will constitute an act of contamination. Holding them elsewhere serves to strengthen the meaning of the boundary at a time when its efficacy is in doubt. It reinforces the fiction that there are no serious terrorists within the United States.

Homeland Security and Ritualism

Kai Erikson in his classic study of the Puritans' actions in confronting religious dissenters and accusations of witchcraft in seventeenth-century New England observed that the affected communities required cleansing rituals of purification.[29] However, he dealt with cases in which those accused of evil acts were already in the communities, which could then concentrate on processing the offenders. The situation with regard to terrorism is quite different. Although some cases have come to light of plots developed by Americans within the United States (e.g., the Lackawanna Six), for the most part concern has been with non-Americans presently outside U.S. territory. Although some have been captured, most are believed still to be at large. Yet even under these circumstances, ritual plays an important role.

We may divide homeland security rituals into several types. One has already been discussed: the detention of terrorists outside the United States. Whatever pragmatic considerations may have led to that decision, the continuation of the practice acts to reinforce the country's boundary by using that boundary as a dividing line between the United States, on the one hand, and the domain of international terrorism, on the other. A second ritual is the complex system of security checks at airports and many public buildings. As airport security checks have become more involved, passengers going through have become more active participants, going through a regular set of movements (removing jackets and shoes, separating liquids from other hand luggage, and so forth; providing fingerprints for non-Americans). A third set of rituals consists of those actions that directly introduce high levels of policing and security into settings where they are not generally found. Examples include the presence of armed troops in airports for weeks after September 11th and roadblocks during periods of high alert when drivers are required to open car trunks. Fourth, the fluctuating, closely watched Homeland Security Advisory System constitutes a signaling ritual for both government agencies and the public, discussed in detail in the next chapter. Finally, a complex set of rituals concerns government restructuring.

Rituals of governmental restructuring typically begin with the impaneling of study commissions or congressional investigating committees, which then produce reports, which become the basis for organizational change. This process began before September 11th with the reports of governmental study commissions, and continued through such bodies as the 9/11 Commission and the congressional investigations of the Katrina debacle. The major result has been a massive, two-pronged reorganization. One prong was the creation of the Department of Homeland Security out of so-called legacy agencies, the largest reorganization since the creation of the Department of Defense. The second was the reorganization of the intelligence community under a new director of National Intelligence (although the intelligence functions of the Department of Defense were exempted). A third aspect, undertaken without any prior commission study, was the creation of the separate detention and interrogation system.

To term acts "rituals" says nothing about their effectiveness. In the case of homeland security rituals, they may or may not actually make people safer. However, their ritualistic character may well make people *feel* safer. In the first place, they provide evidence that government is doing something and the appearance that it is acting on a problem. Second, the actions tend to be in the form of stereotypical problem-solving modalities used to deal with earlier problems: transferring responsibilities to the military, appointing a "czar," or rearranging responsibilities and personnel. It is also possible that some of the rituals may be effective from a security standpoint, as well as from an anxiety-reduction standpoint, although this may be difficult to measure.

A large number of the rituals are directly or indirectly concerned with either maintaining the integrity of borders, controlling who passes across them, or detecting harm doers who may have managed to get onto American territory. In that sense, the rituals act to maintain both the society's safety and its purity, defined as the absence of potential terrorists within its boundaries. This emphasis upon border integrity significantly differentiates homeland security from earlier national defense, which was aimed at preventing foreign attack, not infiltration. It is true that there were concerns about internal threats during World War II. These led to the detention of Japanese Americans, as well as highly publicized vigilance against German sabotage and espionage. In a somewhat similar manner, there was widespread concern in the 1950s about Soviet spying. In both cases, however, these issues were secondary to concentration on the main enemies, other territorial states whose principal means of attack were through their organized militaries.

In the present case, where the adversary is nonterritorial and has no organized conventional military force, the issue of infiltration and what I earlier termed "crowd invisibility" moves from a marginal position to a central position. The terrorist, however, becomes not merely an invader who has secretly crossed into one's territory but one who has desecrated it by his very presence. This idea partly springs from the historical immunity of America from invasion, apart from the British invasion during the War of 1812. But it is also a function of the significance of invisibility in terrorism, both the invisibility of the perpetrator and the possible invisibility of the weapons he may use—an invisibility that links terrorism with another form of invisible but polluting danger, unseen microbial agents that spread disease.

The linkage of terrorism with biological and chemical weapons takes us into an unfamiliar realm. For as soon as the concern about unseen dangers coincides with fears about impurity, we gradually enter a mysterious universe that appears to be governed by malign forces. This is a view of the world profoundly antithetical to that we normally hold; indeed, antithetical to modernism itself. It suggests a world that is archaic, primitive, or magical, a world that is arbitrary and capricious notwithstanding the scientific and technical knowledge associated with the fabrication, use, and detection of such weapons. It is a landscape of fear filled with entities that can neither be seen nor propitiated. A landscape of fear dominated by such uncontrollable, invisible dangers suggests not the present but some primeval age before the scientific "disenchantment" about which Max Weber famously spoke.

Weber's disenchanted world, discussed in Chapter 1, is one in which the behavior of the natural world is reduced to comprehensible physical laws. If one does not personally understand such notions, one can take comfort from the fact that someone somewhere does, and can harness them for the protection and well-being of society. While Weber had in mind the progress of scientific knowledge and technological sophistication, this development has been at least partially reproduced in the dynamics of the state system.

While governments cannot perfectly predict one another's actions, the division of the world's land areas into states, begun in Europe during the Renaissance and ultimately globalized, has reduced international politics to a single "game." Its rules, codified in international law and underwritten by the major powers, were well understood. They permitted a privileged system of interstate communication through the exchange of diplomats. The system went through periodic times of turbulence, but it always reverted to stability in which old norms of statecraft again prevailed and, paradoxically, even structured the conduct of armed conflict.

The rise of potent terrorist organizations re-enchants this world, for such groups are doubly subversive of the status quo. Not only do they desire an overturning of power relationships; they seek it from a position totally outside the state system. It is as though history were rolled back and states suddenly had to confront a pre-state world. They have, of course, sometimes done so in the past, as when they expanded into areas of southern Africa that had no state organizations. But they did so then from the standpoint of undoubted military superiority. They now confront a "re-enchanted," archaic, stateless reality powerful and elusive enough to give them pause.

The threat it may pose is magnified to the extent that it is associated with weapons of mass destruction—particularly those that act in insidious and invisible ways, such as chemical, biological, and radiological weapons. The combination of a stateless political actor with such weapons confront governments with, in a Weberian sense, a re-enchanted world: They must now deal with a shadowy, pre-state adversary with no clearly demarcated territorial location that may possess means of destruction that cannot be readily seen. The images and anxieties of the landscape of fear suggest that whether or not terrorists actually possess such weapons, we are prone to project upon them *belief* in their possession. Thus a world that was once comprehensible and at least moderately orderly has become filled with a mysterious unseen evil force that can be neither understood nor controlled.

Americans suddenly confront a world filled with mysterious, invisible powers. However, unlike those in traditional societies inured to living in an enchanted world, we have long lived in a primarily disenchanted one. As a result, we lack the traditionalist's armory of magic, religious ritual, and placatory gestures with which to keep evil at bay, not to mention the fatalistic acceptance of unseen dangers. It is true, as we have seen, that some rituals have in fact begun to develop, part of what John Mueller calls "security theater." Mueller suggests that even if such measures do nothing to increase actual levels of security, they may still be useful if they make people feel less fearful.[30] The color-coded Homeland Security Advisory System, was never below yellow, suggesting that those who govern are always on guard, assessing risks and alert to danger. Yet given the invisible character of the danger, the protective rituals have not always resulted in a secure public.

Part of the problem lies in the difficulty of tracking an unseen enemy, but part lies in the gulf between victim and terrorist. For victim societies in the West are overwhelmingly made up of individuals whose world is disenchanted. Notwithstanding recent religious developments, the description of the world Max Weber gave ninety years ago is still broadly valid. But religious terrorists, such as al-Qaeda and its imitators, live in a different ideological universe. Their world is enchanted, and explicitly so in its rejection of modernity. Their use of violence without demands, claims of responsibility, or obvious tactical considerations places it outside the rational scientific domain of the disenchanted world, and it is all the more frightening for that reason. Potential victims thus face not merely violence and the threat of violence but the incursion of an enchanted worldview that threatens to re-enchant their own world long after its own disenchantment.

The fear engendered by religious terrorism is not merely a product of the extraordinary commitment its practitioners bring to their mission; it also raises the possibility that presently secularized societies might be returned to a condition before disenchantment occurred, a world where religion permeated all of life before what is now the secular domain existed.

There is surely a link between this fear of a sphere of invisible evil and the simultaneous anxiety about unseen impurities and their carriers. Borders were once a trip-wire that when crossed by the armed forces of another state signaled the beginning of a state of war. We live in a different world now, where wars between states have become exceptional events. Not only have borders become permeable because of the volume of international transactions—economic, cultural, and social—that flow across them, but they have seemingly lost their capacity to clearly signal danger to the security of the state. From this follows the immense expenditure of resources by the Department of Homeland Security in an attempt to give back to borders their original capacity to detect danger. Yet there remains the sense that the invisibility of the danger makes such efforts problematic, that on the other side of the boundary lies a realm of impurity that constantly threatens to seep across no matter how sophisticated the efforts to prevent it.

It is fanciful to imagine that the United States (or any other developed country, for that matter) could seal itself off, as Albania once did during the Cold War. The dream of autarky, still sought by some countries in the early twentieth century, by which a state could make itself economically self-sufficient, is no longer possible. Hence a border is less a barrier than it is a permeable membrane through which millions of transactions pass in both directions. Given the reality of this condition, homeland security presents a virtually insoluble dilemma. It is predicated on the view that the boundary not only defines American territory but also divides a set of domains: purity and contamination, good and evil, the seen and the unseen, and—potentially—the modern conception of disenchantment and the premodern world of enchantment.

As we have seen, the theme of unseen dangers runs through contemporary American thinking about terrorism and homeland security—in its search for technologies that will unmask the hidden terrorist, in its stress on weapons of mass destruction, and in its inconsistent application of all-hazards planning. Yet describing the frequency with which the motif of invisible evil recurs does not explain its prominence. Why do the unseen malefactor and invisible weapons evoke such intense fears and exercise so great a hold over policy? The chapters that follow seek to address these questions in a more systematic fashion, first by examining models of behavior that explain similar social processes, and then by applying concepts from these models to terrorism and homeland security.

seven

TWO MODELS OF NONRATIONAL ACTION

The preceding chapters suggest that our attitudes toward terrorism and homeland security are a mixture of rational and nonrational considerations. The appearance of nonrational considerations in terrorism and homeland security policy is not as surprising as might at first seem when one considers the prominence of unseen dangers, which invite deviations from purely rational analysis. How are we to understand the role nonrational factors play? In this chapter, we shall generate a vocabulary of concepts essential to an understanding of collective reactions to unseen dangers. These will be derived from two models constructed with other kinds of behavior in mind, albeit behavior that, as we shall see, bears some similarities to the responses that terrorism elicits. They are particularly useful because the behavior they examine has distinctly nonrational elements. We shall then take the concepts drawn from these two models and, with some rearrangement, suggest here and in the next chapter how they might explain the unseen dangers problem.

Two Elegant Models of Collective Phenomena

The two models we shall examine are *important* and *elegant*, although neither was formulated with terrorism in mind. The first—from the sociologist Stanley Cohen's *Folk Devils and Moral Panics*—grew out of Cohen's study of widespread fears in England about violence associated with youths who congregated at seaside resorts in the mid-1960s.[1] The second, which appears in the historian of religion David Frankfurter's *Evil Incarnate*, applies to a broader range of cases: ancient Roman fears of subversive cults; fears of witches in contemporary Africa and early modern Europe; and contemporary charges of satanic ritual abuse in child care facilities.[2] Cohen's and Frankfurter's studies have two common characteristics: First, each one deals with threats that have some element of insubstantiality, although, as we shall see, the nature of that insubstantiality is not always the same. Second, in each the societal response was always organized, militant, and significantly out of proportion to the threat. After examining each model, we shall compare them with the case of unseen danger manifested by terrorism.

FOLK DEVILS AND MORAL PANICS

Stanley Cohen chose as his starting point two British youth cultures of the 1960s, known as the Mods and the Rockers. These much-caricatured groups of adolescents were roughly distinguishable by their lifestyle traits. In their less nuanced form, the motor-scooter riding Mods were said to be sharp dressers who favored Italian styles, gathered in espresso bars, and listened to rhythm and blues music. As the name suggests, the Rockers preferred rock music. They also liked motorcycles, wore studded black leather, and preferred the open highway to the city.[3]

Beginning in 1964, some exceedingly minor altercations took place between Mods and Rockers during holiday periods at seaside resorts. These events would have attracted little notice had they not been transformed by the tabloid press into lurid battles. No one reading British newspapers would have had any idea of their true magnitude, for media accounts suggested that ordered society was about to be destroyed by an onrushing hoard of youthful barbarians. Indeed, it was this discrepancy between what had actually occurred and what was reported that drove Cohen's theoretical development. What was portrayed was a series of battles between loutish armies of juveniles, with innocent citizens as victims caught in the middle, when in fact whatever tension existed occurred at the margins of entirely peaceful communities.

Why had the reality come to be so distorted in the reporting? The distortion had occurred because the Mods and Rockers had been transformed into "folk devils"; that is, turned into a stereotyped group "defined as a threat to societal values and interests."[4] They now functioned as a symbol of evil rather than as individuals whose behavior was simply to be noted.

As a source of danger and pollution, their actual actions were less important than the responses mounted against them. What was called for was a
campaign of control and, if need be, eradication, the "moral panic" phase.

A moral panic is not the random, chaotic outburst that the word "panic"
evokes. Indeed, Cohen himself came to have some regrets about the term
because it invited misunderstanding.[5] Moral panics can be highly organized as leaders and opinion-makers mobilize a community to purge the
group that is believed to threaten it. Sometimes those in government lead
the way, but often private citizens mobilize first and pressure the government to follow. That was certainly the case in the Mods and Rockers
episode, where wildly exaggerated press coverage shaped public opinion,
which in turn placed pressure on the police and courts.

Cohen's study first appeared in 1972, only a few years after the events
it analyzed. When he returned to the subject in the third edition, he addressed a question implicit in the original research: Do moral panics occur
only in situations of fantasized danger? For of course there were no pitched
battles between Mods and Rockers; they did not pose a genuine threat to
societal values. Did that mean that folk devils were always, as it were, man-
ufactured out of whole cloth, as the British tabloids had done in the mid-
sixties? Cohen insisted it did not: "Calling something a 'moral panic' does
not imply that this something does not exist or happened at all and that
reaction is based on fantasy, hysteria, delusion or illusion or being duped by
the powerful."[6] Nonetheless, Cohen found it necessary to redefine "moral
panic," and in so doing distinguish it from "ordinary" responses to social
problems. In most respects, moral panics resemble more mundane campaigns: concern about a threat, moral outrage, and a broad consensus that
something needs to be done. But in two respects, moral panics do differ
from ordinary responses: First, they embody a striking disproportionality,
exaggerating the number of cases, the damage, the moral offensiveness, or
the danger. Second, they erupt quickly and just as quickly subside.[7] However, the greater the disproportionality between stimulus and response, the
closer the conception of folk devils comes to fantasy. Put somewhat differently, how insignificant in objective terms must the danger be before we
can truly say that a moral panic is an irrational response to an imagined
threat?

Finally, Stanley Cohen saw moral panics as arising in a relatively limited
number of situations. That is, he saw certain groups as likely targets for designation as "folk devils" and certain putative social problems as probable

catalysts for moral panics. In the end, he settled on seven clusters: violent, young, working-class males; school violence; psychoactive drugs; child abuse, linked to pedophilia and satanism; sex in the media and its relationship to violence; welfare cheats; and refugees and asylum seekers.[8] All of the likely "folk devils," in other word, were members of relatively powerless groups. Many were already socially marginalized, classed as deviants by the majority as well as by the authorities. They posed no real threat despite the disdain they generated. This catalog clearly reflected recent anxieties in Britain and, to a lesser extent, America. That it is in any sense exhaustive is open to question. In any case, it has not prevented others from adding their own claims for moral panics, such as recent condemnation of so-called religious cults in Western Europe.[9] The absence of terrorism on the list is more likely the result of his writing in 2002 (rather than, say, 2005) than it is a consequence of his theory.

Ulrich Beck had not introduced his concept of the risk society (discussed in Chapter 2) when *Folk Devils and Moral Panics* was first published. However, as successive editions of the book appeared, Cohen found it necessary to deal with Beck's ideas. The risk society poses challenges to the moral panic formulation at a number of levels. Beck argued that the present—what he terms "late modernity"—is characterized by chronic emergencies. New technologies are so prone to unintended and unanticipated accidents that large-scale disasters are frequent occurrences in such areas as nuclear power, new drugs and medical procedures, and the environment. Unlike moral panics, these emergencies involve "real" issues less subject to high levels of disproportionality between a catalytic event and the social response. The responses, too, exhibit a different dynamic.

The original description of moral panics was essentially a contribution to the sociology of deviance, in which folk devils were chosen from among suspicious-looking groups in the youthful population, such as the Mods and Rockers, or from others who were dispossessed and relatively powerless. Agents of social control, such as the police, then acted on the fears and anger of the population.[10] Beck, however, paints a very different picture of the risk society. Its calamities are unintentional and often of unknown origin, at least temporarily puzzling even to the scientific personnel responsible for the technical processes that have gone out of control. There is no immediate folk devil. If anything, government officials, far from leading the charge, are often in positions of acute vulnerability, since they are often the ones legally or operationally responsible for the process that has gone wrong. As a consequence, they are obsessed with passing the "hot potato" of responsibility, lest one of them be identified as the culprit.[11]

Cohen doesn't quite know what to do with the risk society. At one point, he suggests that its "inchoate social anxieties" are partially replacing moral panics.[12] He recognizes that there is a major difference between the disasters Beck describes and moral panics. The problems generated in a risk society are *in principle* technical problems, the side effects of poorly understood but extremely potent innovations. But the essence of moral panics is that they are *moral*—they depend upon social judgments about right and wrong conduct, not simply judgments about technical mistakes. The identification of a folk devil is part of the "allocation of blame."[13] Yet Cohen must in the end concede that the same thing often happens in the arena of the risk society. What starts out as a technical issue can become transposed into moral terms, as happened with HIV/AIDS in the history of the pandemic. Beck suggests that such reactions are part of a process of "interpretative diversion," in which anxious populations that are unable to deal directly with their insecurity deflect it, displacing it onto scapegoats in a manner that closely resembles the identification of folk devils.[14] But in the end, we are left not knowing how this happens, or much about the dynamics of moral panics in a risk society.

EVIL INCARNATE

David Frankfurter's comparative study of demonic conspiracy beliefs offers the following scenario: Individuals who claim some professional expertise convince significant numbers of people in their community that a demonic conspiracy exists and that it is spreading organized evil. Those who come to accept this idea believe the problem is so serious that only some total act of purgation will purify the society, for example, a witch hunt, exorcisms, systematic prosecutions, or even extermination. The conspiracy is said to practice peculiarly loathsome rituals that constitute an inversion of the society's own morality. These beliefs become credible because they are buttressed by what appears to be direct testimony from members of the conspiracy who confess, from witnesses who claim to have seen the conspiracy's rituals, and from those who say they were the conspiracy's victims.[15]

The attractiveness of Frankfurter's formulation is that it permits comparison of similar outbreaks in dissimilar societies, across cultures, time periods, and levels of economic development. Whether in ancient Rome, medieval Germany, sub-Saharan African, or contemporary America, the process seems to be the same. The range of situations encompasses rumors about early Christians in the Roman Empire, European and African witch hunts, and allegations of satanic ritual child abuse in contemporary day-care centers. Experts paint a picture of conspiratorial moral inversion, made credible both by their professional credentials and by what Frankfurter calls the "mimetic performance" of those who say they can provide firsthand accounts of the conspiracy's activities. What remains to be done is for the community to mobilize in order to cleanse itself of the demonic pollution.

Much of this may seem similar to Stanley Cohen's model, but the similarities are superficial. There are certainly "devils" in David Frankfurter's model; indeed, the evildoers are often explicitly identified as satanic or demonic. Yet they are not necessarily familiar "folk devils." Cohen suggested that folk devils would always come from identifiable groups, such as young working-class men or immigrants, that the media can quickly grasp. His paradigmatic case of the Mods and Rockers makes that very point. For Frankfurter, matters are more complex, for now the identification of evildoers is in the hands of experts, not the media. They have their own arcane techniques, to which laypeople defer: "In his ability to show the evil system behind inchoate misfortune, he [the expert] offers his audiences the tangible hope of purging it. . . . As he lays out the nomenclature and intentions of the demonic, as he projects order onto incomprehensible current events, he himself gains a preternatural power."[16]

Just as Frankfurter's demons are not identical to Cohen's folk devils, so their purgation only superficially resembles moral panics. The moral panic is intense but also limited. It begins abruptly but also ends abruptly as the community moves on to other things. It is not surprising that this should be the case, since the targets of moral panics are relatively powerless. Not so with the malefactors in *Evil Incarnate*. They are participants in conspiracies, said to be vast and powerful organizations. Not only must individuals be punished, but the conspiratorial apparatus itself must be dismantled, lest it live to fight another day. Because it is invisible, the conspiracy may be omnipresent, still lurking despite the community's rituals of purification. Unlike Cohen's picture of spasmodic outbreaks, Frankfurter portrays campaigns governed by Manichean worldviews in which good and evil confront one another in a cosmic struggle. Such campaigns come to a close only by exhaustion and by a sense that the community is engaged in an act of collective cannibalism in which the innocent can no longer be distinguished from the guilty.

That dismemberment is inextricably bound up with "the performance of evil," the act of making evil tangible by the testimony, sometimes voluntary but often coerced, by the accused. The performances are essential in part because the conspiracies themselves are invisible and might not seem credible without such first-person accounts. These dramatic manifestations are closely linked to rituals of purification that sometimes reintegrate the evildoers back into the community, but can also expel or destroy them. In part, the outcome depends upon a group's capabilities: "[S]tates and large institutions often carry the means for the brutal extermination of evil bodies, while witch-finders operating on smaller, more regional scales may offer more socially agreeable procedures for evil to be cleansed from communities."[17]

In curious ways, the picture Frankfurter paints appears to be an inversion of the analysis of religious terrorism provided by Mark Juergensmeyer in his influential work, *Terror in the Mind of God*. Juergensmeyer, too, speaks of a cosmic struggle, but his "cosmic war" is central to the worldviews of terrorists, not the worldviews of their adversaries.[18] It is the enemies of the status quo who envision a cosmic struggle, whereas in the cases Frankfurter examines, it is the representatives of the status quo who see the world in those terms. There is a second element to the inversion. Juergensmeyer emphasizes the extent to which violence by religious terrorists is "performance violence," "like religious ritual . . . dramas designed to have an impact on the several audiences that they affect."[19] In Frankfurter's analysis, the performance/ritual is undertaken not by the anti–status quo forces of "evil" but by the community as an act of purification. Now in truth the two approaches are not necessarily mutually exclusive. Much of the difference lies in their points of view, with one examining communities obsessed by imagined threats to their integrity and the other seeking to understand how religious terrorists see the world they wish to overturn. Juxtaposed, they appear to be mirror images of one another.

Comparing the Models

The two models—Cohen's and Frankfurter's—have much in common. Both seek to understand and explain community upheavals directed at threats that either have emerged suddenly or have only now been identified. In both cases, the community believes that unless action is taken, its integrity is at risk. In both cases, there are leaders who define and amplify the problem: the media in Cohen's study, experts on evil in Frankfurter's. They take inchoate popular fears and anxieties and give them shape and definition.

But there are also differences. The evildoers that Cohen studies are easily identifiable: they are marginal social groups with little power who are always at risk, such as adolescents, unemployed workers, and immigrants. The situation for Frankfurter is more complex. While the actual victims may belong to vulnerable groups, such as old, unmarried women or Jews, they become targets only after they have become linked to a conspiracy—an invisible, conceptual structure. This is related to what might be termed the "visibility problem." The moral panics model deals with evildoers that are already visible but whose importance has been grotesquely exaggerated. Frankfurter's demonic conspiracy model, however, posits an invisible source of evil—a hidden satanic or demonic source—albeit one that may work through visible instruments or agents. It is made visible through the activity of the experts on evil who explain why superficially innocuous individuals are really dangerous.

When we look for the fit between these models and situations of unseen danger considered in earlier chapters, we face the following problem: Stanley Cohen does not address unseen dangers at all. The problem he must wrestle with is not visibility versus invisibility but the appropriateness of his model for genuine dangers, not merely those inflated by the media. Yet despite the apparent inapplicability of *Folk Devils and Moral Panics*, elements of it may speak to situations of unseen danger: the role of mass communications in defining danger and feeding a community's fears, and the demands the public makes on authorities to safeguard it from an apparent threat.

In the case of *Evil Incarnate*, the enemy is invisible; this is a model built around unseen danger. But it is what I earlier called "attributed danger." That is, the dangers that so exercised populations in Frankfurter's cases were all illusory. They existed in the minds of the "experts on evil" and later in the general population's. However, there is no empirical evidence for their existence that might satisfy an observer outside the groups involved. In the case of tales of satanic abuse in child-care facilities—the only contemporary cases with which Frankfurter is concerned—none has been confirmed. So the model here seeks to explain only misidentified unseen dangers, leaving aside those that are "real." Yet elements of the model can be put to work in broader contexts, notably two features: the emphasis on professional experts on evil to whom the general population looks for guidance in situations of potential danger; and the importance of ritual, the "mimetic performance," in which practitioners of evil, victims, and/or witnesses participate in activities that make danger credible and suggest that the community is on its way to ridding itself of polluting elements.

Applying the Models

Elements of both models can guide us to an understanding of unseen dangers in an age of terrorism. Stanley Cohen's emphasis on the media focuses attention on an element in the generation of a sense of danger that is often overlooked. While individuals may make their own judgments about the constellation of risk, hazard, and vulnerability, those judgments are often significantly mediated by organs of mass communication. Those organs are, of course, critical sources of information, but they may also, however unintentionally, communicate other messages. Cass Sunstein, who is familiar with moral panics without being directly familiar with Cohen's work, regards moral panics as a subtype of what he terms "social cascades." By a social cascade he means the accelerating movements of messages through a population. In its most benign form, a cascade might take the form of an urban legend, a story that might not carry with it any suggestion of fear and moves largely through person-to-person contact. Such cascades can sometimes contain fear-inducing messages. The process imparts a spurious credibility to the message by virtue of the number of people who believe it, although the earlier message-carriers were themselves merely imitating still earlier participants in the cascade. The only difference between social cascades in general and moral panics is that moral panics are social cascades that focus on notably vulnerable groups.[20]

Mass media can amplify the sense of danger by, for example, communicating contradictory or ambiguous messages from public officials. The combination of mass media and the involvement of public officials give added force and sometimes unintended direction to a social cascade. During the Three Mile Island nuclear reactor accident in Pennsylvania in 1979, for example, no evacuation order was given, but in two-thirds of the households within five miles of the plant, at least one person evacuated. When questioned afterward, 80 percent said they did so because of the confusing information they received from public officials.[21] As we have already seen, mass media, including forms of popular entertainment, also inadvertently transmit stereotypes of danger and evil that we unconsciously impose upon ambiguous and stressful situations. Thus the swarthy Middle Easterner with an exotic name has become a stock villain populating television programs and Hollywood films, and while, like all stereotypes, this arises from an initial factual basis, it also leads to wild overgeneralization in the application to everyday life.

"The war on terror" has become a big story for journalists, perhaps one of the biggest stories of the early twenty-first century. Like all "big stories," this one affects news judgments, which in turn affect public attitudes. It crowds out other stories, preempting reports that may be equally, perhaps more, important in terms of subsequent consequences. It also leads to exaggerated coverage of related events. Just as a major airplane crash leads to overcoverage of minor accidents soon afterward, so concern about mass-casualty terrorist attacks leads to heavy coverage of reports dealing with minor incidents—for example, plots uncovered before any operational preparations could be undertaken.

Saturation media coverage can also give a story an element of seeming disproportionality. For example, during the Washington-area sniper incidents in the fall of 2002, the level of public anxiety was so high that many routine events were cancelled. Yet the actual risk of death or injury was less than in many activities of daily life. This notwithstanding the fact that "the real risk could not possibly have been sufficient to justify the high levels of anxiety and fear, which, for many, bordered on hysteria."[22] Yet unlike the utterly insubstantial seaside disputes that served as the basis for the British tabloids' Mods and Rockers headlines, there *was* a real threat here, albeit an exaggerated one. The disproportionality in this case may have been due less to media hype than to the invisibility of the shooters. As far as the public was concerned, the shots came from nowhere, mysteriously killing random victims in well-lighted public places. The risk to any single individual may have been trivial and thus no justification for the massive press coverage. But the fact that the killers were *unseen* in locales where everyone else was visible gave to the incidents a terror that exceeded that which the number of victims warranted.

John Mueller, in his contrarian examination of the "terrorism industry," argues that communications media are complicit in spreading exaggerated conceptions of the danger terrorists pose. Thus the twenty-three terrorism alerts that were announced between 2001 and 2004 were all treated as major news stories by television evening news programs, but the same programs gave comparable coverage to only 13 percent of the subsequent reductions in alert levels.[23] In similar fashion, major media give heavy coverage to those who make dire predictions but rarely re-interview prophets when their predictions turn out to be incorrect.[24]

Mueller describes a post-9/11 "coterie of risk entrepreneurs," individuals in both the public and private sectors whose livelihoods depend upon the salience of terrorism as a public policy issue.[25] In somewhat the same vein, there can be "worst-case entrepreneurs," public officials who emphasize the risk of terrorism and the intensity of public outrage.[26] In this case, they do so less for pecuniary reasons than because of concern for political survival or genuine fear. However, both sets of entrepreneurs develop symbiotic relationships with the media who amplify their warnings, in part because the warnings feed the media's need for sensational narratives.

Thus there is a distinction between Stanley Cohen's brief, episodic panics and the broad-based hysteria driven by unseen dangers. Cohen's panics can be brief precisely because the causes are not invisible. The agents are visible, readily identifiable groups, and relatively powerless ones at that. As soon as the society's agents of social control are seen to have mobilized, the media campaign and public concern move on to other matters. But when the evil is unseen—whether in the form of the Washington snipers or a terrorist threat—the way lies open for a prolonged period of chronic hysteria.

We can also learn from Frankfurter's emphasis on the role of experts on evil, the professionals to whom the community looks for guidance in identifying danger. Unlike conventional military defeats, terrorist attacks are increasingly regarded as failures of expertise—failures to understand arcane belief systems, unfamiliar cultures, or novel modes of organization. The cliché "connecting the dots" is merely a catchphrase for the role of experts in creating a coherent narrative out of what the layperson might consider merely random pieces of information, a task we shall examine in detail in the next chapter. The role of the expert becomes all the more important in situations where evil is equated with invisibility. For the terrorism expert is believed to be the person who by dint of special training and techniques can enter the realm of the unseen. He or she can then reveal or make visible what cannot be seen either by the general public or by non-expert policymakers.

Doubts about the adequacy of such expert capabilities were already rife even before the September 11th attacks. Prior to 9/11 these issues were being dealt with more or less simultaneously by two study commissions. The U.S. Commission on National Security/21st Century had been chartered by the secretary of defense in 1998. It was popularly known as the Hart-Rudman Commission, after its co-chairs, former senators Gary Hart and Warren Rudman. As its name indicates, its mandate covered a wide range of security issues, but terrorism and homeland security were prominent among them. The following year—1999—Congress chartered the Advisory Panel to Assess Domestic Response Capabilities for Terrorism Involving Weapons of Mass Destruction, commonly referred to as the Gilmore Commission, after its chair, former Virginia governor James Gilmore.

Both commissions had submitted recommendations dealing with the organization of government terrorism capabilities prior to September 11, 2001, so that alternative models were "on the table" at the time of the attacks. Without going into a detailed analysis of the two proposals, they can be roughly characterized in the following manner: Both commissions acknowledged that there were severe problems, particularly at the federal level, with the organization of governmental resources to detect, defend against, and respond to terrorist threats. Despite their shared diagnosis, however, they reached different conclusions concerning the proper remedy. The Gilmore Commission opted to leave standing the existing array of government agencies concerned with terrorism but to impose upon them a coordinating mechanism situated in the White House. They proposed a National Office for Combating Terrorism in the executive office of the president with budgetary authority over federal agencies.[27] The Hart-Rudman Commission, on the other hand, opted for a radical reconfiguration in which a number of agencies would be moved from their original locations into a new cabinet-level department. Its plan for "organizational realignment" called for the creation of a National Homeland Security Agency including FEMA, as well as the Coast Guard, Customs Service, and the Border Patrol.[28] Although in the immediate aftermath of 9/11 it appeared that the Gilmore Commission's model might be adopted, with the passage of time, pressure for a new department became unstoppable and so the Department of Homeland Security was established in 2002, generally along the lines the Hart-Rudman Commission had suggested.

The DHS became the repository for expertise concerning ways for distinguishing terrorists from law-abiding individuals, and weapons from innocent cargo. This does not, of course, exhaust the department's responsibilities, but it constitutes the core of its explicit and implied tasks laid out in its mission statement: "We will lead the unified national effort to secure America. We will prevent and deter terrorist attacks and protect against and respond to threats and hazards to the nation. We will ensure safe and secure borders, welcome lawful immigrants and visitors, and promote the free-flow of commerce."[29] Nowhere was the department's claim to expertise concretized more vividly than in the color-coded Homeland Security Advisory System.

The Homeland Security Advisory System: Making Invisible Threats Visible

The Homeland Security Advisory System, in the minds of most Americans, constituted a summarization of the Department of Homeland Security's expert judgment about unseen dangers. However, the system did not begin this way. Its origin, like much else concerning homeland security, lay in a Homeland Security Presidential Directive, in this case HSPD-3, which was issued in March 2002, before the Department of Homeland Security was even established. At that point, it appeared that something like the Gilmore Commission's model might be taking shape in the form of an assistant to the president for homeland security. He was, in fact, Tom Ridge, shortly to become the founding secretary of homeland security when the department was established. All that, however, still lay in the future when HSPD-3 was drafted.

HSPD-3 established the now-familiar color designations for rising threat levels: green, blue, yellow, orange, and red. However, in significant respects the original description of the system differs from the way it was subsequently understood. It was originally intended less as a way of communicating with the public than as "a comprehensive and effective means to disseminate information regarding the risk of terrorist attacks to Federal, State, and local authorities," so that "[a]t each Threat Condition, Federal departments and agencies would implement a corresponding set of 'Protective Measures.'" In other words, each color was a signal for action to governmental organizations. The assignment of threat condition was to be made by the attorney general, in consultation with the presidential assistant for homeland security.[30] Notwithstanding the text of the directive, however, when Tom Ridge introduced the scheme publicly on March 12, 2002, he emphasized the system's role as a way of reaching the public, a function played down in the document itself: "The Homeland Security Advisory System is designed to measure and evaluate terrorist threats and communicate them to the public in a timely manner."[31]

Although green meant low and blue symbolized guarded, the security level was never below yellow, or elevated, in the six years the advisory system existed. It was red only once, in 2006, in response to threats against flights from the United Kingdom to the United States. Otherwise, it fluctuated between yellow and orange (high), going back and forth sixteen times between 2002 and 2006.[32]

In one respect, HSPD-3 conflicted with the approach Michael Chertoff brought into the DHS when he became secretary in 2005. The presidential directive used "threat" and "risk" almost interchangeably: "The higher the Threat Condition, the greater the risk of a terrorist attack." It defined risk as "the probability of an attack occurring and its potential gravity,"[33] although, as was pointed out earlier, it would almost certainly be impossible to calculate probability for a mass-casualty attack. However, in an important early speech, Secretary Chertoff attempted to separate threat from risk and place his department on the side of a risk-based approach. Threats, he said, "should not be automatic instigators of action." Instead, risk should be assessed by looking simultaneously at threat, vulnerability, and consequence.[34] Whether Chertoff's formulation affected assignments of threat level, however, is something known only to those inside the department.

What is clear is that the color-coded threat level advisories quickly assumed a public salience almost certainly not contemplated when the presidential directive was drafted. The creation of the Department of Homeland Security was not the only innovation that was stimulated by terrorist attacks. The post-9/11 period also saw the creation of such entities and offices as the National Counterterrorism Center, Northern Command (NORTHCOM) in the Defense Department, and the director of National Intelligence. But the DHS was unique in the variety of its tasks that involved direct contact with the general population (for example, at airport checkpoints) and in the degree to which it continually communicated to the public. As a result, no matter what expertise might exist elsewhere, either in the government or in the private sector, the department emerged almost by default as the public voice of expert knowledge on the invisible terrorist threat. Therefore, in the absence of any summarization of terrorism-related information from any other governmental source, the threat advisory level—

despite occasional ridicule from late-night television comedians—became the single best known and easily understood source. It in effect answered the question, How frightened should I be? Level changes became major news stories, particularly the threat elevations. The media, without knowing the basis for the threat judgments, communicated those judgments to the general community, amplifying them in the process. They thus functioned somewhat in the manner of the press in Stanley Cohen's description of moral panics.

The color-coding also neatly juxtaposed the realms of the seen and the unseen, transforming the invisible enemy into a vivid block of color. Since the level had never been blue, let alone green, yellow became, as it were, "the new green," the normal state of affairs—at once relatively stable and a source of chronic anxiety. The Department of Homeland Security advised that "[a]ll Americans should continue to be vigilant, take notice of their surroundings, and report suspicious items or activities to local authorities immediately."[35] Experts in evil, as David Frankfurter would describe them, have determined that invisible malefactors still lurk, albeit not always with the intention of inflicting immediate harm, and the appropriate color has been assigned.

The issues surrounding the threat advisory system would not have assumed so large a place were it not for the peculiar character of the 9/11 attacks, which had the effect of obliterating the distinction between victims and spectators. In his widely praised study of a 1972 flood that destroyed a West Virginia community, Kai Erikson observed:

Among the symptoms of extreme trauma is a sense of vulnerability, a feeling that one has lost a certain natural immunity to misfortune, a growing conviction, even, that the world is no longer a safe place to be. And this feeling often grows into a prediction that something terrible is bound to happen again. One of the bargains that men make with one another in order to maintain their sanity is to share an illusion that they are safe even when the physical evidence in the world around them does not seem to warrant that conclusion. The survivors of a disaster, of course, are prone to overestimate the perils of their situation, if only to compensate for the fact that they underestimated those perils once before; but what is worse, far worse is that they sometimes live in a state of almost constant apprehension because they have lost the human capacity to screen the signs of danger out of their line of vision.[36]

In the context of our discussion, this remarkable passage gives rise to two important implications.

First, because the September 11th attacks were covered by television in real time and occurred over a sufficiently long period to acquire a mass audience, millions of people outside the greater New York City and Washington, D.C., areas became, as it were, vicarious victims. The sense of victimization extended beyond those who worked in the World Trade Center towers and the Pentagon, and those related to the passengers on the airliners, and even beyond those living and working in Lower Manhattan and Arlington, Virginia. This vicarious victimization was significantly reinforced by the fact that the events preempted virtually all programming on major television channels, caused the cancellation of many community events all over the country, and caused the unprecedented cessation of commercial air service. We know also that psychological trauma symptoms not only varied with distance from the attack sites but increased with the number of hours individuals watched television coverage.[37] These findings mimic those of studies conducted after the 1963 assassination of President John F. Kennedy[38] and strongly suggest that certain forms of media coverage of traumatic national events can induce trauma symptoms in those not in physical proximity to the events themselves. While Erikson in the observations above had in mind direct physical survivors of a disaster, it is not unreasonable to think of the American population in general as disaster survivors following 9/11, and therefore in precisely that condition of vulnerability of which he speaks. Our collective "illusion of safety" had been shattered and with it came "a growing conviction . . . that the world is no longer a safe place to be." The color-coded warnings were therefore more than warnings; they were expert validations of inner mental states.

Second, Erikson speaks of an overestimation of perils that follows what had previously been an underestimation of perils—an entirely understandable act of compensation. It is, however, a process that falls not simply upon the victims (the population Erikson was primarily concerned with), however one chooses to define them. It also falls upon the experts, for it is often the failure of their expertise that causes the underestimation of perils. Much has been made, by the 9/11 Commission and others, of the failure of experts in the intelligence community to foresee the attacks. Yet like Cassandra, the ancient prophetess cursed by Apollo with the gift of making accurate forecasts that no one would believe, there were some who made accurate predictions. Richard A. Clarke, within days of the presidential inauguration in January 2001, had written a memorandum to Condoleezza Rice, then national security advisor, in which he insisted without much success that the fight against al-Qaeda be made a top priority.[39] It is scarcely surprising, therefore, that post-9/11 experts on evil would make precisely the compensatory move that Erikson indicates: they would never again act as though the world were a safe place.

Hence in addition to the *episodic* amplification of threat that Stanley Cohen makes part of the moral panic process, one would also expect that postdisaster situations would create a form of *structured* amplification. Here the primary agents of amplification may not be the media, as Cohen might suppose, but are likely to be Frankfurter's experts on evil, anxious to avoid the underestimation that characterized their predisaster forecasts. They operate in the public sector and derive their prestige both from their expertise and from their official positions. They begin the process of amplification by pointing out dangers and indicating the threat level. The media then continue by spreading their message. Having fallen into the trap of false negatives, those with expertise are more than willing to risk false positives, not only because their self-interest favors it, but also because they now genuinely believe the world is a much more dangerous place than they once thought. This may have paradoxical consequences. Thus, one unintended result is the often remarked upon "alert exhaustion," when the general public ceases to take warnings seriously and lapses into complacency.

Cohen could characterize the panics as episodic because crises of any kind are by their nature discontinuities that for a relatively short time interrupt the normal flow of events. However, when experts on evil (to use Frankfurter's term) engage in the structured rather than episodic amplification of warnings, we are on different terrain. It suggests a condition of chronic crisis. This, of course, sounds like an oxymoron. A genuine crisis cannot continue indefinitely. Yet the structured amplification of danger after 9/11, by normalizing danger, has gone far toward creating an ambiance of chronic crisis. The threat level never dipped below yellow, and the "war on terror" was projected to continue indefinitely into the future. Yet the "war on terror" both is and is not a "moral panic." It clearly includes the moral dimension Cohen regarded as vital, the sense that the conflict engages critical issues of right and wrong. But eight years after September 11th, whatever presently exists in the United States can scarcely be called a panic. What may appear from one perspective an atmosphere of chronic crisis is from another a new status quo.

Experts, the Media, and the Creation of Invisibility: The Cases of Eric McDavid and William Krar

As we have seen, widespread concern about the danger of terrorism has led to the empowerment of experts to whom both policymakers and ordinary citizens defer in seeking to know the identity of dangerous individuals and organizations, and the likelihood that they will act. Media of communication—television, newspapers, magazines, radio, and websites—spread and therefore amplify these judgments about danger. However—and this appears counterintuitive—the process can run in reverse. That is, those who might be the subject of such amplified warnings may be ignored, both by the experts on evil and by the mass media who report their judgments, even in cases where no attempt is made to keep information secret. Situations that on their face might be thought likely to call forth significant governmental and media activity sometimes pass with virtually no notice. Put somewhat differently, apprehended terrorists whose arrests and alleged acts or plans are matters of public record may simply vanish. Although plainly visible, they become effectively invisible.

The process through which invisibility is conferred upon such individuals is not the work of some nefarious government plan. Rather, it is the result of the convergent disinterest of so many parties, both public and private, that unless one happens to live in the region where terrorists' cases are processed, one is likely to know little or nothing about them. Paradoxically, one finds dramatic terrorist cases that were fully covered in local media in areas where prosecutions occurred but were virtually ignored by national reporters. They are not, therefore, truly unseen dangers. These are, after all, individuals who have been arrested and run through the judicial system. But insofar as the vast majority of the public is concerned, they are nonexistent and therefore invisible. Two cases will illustrate the process.

On September 27, 2007, Eric McDavid of Foresthill, California, was convicted in federal court of conspiracy to use fire or explosives to damage or destroy property, in this case a range of targets that included the United States Forest Service Institute of Forest Genetics, the Nimbus Dam and fish hatchery, cellular phone towers, and power stations.[40] Two of the co-conspirators had pled guilty in return for lighter sentences and their agreement to cooperate with the government. McDavid was apparently a member of the Earth Liberation Front (erroneously identified as the "Environmental Liberation Front" in a press release from the U.S. Attorney). In May 2008 he was sentenced to nineteen years and seven months in prison, plus thirty-six months of supervised release, almost the maximum time allowable under Federal Sentencing Guidelines.[41] Although there were no actual attacks on the targeted facilities, the three conspirators engaged in reconnaissance of the sites, bought components for an explosive device, and began to fashion the device.[42] Nonetheless, except for coverage in local media, the episode passed unnoticed as far as the country at large was concerned. It is true that the case was widely noted on the web, but almost all the stories were on sites maintained by organizations of activists sympathetic to McDavid's cause, such as Earth First!.[43] For others, it is truly as though the case did not exist and Eric McDavid were invisible. The most obvious reasons for the general disinterest was the domestic origin of the case and the ideological basis for the activities of McDavid and his colleagues. Except for some areas of the West, environmental terrorism is not part of most Americans' landscape of fear.

The next example is even stranger. On November 13, 2003, the U.S. Attorney's Office for the Eastern District of Texas issued a brief press release—scarcely more than half a page—announcing the guilty pleas of William J. Krar and his common-law wife, Judith L. Bruey. Krar had pled to one count of possessing a dangerous chemical weapon and his wife to conspiracy to possess illegal weapons. However, the brief description of the case in the release concealed a complex story. Krar had sent a package in January 2002 to an associate, Edward Feltus, in New Jersey, but it had been misdelivered to a home on Staten Island. The recipient opened the package and found that it contained a number of false documents: a Social Security card, a Vermont birth certificate, a North Dakota birth certificate, a Defense Intelligence Agency identification card, and a United Nations Multinational Force identification card. He notified authorities.[44]

This incident set in motion a protracted investigation that eventually led to a search of Krar's home and storage locker. The locker contained an extraordinary arsenal: 78 firearms of various types, 3 machine guns, silencers, 100,000 rounds of ammunition, 60 pipe bombs, "a remote-controlled briefcase device ready for explosive insertion," a fabricated landmine, grenades, 67 pounds of ammonium nitrate explosive, 66 tubes of liquid nitromethane explosive, military detonators, blasting caps, and atropine syringes.[45] But the most remarkable discovery was the ingredients for chemical weapons, sodium cyanide and hydrochloric acid. Some had already been assembled as a bomb in the form of "a green metal military ammo box containing 800 grams of pure sodium cyanide and two glass vials of hydrochloric acid." The device could produce enough hydrogen cyanide gas to kill more than 6,000 people under optimum conditions, or, under an alternative calculation, half the people in a $40\times40\times9$-foot room.[46] Brit Featherston, as assistant U.S. Attorney, suggested to KLTV in Tyler, Texas, "We have to figure out the actual destination of these bombs or any of the devices . . . but I don't think you possess these weapons for defensive reasons."[47] There was racist literature present as well, including William Pierce's two racist novels, *The Turner Diaries* and *Hunter*.

News of the discovery of the arsenal was widely reported by media in Texas. However, it was ignored everywhere else in the country. It was not reported by the *New York Times*, the *Washington Post*, the *Los Angeles Times*, CNN, Fox News, or MSNBC.[48] It was not the subject of a news conference by either the U.S. attorney general or the director of the FBI.[49] The Krar case did not surface in the national media until two months later when it was the subject of an interview on CNN's "American Morning" program on December 30. Soledad O'Brien questioned Brit Featherston. "This case is so bizarre and shocking," she said. "Why do you think it's flown under the radar for the bulk of the media?" In his disingenuous response he blamed the lack of interest on the war in Iraq and the fact that the investigation was still ongoing.[50]

Krar has said nothing about why he had the weapons or what he was planning to do with them. He was sentenced to eleven years in prison, his wife to four years, nine months. His only comment was: "For the record, I'm neither a terrorist nor a separatist. I've never desired to hurt anyone or the country that I love."[51] However, that scarcely disposes of so strange an episode. When the case finally surfaced in the *New York Times*, it was in Paul Krugman's column, where he observed, "[I]t's hard to believe that William Krar wouldn't have become a household name if he had been a Muslim or even a leftist. . . . [I]s Mr. [John] Ashcroft neglecting real threats to the public because of his ideological biases?"[52]

In effect, William Krar had become invisible, at least outside of Texas, even though the facts of the case were a matter of public record. The Justice Department chose not to publicize Krar's arrest despite the extraordinary quantity of weapons and despite the fact that they were seized before any acts of violence were committed. National media chose not to treat the arrest as a national news story, despite the fact that the weapons cache exceeded in size that of any found since September 11th. By a series of independent decisions made in government and media offices, William Krar became almost as invisible after his arrest as he had been before it. It is as if the elaborate system of risk amplification put in place after 9/11 had gone into reverse, de-amplifying what on its face appeared to be a major terrorist threat avoided; the more so since sodium cyanide itself is considered a chemical weapon. What might have caused such paradoxical behavior?

One possibility is that William Krar did not fit the current stereotype of a terrorist. He is a native-born American, presumably Christian. There is considerable circumstantial evidence of his right-wing politics: not only the literature confiscated but also that he had paid no federal income taxes since 1988 and his associate in New Jersey, Edward Feltus, was a member of a militia group. As Paul Krugman suggested, the absence of left-wing or, especially, Muslim associations made him a poor candidate for the terrorist label. Further, even though acts and threats of violence have continued from the extreme Right, there has been a sea change in American public and governmental opinion. The obsession with paramilitary groups that followed the 1995 Oklahoma City bombing has disappeared. In its place has come a fixation upon the dangers posed by radical Islam. Had William Krar been discovered, say, in 1996 or 1997, no doubt his arrest would have led the national news. Six or seven years later he was a quaint anomaly. Even his possession of a large quantity of deadly poison did not lift him above the routine.

Another, related possibility is that Krar was regarded as a secondary danger and therefore someone who did not warrant significant attention. He would have constituted a primary danger in the 1990s, but in a different context, defined by radical Islam, he was perhaps judged to be a lesser threat. He was also, as far as we know, not connected with an organization, which may also have relegated him to a category of minor dangers, although he had a long history of associations with militia groups.[53]

It is difficult to know what danger Krar may have posed. However, the volume and variety of weapons certainly make a prima facie case for dangerousness. But since he and his wife pleaded guilty, there was no trial at which this question might have been pursued. The federal investigation is said to have proceeded, but if any additional information was found concerning his motives, it has not been made public. The few references to him in national media in 2003 and 2004 were not followed up, and his case disappeared from view, the result of a tacit social decision that he was unimportant. Just as there can be social judgments about significance, such as in moral panics, so there can be judgments about insignificance. Stanley Cohen made the point that judgments about significance that eventuate in moral panics often have nothing to do with real danger, since the objects of panic fears rarely have the capacity to do much harm. He did not explore, because he was not interested in, situations where a consensus is reached that a situation is unimportant and thus not worth the community's collective anxiety. But as we have seen in the cases of Eric McDavid and William Krar, such instances do exist, and in them, too, the issue of real capacity to harm may be irrelevant to the community's decision.

It is as if the issue of whether or not to amplify danger warnings is at least partially decoupled from an objective analysis of dangerousness. Unlike McDavid, whose arrest was facilitated by an informant within the cell, William Krar operated alone. This means there can be warnings of danger in times of relative safety, and no or few warnings at times of danger. The former is understandable, since warning systems are biased toward false positives. The bias is understandable, because those in positions of accountability know that their positions are safer if they overwarn. But the latter—ignoring a dangerous situation—appears counterintuitive, for it suggests a bias toward false negatives. Why would those in positions of accountability appear less than hypervigilant? To be so suggests their willingness to take risks with their job security as well as with the safety of their society that appears inconsistent with the mind-set of most public servants, particularly if we leave aside cases of incompetence or corruption. Yet there are many cases of warnings that either were not made or were made and not heeded, such as Richard Clarke's memo about al-Qaeda.

What appears to be happening in most of these cases is that decision-makers are, like all of us, in a condition of limited information-processing capacity that results in differential focusing, what Richard Posner calls "economy of attention."[54] If those limited capacities have been preempted by other matters that have already been defined as problems of primary importance, the psychic cost of rearranging priorities is likely to be too great, and the warning will probably be ignored or at least relegated to a subordinate category of significance. In the cases of McDavid and Krar, who had of course already been apprehended, the issue was publicizing their arrests and what was known of their conduct. Yet problems connected with Islamic terrorism had, especially since 9/11, claimed so much attention that short of redefining post-9/11 counterterrorism priorities, the fate of Eric McDavid and William Krar and what might be said about them to the public were deemed to be matters of no great importance—which allowed them to slip into an obscurity, which rendered them effectively invisible.

Cohen's and Frankfurter's models leave us, then, with a kind of vocabulary that can be utilized to understand a society's response to threats. From Cohen we draw two essential ideas: the phenomenon of the *moral panic* and the importance of *disproportionality*. The former suggests the intensity of the desire to rid society of a perceived evil, while the latter points to the emphasis on responses that are out of proportion to their causes. From Frankfurter comes the critical idea of *experts on evil*, those who can make sense out of the unseen world from which threats ultimately emanate. We will bring these concepts together in the context of terrorism and homeland security in the next chapter.

eight

EXPERTS, NARRATIVES, AND THE PUBLIC

We all tell stories about the world. When danger appears, the need for such stories grows, in order to explain why a world that once seemed safe and orderly now seems to be in jeopardy. As we saw in Chapter 4, many such stories already exist in the domain of popular culture, ready to be appropriated. But, as we shall see now, the situations in which laypersons and experts tell stories are not always the same, nor do laypersons and experts tell the same stories. We have already seen the central role occupied by experts on evil, those whose skills allow them to perform the critical function of recognizing and defining social danger, especially when the causes of that danger appear to be unseen. Hence it becomes essential to understand both their narratives and those of the larger public.

In the discussion that follows, we will examine the role stories play in situations of danger, and the way they function for both potential victims and outside experts. Then we will look at the role of narrative more generally and the difference between two types of narratives, the *narrative of centralized control* and the *narrative of emergent behavior*. We will look at the manner in which these two narratives might be applied to terrorism, and, more specifically, their application by terrorism experts to contemporary Islamic radicalism.

Routine and Nonroutine Risks

First, however, we need to distinguish ordinary from extraordinary dangers. Ordinary dangers are not necessarily those that inflict less harm. In scale and destructiveness, ordinary dangers may still legitimately be considered disasters. However, their ordinariness lies in the fact that as a result of location, history, or other factors their appearance is predictable or can be readily anticipated. For example, a city that lies near the path frequently taken by hurricanes can expect to be hit at some time and hence can face the "ordinary" danger of a hurricane, yet the ordinariness of the danger does not preclude the possibility of heavy loss of life and property. On the other hand, there may be other dangers that can be neither predicted nor even reasonably anticipated: the outbreak of a hitherto unknown disease, for example, or a mass-casualty terrorist attack by a tactic not previously utilized. These, too, are disasters, but they are also extraordinary dangers for which the past provides little or no guidance.

Where ordinary risks are repeated over long periods of time, the population develops its own expertise or "local knowledge" about how the danger should be confronted. Social scientists have often reserved this term for the disaster-coping practices of indigenous, non-Western peoples.[1] However, it may easily be found among the general public in developed countries as well, where, as a result, people listen to experts with a certain skepticism and do not always defer to their judgment. This is often the case with natural disasters that occur on a regular basis, such as hurricanes and forest fires. Affected communities accumulate a kind of folk wisdom or local knowledge, as well as a repertoire of defensive practices believed to work effectively in times of danger. These largely oral traditions in effect make every potential victim an expert who feels capable not only of dealing with an emergency but of independently evaluating the views of professionals. This explains why there is sometimes noncompliance in the face of evacuation orders. The noncompliers are neither irrationally stubborn nor merely eccentric. Rather, they consider that their knowledge base, resting as it does upon personal and communal experience, provides them with grounds for challenging the validity of advice or orders from "outsiders." By the same token, where there is compliance, it, too, is likely to be grounded less in deference to expertise than in the fact that expert judgments happen to be consistent with compliers' own and their community's knowledge. In each case, behavior will have been grounded in stories that have been passed on, in the form of personal anecdotes, secondhand accounts, and legends about previous disasters and the manner in which they were faced.

Recourse to local knowledge, however, is of little or no value for extraordinary dangers whose novelty places them outside personal and communal experience. New or exotic risks recast the relationship between laypersons and experts. These differences became clear in research that examined the different ways in which experts and nonexperts conceptualized potentially dangerous situations. While the research focused on the dangers posed by electromagnetic fields, it is highly suggestive of the general manner in which people handle unfamiliar risks. In such cases, members of the general public have neither their own nor collective memories to fall back on. There is no local knowledge. On the other hand, there may be a good deal of expert knowledge. That expert knowledge seeks to establish chains of cause and effect concerning fundamental types of risk: whether a hazard exists; whether an accident is possible; whether there is exposure to a dangerous agent; whether there is evidence of damage; and whether an accident has occurred.[2] Consequently, in such situations researchers found that experts were likely to address potential victims not in terms of compelling narratives but rather by providing answers to specific questions. However, the situations they examined were, as we shall see, relatively localized problems: those characterized by scientific or technological innovation, the by-products of technological processes, or new disease entities—in other words, in general, with the exception of new diseases, they constituted the results of Ulrich Beck's "risk society." These are the situations of modernity fraught with danger and unpredictability where experts are anxious to shift the "hot potato" of responsibility.

On the other hand, it also turned out that laypersons, confronted with the same situations, did construct stories. Where risks were novel, they could not construct stories based on the past. They therefore constructed them differently, based on such stereotypical motifs as "Things can happen sooner than you think"; "Who is to say there isn't any . . . ?"; "We are all victims already"; "Don't let them get away with it"; and "It was bound to happen sooner or later."[3] These are essentially hypotheticals, projecting the danger into the near-term future as a counterweight to the confidence of experts. While experts might use knowledge claims to attempt to de-amplify risk, laypersons employed story lines to amplify it.[4] Where hurricane and forest fire victims are often skeptical of experts based on their own claim to equal or superior knowledge, potential victims of novel risks can make no such claim, yet they, too, are likely to manifest skepticism, a skepticism that breeds fear.

What accounts for such skepticism? In the first place, the dangers involved are likely to be in close physical proximity to the potential victims. For example, dangers believed to be associated with nuclear power plants, environmental pollution, genetically modified crops, and cases of BSE exist because the causes of those dangers are in the immediate vicinity of those who believe they might be victims. All are either immediately close to populations or likely to be so through food distribution chains or other mechanisms. The dangers therefore cannot be discounted because of remoteness. Second, these are overwhelmingly anthropogenic—humanly caused—disasters rather than results of the natural world. As such, they are likely to be targets for attributions of responsibility and blame. Finally, there is also the issue of the degree of confidence nonexperts repose in experts. Confidence in expertise becomes vulnerable when claims are made about rare or novel events and processes. That lies at the heart of Beck's analysis of the risk society, for he argues that as technical options grow, so, too, does the incalculability of their consequences.[5] Scientific expertise may create means, but it cannot necessarily determine the total variety or likelihood of ends. Accurately predicting consequences becomes increasingly difficult, and there is always the possibility that something new will exceed the ability of its creators to control it. In similar fashion, Richard Posner reminds us that when attempting to assess the likelihood of rare events, such as those involving mass casualties, it is impossible to calculate probabilities, and thus quantify risk.[6] Attempts by experts to mollify potential victims by assuring them that all possible outcomes have been foreseen and that there is no chance of error or accident will, therefore, be met by well-grounded doubts.

Terrorism, Experts, and Public Attitudes

As we have seen, when the general public is faced with novel risks associated with nearby potentially dangerous technological processes, it often tends to amplify them through the construction of frightening stories, while experts try to reassure them by marshalling soothing facts and arguments. However, when the issue is another novel risk—mass-casualty terrorism—a significant reversal can occur: *The public grows gradually complacent while the experts construct ever more frightening narratives.* Much of the remainder of this chapter will be taken up with examining how and why this curious reversal takes place.

While the American public appears generally skeptical about the effectiveness of homeland security measures, there has been a continuing drop in fears of an imminent terrorist attack. CNN polls conducted since 2001 show that in recent years these fears have substantially declined. A majority of Americans questioned between 2002 and 2006 believed a terrorist attack was imminent. However, by 2007 the number had declined to 41 percent, and in 2008 it dropped to just 35 percent.[7] However, polling data, at least through 2005, show doubts about the effectiveness of the government's efforts to protect Americans, just as more recent data confirm the reduced significance of terrorism fears. The number of people expressing significant confidence in prevention dropped from 69 percent to 59 percent immediately after the Hurricane Katrina debacle. Not surprisingly, more than half the population questioned "their government's ability to prevent terrorism in their own communities," although at the same time only 14 percent believed an attack was likely to take place soon in their own community.[8] Even if this trend persists, it would coexist with a greatly reduced belief that an attack would actually take place. Terrorism was not a salient issue during the 2008 presidential campaign, with only about 10 percent of Americans indicating that it would decide their presidential vote.[9] Polls taken in October and November 2008 showed only between 9 percent and 13 percent of voters identified it as their most important issue.[10]

A similar, if somewhat more nuanced, view emerges from a series of Pew surveys. In the early summer of 2002—nine months after the attacks and just after the arrest of Jose Padilla in connection with an alleged "dirty bomb" plot—20 percent of voters wanted terrorism discussed in the congressional election, the same percentage that desired discussion of the economy.[11] When annual Pew surveys asked respondents to identify the most important problem facing Americans, the percentage naming terrorism began to drop, from 24 percent in 2002, to 16 percent in 2003 and 14 percent in 2004.[12] On the other hand, judgments about terrorists' capabilities have remained relatively constant since 2002. Most see their capabilities as the same as on 9/11, although the percentage regarding the capabilities as greater has fallen, from 22 percent in 2002 to 18 percent in 2008.[13] Regarding the question of whether terrorism was "very important" to one's vote, the percentage has fallen from 77 percent in 2004 to 68 percent in 2008. Dramatic events such as the frustrated plot to bring down transatlantic airliners, the London transit bombings, and the Madrid train bombings did increase the proportion of interviewees who reported being "very worried" about terrorism. However, the increases from before to after each event were, respectively, from 17 percent to 25 percent; from 17 percent to 26 percent; and from 13 percent to 20 percent. Thus, dramatic threats or attacks could increase the very worried by 7–9 percent but expanded that segment to only about one-quarter of the total sample.[14]

While terrorism has moved steadily off of the public's "radar," replaced by such issues as the economy, it continues to occupy a significant place on the agenda of experts, both in and out of government. As we shall shortly see, it is they, rather than the general public, who construct narratives of fear, and it is therefore to the role of narrative that we now turn.

Two Kinds of Narratives

The reversal, in which experts rather than laypersons tell stories about terrorist threats, compels us to look more broadly at the nature of narrative. The public does not tell stories about terrorism because, unlike such novel risks as nuclear power plants and environmental pollution, terrorism is not viewed as a proximate threat. If it comes, it will come from some far distant place, oceans and continents away. Its source lies in unfamiliar societies and cultures. The United States, unlike for example the United Kingdom, does not contain large, residentially concentrated communities of immigrants from Muslim countries, nor are its Muslim citizens for the most part unintegrated and radicalized. The number of Americans associated with radical Islamic groups has been small.[15] Hence, the public's need to construct such a narrative is greatly reduced. For those, such as experts, who deal professionally with distant threats on a daily basis, however, the need for a narrative is much greater, and the psychological, if not the physical, distance is much smaller. The danger to them seems proximate. For them, two types of narrative are potentially available: the *narrative of centralized control*, and the *narrative of emergent behavior*.[16]

According to the narrative of centralized control, the behavior of any collectivity is the result of a "guiding entity." The behavior of both the mass and the elements in it are, therefore, the effects of an external cause. This causal agent thus controls an array of actors that may appear to behave independently but in fact do the bidding of a directing force. This story line is often applied even in cases where it is known to be false, as when a president is credited or blamed for economic conditions over which he has little or no control. Yet that causal link is imputed as part of a narrative of centralized control.[17] Such narratives can, of course, be modified by the inclusion of elements of chance, while still preserving a narrative thread. However, the greater the element of centralized control, the more cohesive the story.

The narrative of emergent behavior is quite different. Emergent behavior is "the coming into being of objects or patterns that are not the result of a centralized authority or plan or guiding hand or pacemaker or any other kind of overarching control, much less an intention, but instead are the result of innumerable local interactions."[18] These might include examples as disparate as the stock market, mobs, or flocks of birds, for in each case the patterning is the spontaneous result of hundreds or thousands of independent behaviors. This is distinct from the concept of "swarming" as a strategic principle, in which a fighting force consciously attacks from many different directions.[19] In the case of genuine emergent behavior, what develops without conscious intent is a collective behavior greater than the sum of the individual actions. The idea that some form of order might emerge without centralized control is antithetical to the belief that order must be imposed or directed, and thus introduces a radically different "story line." Yet trying to find the story line is neither simple nor easy, since there are in fact a great many independent stories that must be traced, and their interdependence is essential to produce the outcome. Where the narrative of centralized control minimizes the number of causal factors in its attempt to explain effects, the narrative of emergent behavior multiplies the number of causes. Where the one is parsimonious, the other appears messy and untidy.

Both types of narratives might in principle be applied to terrorism. A terrorist narrative of centralized control, for example, would tell a story about an organization capable of dispatching members to carry out attacks against distant targets, circumventing the defensive measures of government intelligence services, law enforcement agencies, and military organizations. By contrast, a narrative built around emergent behavior would tell a very different story, in which wholly independent individual terrorists or autonomous cells would carry out opportunistic attacks against similar targets that combined to create the appearance of a coordinated force. Clearly, the choice of story line would be dictated in part by the facts available. However, where terrorism is concerned, the facts are often incomplete, contested, or subject to interpretation, so that no single "reading" is self-evident in the process so often termed "connecting the dots," so that the choice of narrative is in large part an interpretive decision.

The narrative of central control is the more familiar, in part because it is built into the language of international relations in which we adopt the convenient fiction that each state speaks with one voice; this despite the fact that governments in reality are pulled in different directions by competing factions, interest groups, political parties, and rival leaders. However, for the ease of diplomacy, it becomes advantageous to pretend that these conflicting forces do not exist and to ascribe the actions of the state to a monolithic governing apparatus.

What might be termed a pathological variation of the narrative of centralized control appears in conspiracy theories in which a wide range of consequences are attributed to a powerful hidden organization. From a conspiracist viewpoint, nothing happens by accident, everything is connected, and nothing is as it seems.[20] By definition, a conspiracy is invisible and acts by stealth. The ultimate conspiracy theory would describe an unseen organization that controlled everything, and thus would constitute the consummate version of a narrative of centralized control. The potential for an overlap between conspiracy theories and narratives of terrorism is obvious, for terrorist organizations, too, seek invisibility and attempt to act in ways that frustrate detection. Hence they mimic the organizations described in conspiracy theories. The danger, however, is that descriptions of terrorist organizations will take the form of conspiracy theories. This danger is increased by the degree to which reliable information about the organizations is unavailable and the lacunae filled in with speculation, surmise, or data of doubtful reliability. In addition, terrorists may spread disinformation about their capabilities that make them appear far more powerful than they are. Terrorist organizations may be conspiracies, but explaining their activities by recourse to conspiracy theories is fraught with dangers, for conspiracy theories are closed systems of ideas that purport to explain even as they shut themselves off to data inconsistent with their fundamental assumptions.

Government Chooses a Narrative

At this writing, the current official narrative concerning the terrorist threat is a narrative of centralized control. It may be found most prominently in the National Intelligence Estimate, "The Terrorist Threat to the US Homeland," issued in July 2007. Such documents are "the Intelligence Community's most authoritative written judgments on national security issues." Concerning al-Qaeda, the estimate concluded: "Al Qa'ida is and will remain the most serious terrorist threat to the Homeland, as its central leadership continues to plan high impact plots, while pushing others in extremist Sunni communities to mimic its efforts and to supplements its capabilities. We assess the group has protected or regenerated key elements of its Homeland attack capability, including a safehaven in the Pakistan Federally Administered Tribal Areas (FATA), operational lieutenants, and its top leadership."[21] The drafters of the estimate also believed that the organization would continue to seek attacks on U.S. targets that would produce "mass casualties, visually dramatic destruction, significant economic aftershocks, and/or fear among the US population." Al-Qaeda would continue trying to secure weapons of mass destruction (CBRN) and would use them if available.[22] These conclusions were reinforced the following year by Admiral Michael McConnell, then director of National Intelligence (DNI), in testimony before the Senate Select Committee on Intelligence. He repeated and elaborated upon all the major judgments in the National Intelligence Estimate.[23] Much the same picture was painted in a fall 2008 speech by General Michael Hayden, then director of the Central Intelligence Agency: "[T]here is no greater national security threat facing the United States than al-Qa'ida and its associates. Bin Laden has said repeatedly that he considers acquisition of nuclear weapons 'a religious duty.' And we know that al-Qa'ida remains determined to attack our country in ways that inflict maximum death and destruction."[24]

Both the National Intelligence Estimate and the lengthy testimony of the DNI mentioned terrorism by groups other than al-Qaeda. However, it was clear from both that these were considered decidedly secondary threats. It was a revived and centrally directed al-Qaeda, operating from bases in Pakistan, that, in their view, constituted the most profound threat to the United States.

The Narrative of Centralized Control Is Challenged

The most sustained attack on the application of the narrative of centralized control to contemporary transnational terrorism appeared in Marc Sageman's 2008 book, *Leaderless Jihad*.[25] Sageman was already well known as the author of an earlier volume, *Understanding Terror Networks.*[26] *Understanding Terror Networks* was in fact itself a narrative of centralized control, based on data about the backgrounds and interactions of 172 Islamic terrorists. From his analysis, which extended from about 1980 through the 2001 attacks, Sageman had concluded that the "global Salafi jihad" was directed by al-Qaeda. At its core was a "Central Staff" made up of thirty-two members of the sample, including Osama bin Laden and his circle in Afghanistan. In addition, there were clusters of Maghrebi Arabs (fifty-three); Core Arabs, from Egypt and the Gulf region (sixty-six); and participants from Southeast Asia (twenty-one).[27] The Central Staff, although they themselves did not directly engage in terrorist operations, were linked through lieutenants to those who did, and funded their operations.[28] The Central Staff stood, as the name implies, at the center of networks of terrorists. At the time of publication, Sageman was unsure what al-Qaeda's post-9/11 role would be, since attacks and arrests had weakened the organization. Nonetheless, he left open the possibility that "the survival of many central staffers . . . still makes the global jihad a potent threat." Yet he thought it more probable that the Central Staff would be more an inspiration than a controlling force.[29]

However, the picture he painted four years later in *Leaderless Jihad* constituted a dramatic departure, for he now asserted that Islamic terrorism had devolved into a collection of spontaneous, self-organizing, and uncoordinated groups—in other words, he now told a narrative of emergent behavior. His very title suggested a radical reorientation, for it alluded not to radical Islam but to the white supremacist movement in the United States.

The phrase "leaderless resistance" was first popularized on the American extreme right through an essay of the same name by Louis Beam, a former Klan leader later associated with the racist and anti-Semitic theology known as Christian Identity. Beam had borrowed the phrase from a shadowy Cold War figure, Colonel Ulius Louis Amoss, who may or may not have worked for the Office of Strategic Services during World War II but unquestionably ran a private intelligence service afterward.[30] In Beam's view, any dissident organization, even when built on a cellular model, was in danger of penetration by the government. Consequently, the only armed resistance that could be safely pursued would have to be conducted by independent, unconnected individuals or very small coteries acting on their own.[31] Beam's ideas first reached a significant audience when his essay was circulated in October 1992 at a "Meeting of Christian Men" convened in

Estes Park, Colorado, by the Christian Identity preacher Pete Peters. The aim of the meeting was to protest the killing of the wife and son of Randy Weaver, a Christian Identity believer involved in a protracted armed stand-off with the FBI at his remote Idaho cabin. The meeting was attended by an array of important antigovernment militants, including figures in the militia movement.[32] Beam's essay was read not only against the background of the Weaver affair but in the context of a long period of intense government pressure on the extreme right that began with the smashing of the insurgent group known as The Order in the mid-1980s. Thus, although "leaderless resistance" was advanced by Beam as a strategic principle, it was, as Jeffrey Kaplan has observed, "[m]ore a mark of despair than a revolutionary strategy."[33] Subsequently, Beam's essay was linked to the website of the Army of God, the most radical and violent fringe of the anti-abortion movement.

Sageman had something different in mind. Where Beam argued that independently organized violence should be pursued intentionally as a conscious strategic principle, Sageman asserted in 2008 that it had emerged spontaneously among Islamic terrorists: "The present threat has evolved from a structured group of al Qaeda masterminds, controlling vast resources and issuing commands, to a multitude of local groups trying to emulate their predecessors by conceiving and executing operations from the bottom up."[34] This required an explicit rejection of the National Intelligence Estimate as inflated and based upon anecdotal evidence.[35] Al-Qaeda might have influence in the tribal areas of Pakistan and adjacent areas of Afghanistan, but the blows inflicted since 9/11 had so degraded communications that the organization's Central Staff could no longer exercise command and control functions.[36] In its place was an uncoordinated array of imitators, former affiliates, and wannabes each making its own decisions about targets and means. In short, the earlier narrative of centralized control had been replaced by a new narrative of emergent behavior.

Leaderless Jihad was sharply attacked in a review essay that was noteworthy for both the author and the venue. Its author was Bruce Hoffman, a distinguished terrorism scholar formerly at Rand and now at the Georgetown School of Foreign Service and it appeared in *Foreign Affairs*, which reaches a cross-over readership of government officials, academics, and opinion-makers. Hoffman accused Sageman of a "fundamental misreading of the al Qaeda threat" in his assertion that a centrally directed terrorist organization had been superseded by an uncoordinated array of local groups.[37] He pointed out that Sageman's position "flies in the face of the two most recent authoritative analyses of terrorist threats to the United States." That referred, of course, to the National Intelligence Estimate of July 2007 and the McConnell testimony before the Senate Select Committee on Intelligence.[38]

Yet another exchange followed, in which Sageman asserted that he had never claimed that the al-Qaeda central organization was without capabilities or had given up on its goal to attack the United States and Hoffman largely restated positions he had taken earlier.[39] This exchange, in the pages of the most prestigious American foreign policy journal, placed in sharp opposition two different narratives of Islamic terrorism. The narrative of centralized control was represented by official documents of the intelligence community, as well as by Hoffman's review of *Leaderless Jihad*. Indeed, the narrative of centralized control had been Sageman's own narrative in *Understanding Terror Networks*. This narrative, however, was now challenged by Sageman himself in *Leaderless Jihad*. The Hoffman-Sageman exchange attracted considerable attention outside the relatively small circle of terrorism scholars. One blogger called Sageman and Hoffman "the Hatfields and McCoys of Counterterrorism."[40] Yet Sageman was scarcely the first person to suggest that the narrative of centralized control might not be the only way to understand Islamic terrorism. An analysis of the April 2004 Madrid train bombings alluded to the Sageman-Hoffman debate when it concluded that "[t]he attacks were 'bottom-up' rather than top down" but added that awareness of al-Qaeda provided "impetus, inspiration, and legitimacy."[41] Years before, Brian A. Jackson had observed that "al-Qaeda" had long been a malleable concept whose meaning shifted with the context and user.[42] Yet not until Sageman's 2008 book was the polarity of competing narratives so starkly evident.[43]

Competing Narratives and the Issue of Unseen Dangers

The dustup between Marc Sageman and Bruce Hoffman, unimportant in itself, was significant because it demonstrated the existence and incompatibility of two narratives about Islamic terrorism. The narrative of centralized control clearly enjoyed the support of the intelligence community and, presumably, of others in the executive branch. It is also the easiest to understand, since it posits a clear, relatively simple line of causation. The narrative of emergent behavior, manifested in Sageman's recent book, is not only "heretical" in the sense that it runs counter to official pronouncements; it is also more difficult to grasp. That is in the nature of emergent behavior story lines, in which separate, largely independent actions aggregate to form a pattern that the individual actors did not plan or intend. The multiple lines of causation present a picture that is, at least at first glance, chaotic.

There are also important implications for the issue of unseen dangers. These implications go to the very raison d'être of American homeland security policy. On the seventh anniversary of the September 11th attacks, the Department of Homeland Security issued a fact sheet about its progress and priorities. Of the five priorities listed, the first two were based on the assumption that threats would come from the outside by stealth or subterfuge. Thus the section "Protecting the Nation from Dangerous People" begins: "DHS prevents the entry of terrorists and criminals while facilitating the legitimate flow of people by strengthening interior security efforts and continuing to increase security at America's borders." The second priority, "Protecting the Nation from Dangerous Goods," begins: "As a part of its risk-based approach, the department is focused on programs to identify, track, and intercept nuclear and radiological components and systems at ports of entry and in transportation systems with U.S. borders. The department is also intensifying efforts to strengthen capabilities that reduce the risk of a biological attack in the United States."[44] The conclusion is inescapable that homeland security policy is founded on the fear that invisible terrorists utilizing invisible weapons of mass destruction, based outside the United States, will somehow manage to penetrate American borders. Only a centrally directed organization would possess sufficient resources and capabilities to engage in such a mass-casualty attack. It is little wonder therefore that those preoccupied with fears of unseen dangers would gravitate toward a narrative of centralized control. At the same time, a narrative of centralized control is subtly reinforced by the stereotypical stories found in popular culture, in which evil comes not through a cascade of independent acts but through the planned efforts of hidden but highly organized malevolent forces.

As we have already seen in Chapters 5 and 6, long before 9/11 there were two widely diffused, preexisting stories about evil. One was the story of the border-crossing cultural alien bearing invisible but destructive pathologies, whether in the form of diseases or alien beliefs. The other was the story of the hidden villain in a remote fortress, with access to high-technology weapons. They both could be readily assimilated to the narrative of centralized control, in which an invisible organization with weapons of mass destruction is infiltrating its members into a complacent America.

A narrative of emergent behavior, by contrast, presents significant difficulties. One, of course, is that the small, local terrorist groups implied by this narrative are unlikely to have significant resources, and particularly not those necessary to procure and employ high-technology weapons of mass destruction. Secondly, this narrative also implies the geographical dispersion of autonomous, locally based terrorists. Instead of being coordinated arms of a far-flung network, following the orders of a distant command, terrorists would decide for themselves what to attack in the countries where they reside. In keeping with his emergent behavior narrative, Sageman pointed to what he calls an "Atlantic divide"; that is, the differential rates of radicalization among Muslims in Western Europe and the United States, far higher in the former than in the latter, are such that "the rate of arrests on terrorism charges per capita among Muslims is six times higher in Europe than in the United States."[45] Local, self-organized groups of Islamic terrorists are most likely to arise where there are large, residentially segregated, alienated Muslim communities, a relative rarity in the United States but common in Western Europe.

To be sure, neither narrative is unproblematic when applied to terrorism. As of this writing, there has been no post-9/11 mass-casualty terrorist attack in the United States. However, it is not unambiguously clear why this is the case. It may be because of the effectiveness of homeland security measures, either as deterrents or as screening measures. It may be because law enforcement, military, or other measures either within the United States or far outside U.S. borders caused missions to be crippled, cancelled, or compromised. Or it may be because some structural change in Islamic terrorism of the sort Sageman describes has made such attacks much less likely. Thus it cannot be said with certainty whether the narrative of centralized control is correct or incorrect. Even if it were, a real-world narrative of centralized control would deviate from the ideal type, inasmuch as no central authority ever has complete control over its subordinates. Particularly in the case of a clandestine organization operating over a large area with difficult and intermittent communications, those at the farthest operational reaches will likely have substantial autonomy. Indeed, we know this to have been the case for the 9/11 hijackers. While operational personnel will carry out the general mandates they have been given, those in command are unlikely to be able to monitor their day-to-day behavior or prevent them from engaging in improvisations.

As to the narrative of emergent behavior, when it is applied in a real-world context, as it is by Sageman, it, too, appears in what might be termed a diluted or impure form. That is because in its pure form such a narrative requires that each actor behave with total independence, completely unaware either of the behavior of others or of any common goal. The common goal should arise spontaneously from unintentionally converging behaviors, in the manner of Adam Smith's "invisible hand" that secures market coordination. However, the local terrorists in *Leaderless Jihad*, even though they make their own operational decisions, must be presumed to know something about others in the armed jihad movement. They are conversant with the Internet, monitor militant websites, and read a common literature. They are al-Qaeda wannabes who share a set of general common goals. In that sense, they are very like the white supremacists Louis Beam addressed in his 1992 leaderless resistance essay, who might never have met or contacted one another but inhabited the same subculture.

Narratives as Templates

Narratives exercise a special attraction as an explanation for terrorism that goes beyond the generic function stories perform in making sense of distressing events. First, in common with other anthropogenic disasters, terrorist attacks lack a commonly accepted narrative of causality. Natural disasters, as we saw in Chapter 2, were once attributed to God and human sinfulness. Later, a new narrative acquired general acceptance, built around morally neutral natural processes separated from human sinfulness or divine punishment. Humanly caused calamities, on the other hand, present a blurred picture, with their complex mixture of intention, accident, and negligence, modified by technology and culture. Thus, as we have also seen, competing explanatory narratives may exist where catastrophes flow or are believed to flow from human action. Such is the case, of course, with terrorism, where, as with other anthropogenic disasters, there is no single consensually validated narrative to explain its occurrence.

Terrorist attacks and the groups that commit them are often made more frightening by the absence of reliable information. The intentions and capabilities of terrorists are usually known (if they are known at all) through a combination of facts, rumors, and speculation. Unlike states that have a tangible existence on a piece of territory, terrorist groups inhabit a non-territorial shadow world. But the greater the sense of threat, the greater the desire for understanding and the greater the appetite for information. Consequently, those who feel threatened by terrorists can scarcely say that they will simply wait until some future day when more information is available. They work with the information they have or with what is thought to be information. That information is useless unless some sense can be made of it. The process might more properly be described as finding a narrative that appears to incorporate and give shape to the facts that are available.

However, those who by virtue of official position or function are called upon to construct such narratives do not do so with a tabula rasa. Like others around them, they already carry an array of images and beliefs, of which they may not even be fully conscious, that can subtly push them toward one narrative or another. Some of the influences that come from popular culture and are least likely to enter conscious awareness have already been discussed. Yet the overall cultural ambiance, including even the fictional tales that surround us, can make one narrative appear more plausible than another, especially when the information available is spotty and of uncertain reliability. A narrative template not only arranges facts in a coherent pattern; it also can provide a compelling way of addressing lacunae in the facts by suggesting the kinds of information that may not in fact be available now but would, if available in the future, fully confirm the story being told.

Narratives and Moral Panics

Recall that moral panic (discussed in Chapter 7) describes a campaign in which a society seeks to rid itself of some greatly feared evil. It is intrinsic to this concept, however, that the magnitude of the evil is inflated beyond the degree of danger that might appear to an unbiased outside observer. Recall also that the cases Stanley Cohen, the theorist of moral panic, examined, such as wayward juveniles, posed little or no real danger, and that he finessed the question of whether there could be a moral panic in the face of a genuine, albeit exaggerated, danger. The question now arises whether this concept can be applied to the fear of terrorists and the weapons of mass destruction they might possess.

When Cohen first introduced moral panic, it was taken to be a fear that gripped the general public, stimulated by sensational media coverage, which then resulted in the mobilization of such social control forces as the police and courts. Clearly, moral panic in this form has little relevance to terrorism. We have already seen that with the passage of time since September 11, 2001, fear of terrorism has declined, as has the sense of terrorism as a salient issue for the American public. As of this writing at least, there is little reason to believe that public pressure for a counterterrorism "crusade" will develop, nor is there evidence that mass media are attempting to stimulate a higher level of popular anxiety. Hence the moral panic model in its original form does not appear to be applicable.

However, might it be applicable in a modified form to the experts who construct terrorism narratives? The same chapter in which we examine the moral panic model also examines David Frankfurter's description of how a community might become gripped by fear of invisible evil. In his conceptualization, however, experts play a pivotal role, for without them the fears can find no focus. Their function is to define the danger by making the invisible, visible and giving the enemy a face. This model cannot be transferred to terrorism intact, given the emphasis it places on public panic, but the catalytic function given to "experts on evil" suggests a way in which elements of both this and the moral panic model might be brought together.

Experts possess functions with regard to terrorism beyond those they perform concerning any other anthropogenic disasters. They define causes, expected magnitudes, likely occurrence, and best defenses. They control access to information about them. They also do so, at least in the United States at present, largely isolated from the concerns of a public which has grown ever more complacent as the tragedy of 9/11 has receded into the past. Many of these experts are in government agencies, but many of those outside—in universities and think-tanks—are supported by government grants and contracts.[46] Thus the domain of terrorism expertise has an autonomous character different from that of other groups with special disaster competence.

The bounded character of the world of terrorism expertise opens the possibility that this community not only might engender community fears—moral panics—but might itself become the very terrain on which a moral panic could be engendered and spread. That is not to say that such a panic would be without foundation. As has already been noted, the implication that moral panics only could be caused by baseless fears must be laid aside. Fears may be simultaneously well grounded *and* disproportionately great. That is, after all, the central thesis of John Mueller's critique in *Over-*

blown. Mueller does not deny that there is a terrorist threat, only that its magnitude has been greatly exaggerated and that the measures taken to defend against it have sometimes been destabilizing and counterproductive.[47]

In creating and sustaining a moral panic, a narrative of centralized control is highly functional. It posits a mode of coordination that links what might otherwise appear to be isolated and unconnected events, thus magnifying the events' significance. The narrative, as a template, becomes a pattern that not only absorbs and classifies information as it arrives but also identifies other pieces of information that presently do not exist but "must" exist, since the template requires their presence. Finally, the narrative provides clear policy direction, since the enemy can now be associated with the controlling entity.

This is particularly important where dangers are unseen. Where terrorists cannot be reliably distinguished from others; where there are suspicions that sleeper cells may have been planted; and where there is a pervasive fear that terrorists will acquire or have acquired weapons that have invisible characteristics, such as chemical, biological, and radiological—here the narrative of centralized control imparts to the intangible a measure of tangibility. If the enemy cannot be seen, at least its organization can be described and, perhaps, even be physically located.

By contrast, the narrative of emergent behavior provides none of these advantages. It portrays terrorism as the product of a large number of independent decisions, so that what appears to be a campaign is only an illusion, the consequence of separate, albeit mutually reinforcing, initiatives. The result is to both increase and reduce invisibility. On the one hand, from a macro-cosmic standpoint, invisibility appears greater, for the sum total of terrorism becomes more difficult to trace to its multiple sources. To the extent that there is concern about weapons of mass destruction, the large number of possible directions from which threats might come makes the search for such weapons even more difficult. On the other hand, each individual organization or cell may at the same time become somewhat more visible, since it is likely to be embedded in a local community where its affiliations can at least in principle be known or traced. This slight advantage, however, is unlikely to outweigh the much greater advantages possessed by the narrative of centralized control, with its capacity to draw many potential strands into what is, in effect, a parsimonious, single-variable theory. In any case, locally based terrorists are less likely to have the resources necessary to create or procure weapons of mass destruction.

Narratives and Truth

None of the foregoing discussion should be read as suggesting that one narrative is more likely to be true than the other, only that one is more likely to be *chosen* than the other. In other words, it is possible that under some circumstances the narrative of centralized control may seem to fit known facts better, may fit developing facts better, and/or may yield policies that seem to provide better outcomes. While supporters of the narrative will usually argue that it should be chosen for these reasons, it is likely to have acquired supporters on other grounds: because it is easy to grasp, because it conforms to preexisting stereotypes of evil present in stories that are already widely known, because policies based upon it can be formulated without undue difficulty. By contrast, the competing narrative of emergent behavior appears confusing, with its welter of independent, separately directed "nests of vipers" that must be wiped out, as opposed to the centralized control narrative's "octopus" that can be destroyed with a single stroke properly directed. In addition, the narrative of emergent behavior conjures up a landscape of fear that is as disorderly as it is disorienting. Independent decisions may coalesce into a pattern, but preventing that pattern from emerging requires information, resources, and mobilization that may be beyond even the capacities of a great power.

Hence there is a built-in bias favoring one type of terrorism narrative over the other, relatively independent of their respective validities. This bias reflects not only the considerations already mentioned but also a more subtle one flowing from the structure of international relations. Governments, habituated to dealing with other states, have long reified them, treating these artificial entities as "group persons" capable of acting in a singular, unified manner in their interactions with other states.[48] States may be artificial in a legal sense, but they are also tangible to the extent that they are identified with distinct territorial locations. Nonstate actors, on the other hand, particularly those that are in armed conflict with the existing political order, have no such determinate territorial locations. They can be everywhere and nowhere. However, opting for the narrative of centralized control endows terrorists with at least some of the attributes of states, notably the capacity to make and implement policies binding upon all their members. To that degree, it gives to an invisible danger some of the characteristics of the visible and known. In that sense, the narrative of centralized control "domesticates" terrorism by conceptualizing terrorist violence as the outcome of a decisional process not unlike the process that occurs within states, a process governments already know and with which they are already comfortable. Only the attribute of territoriality is still missing.

Thus the narrative of centralized control lies within policymakers' and analysts' "comfort zone." Where only a partial array of facts is available, and those of perhaps dubious reliability, it is not surprising that they will be accommodated in the story that both tellers and listeners find easier to understand. Those who offer another story, such as the narrative of emergent behavior, will find it a "hard sell," as Sageman has. It is the kind of story that requires concentration, because the narrative line is less clear and it has fewer resemblances to other stories about evil and invisibility with which we are already familiar. Hence its truth value will be questioned.

Because so much of the contemporary landscape of fear is constructed around the concept of invisibility, responses to it will not always be rational, for unseen dangers tend to evoke reactions of primordial dread. A landscape once thought predictable and secure suddenly becomes filled with intimations of unexpected and unidentifiable danger. The immediate aim is to make the unseen visible. However, as we have seen, the ability to do so is significantly limited by both the available information and the technology of detection. In a situation where one believes one is confronting a faceless adversary, there is a felt necessity to put together a narrative of the enemy. That narrative tends to be a narrative of centralized control, since it is simple and gives to the enemy an organizational form that compensates for his insubstantiality. It is also subtly reinforced by such earlier stories as the pathology-bearing immigrant and the high-tech villain that already pervade the culture.

Mass-casualty terrorist attacks can legitimately be considered low-probability/high-consequence events. However, the thesis advanced here has been that the intense concentration upon them by American homeland security policymakers cannot be ascribed solely to their low-probability/high-consequence character. Rather, it flows neither wholly from considerations of *probability* nor from *consequences* but from a third characteristic: the attacks' presumed *invisibility*.

The preoccupation with invisibility manifests itself in an obsessive concern with secreted weapons that operate in ways that transcend the capabilities of the unaided human senses, as undetectable poisons, microbes, or radiation. The same preoccupation with invisibility manifests itself in the fear of the terrorist who can melt effortlessly into the population, feigning innocence until ready to strike. The combination of the undetectable terrorist and the undetectable weapon of mass destruction has become an idée fixe.

Given the fact that no nonstate group has even attempt to use a CBRN since the religious sect Aum Shinrikyo employed sarin gas in 1995, it seems on its face difficult to explain this intensity of concern. The preceding chapters have suggested that the reason lies less in a weighing of evidence than in the primal anxiety evoked by unseen evil, a fear deeply rooted in the culture and thus not necessarily connected to any empirical evaluation of its likelihood of occurrence. It is that landscape of fear that resides within us that determines how we construct our picture of the landscape of fear outside.

One explanation might be policymakers' desire to avoid the complacency that prevailed before September 11th and that permitted warnings of an imminent al-Qaeda attack on American soil to go unheeded. The current fixation on weapons of mass destruction in the hands of terrorists concentrates on unlikely scenarios, perhaps compensating for the previous failure to consider the unlikely scenario of airplanes used as projectiles. However, there are a host of other unlikely scenarios that do not receive the same degree of attention accorded to biological and chemical weapons—for example, the possibility that conventionally armed terrorists might attack a crowded shopping mall. These alternative scenarios receive short shrift because they lack the requisite mystique of invisibility. Invisibility and centralization mesh to tell a compelling and frightening story. For those who have come to believe that the world is a very dangerous place—and, as we have seen, that includes most terrorism experts who shared in the shock of 9/11—it is the only narrative that makes sense.

EPILOGUE

Few events as brief as the September 11th attacks have stimulated such broad changes in the national government. Some of these consequences were the result of decisions taken quickly, in a semi-improvisatory way, during the first days and weeks after the attacks, but they often resulted in patterns of behavior that were subsequently institutionalized. Some of the outcomes are obvious, such as the protracted wars in Afghanistan and Iraq. The former would surely not have been undertaken otherwise, and the latter, while it might have happened eventually in the absence of the attacks, was clearly facilitated by the post-9/11 atmosphere.

Other consequences were organizational. They include the development of a system of detention for suspected terrorists and terrorist supporters outside the United States, in the expectation that they would also be outside the jurisdiction of American courts. Two parallel systems of detention arose, one administered by the army, the other by the Central Intelligence Agency. In conjunction with the creation of external detention, a conscious decision was reached for the first time to utilize torture as an instrument of national policy, although cloaked in legal rationalizations. The passage of terrorism-related legislation had been a standard response to earlier attacks against Americans and American installations, but no previous measure approached the scope of the USA PATRIOT Act passed after 9/11. The intelligence community outside the Department of Defense was reconfigured by the Intelligence Reform and Terrorism Prevention Act of 2004 in an attempt to avoid the compartmentalization and mishaps that had permitted the attacks. The president ordered sweeping forms of surveillance performed by the National Security Agency (NSA), some of which, such as "warrantless wiretapping," were subsequently revealed but some of which remain classified. A new military command, NORTHCOM, was created in October 2002 with the central mission of homeland security. And, most ambitious of all, the Department of Homeland Security was brought into being in 2003 in the greatest effort at federal government reorganization since the creation of the Defense Department in 1947.

These transformations were not all equally well entrenched, as became evident when the Obama administration took control in early 2009. The CIA prisons were closed. A firm commitment was made to close the detention facility at Guantanamo Bay, and "enhanced" means of interrogation were repudiated. While the new administration was not as forthcoming as some had hoped in making information available about the use and justification of torture, significant new documentation was released, particularly about the involvement of the CIA. Combat forces in Iraq were redeployed and drawn down, although with the likelihood that a significant American military presence would remain for many years. At the same time, consistent with campaign promises, President Obama ordered additional combat forces to Afghanistan. The Department of Homeland Security showed no signs of contracting. Indeed, an immense, $3.4 billion campus remained under construction on the grounds of St. Elizabeth's Hospital in Washington. However, under a new secretary, Janet Napolitano, the department's mission began to broaden significantly. Secretary Napolitano's most significant early initiative was her creation of a bipartisan task force to review the color-coded Homeland Security Advisory System, the department's best-known feature.[1] In January 2011, she announced that the color-coded system would be replaced by more specific alerts, sometimes directed to the public but sometimes directed only to government agencies.[2]

We can thus see changes of substantial magnitude as a result of the attacks. Although some might be undone with the stroke of a pen, many cannot. They have developed a momentum of their own, since they involve substantial movements of people, materiel, money, and political power. The changes have all been based at least in part upon beliefs about the kinds of unseen dangers discussed in the earlier chapters, dangers thought to be posed by invisible adversaries who might wield invisible weapons. In retrospect, at least some of those responses now seem disproportionate to the threat.

The disproportion in the distribution of attention and resources reflected states of mind in the fall of 2001 and beyond. Fear, bordering on hysteria, was rampant, with widely reported speculation that al-Qaeda had already planted second-strike sleeper cells. It was speculation most Americans were prepared to believe. The enigmatic anthrax letters seemed only to confirm these rumors. It seems entirely reasonable to assume that the psychological atmosphere among policymakers was no different than that prevalent in the general population. Indeed, emotions in government circles likely ran higher, given the fragments of intelligence to which their members were privy.

Given what had occurred, these feelings were understandable. They did not, however, provide the soundest basis for the formation of policy, and certainly not for the massive changes in governmental structure and functioning that occurred, particularly between late 2001 and 2004. Action at times of high emotion carries the risk of excess or rashness, causing us to do what in calmer moments we might regret; the same danger, magnified, accrues to communities under like circumstances. Yet it is clear that inaction was impossible, for neither inaction nor even significant delay was a politically acceptable option. The question, then, becomes not whether action should have been taken but what kind it ought to have been.

It is easier to say now what might or might not have been done, because we now have the luxury of reflection. But another, more useful way of putting it is to say that sufficient time has elapsed to see some of the consequences of earlier decisions. The more radical or sweeping a decision, the more significant its consequences are likely to be. Since that is the case, it surely would have been desirable to do what was immediately necessary and then assess the consequences before doing more, rather than set in motion large or extreme plans that might give rise to unwanted or unintended effects.

Such effects were especially likely in a situation where the nation was, as it were, battling shadows. The invisibility of the adversary carried the danger that potential victims would project upon the enemy characteristics, capabilities, and intentions that it did not possess, and—further—make policy on the basis of those putative characteristics, capabilities, and intentions, only to learn much later of their insubstantiality. Overreaction to terrorist threats has been common. It usually takes the form of excessive repression by target governments, as they lash out against imagined enemies. Indeed, some terrorists have sought to manipulate this temptation by deliberately provoking states, in the hope that increasingly repressive actions might stimulate a popular uprising. However, in the 9/11 case, although there were some unnecessarily harsh actions taken against American Muslims, in general excesses were not in the direction of repression of the American population. Rather, they lay elsewhere, in the treatment of detainees, almost none of whom were American citizens; in the expansion of governmental investigative and security powers; and in the creation of a large and cumbersome homeland security bureaucracy.

The rationales for these measures were that they would produce better-quality intelligence, efficiently integrate previously disparate security efforts, and reduce the rivalries that had earlier set agencies against one another. It is obviously impossible to fully judge the quality of intelligence on the basis of the public record, nor is there any way to know how intelligence agencies might have performed after September 11th absent the changes that were made. An examination of the president's NSA surveillance program by inspectors general from five departments and agencies suggests, at best, mixed results. Higher-ranking officials made the most positive evaluations, while those in middle-level positions often complained of insufficient detail, lack of access to the material, or an inability to link it to specific successes.[3] As to turf wars, these have scarcely ended. Instead, the boundaries dividing bureaucratic turfs have been redrawn, and the players realigned.

How might events have played out differently? As suggested earlier, more modest changes might have been made gradually, so that their effects could have been monitored. Yet, although this surely would have been the more rational course, it also might not have been politically viable. Instead, the demand for immediate and sweeping action at any price might have been unstoppable. The beliefs that action is always better than inaction, and that more action is always better than less, are often too strong to withstand in a crisis environment. Many steps that were taken, not all of them clearly thought through, were likely inevitable. What was left in the domain of choice was, perhaps, the ability to choose those that could more easily be modified or foreclosed in the future, instead of those likely to be frozen in place for years to come or those whose consequences might be difficult to unravel.

Shortly after the end of the Second World War, the great constitutional scholar Edward S. Corwin delivered a set of lectures on total war and the Constitution at the University of Michigan Law School. Looking back at the centralization of power that had taken place in wartime, he feared that the resulting erosion of constitutional protections and limits would prove irreversible. As the law school's dean paraphrased Corwin's fear, he wondered "how far we can continue to progress in the direction of conferring upon administrative officials more and more virtually unreviewable discretionary power over the lives and activities of men without finally reaching a state of absolutism that can no longer be called a liberal democracy."[4] We now know, of course, that Corwin's pessimism of more than sixty years ago was misplaced. The emergency measures that he feared might become a permanent fixture of American life were largely dismantled. However, aggrandizement of power predicated upon invisible threats constitutes a very different kind of danger. For the expansion of governmental authority during World War II was based upon enemies that could be seen, engaged, and definitively defeated, and once the conflict ended, so too did the sense of crisis and the expedients associated with it. When, however, the cause of the crisis is deemed to be unseen, and the crisis itself—what was at first called "the global war on terror"—is said to be a battle that will go on indefinitely, the temptation exists to leave in place what might otherwise be temporary. When does an unseen danger cease to exist? As we have seen, that is as much a question about the perceptions of those who regard themselves as potential victims as it is a question about an objective reality. As long as the problem of terrorism is dominated by fear of the unseen, subjective considerations are likely to have the upper hand. As a result, the policies and governmental structures that persist are likely to be not only those that deal with "facts on the ground," as it were, but also those that are most responsive to the emotional factors put in play by the fear of unseen danger.

What Went Wrong?

When we look for defects in the homeland security response after September 11th, the factors fall under two broad headings, the organizational and the attitudinal. Let us begin with the organizational.

The changes that were made after September 11th were supposed to reduce duplication among federal agencies that dealt with terrorism in an effort to end turf wars among federal agencies and improve efficiency. In the end, many of the changes had precisely the opposite effect: They replaced some forms of redundancy with others, leading to new turf wars and different types of inefficiency. For example, consider two of the more prominent new counterterrorism entities, the Department of Homeland Security and the Department of Defense's NORTHCOM. Each had a general mandate to defend U.S. territory, yet no clear effort was made to demarcate their respective jurisdictions. Since NORTHCOM had relatively few forces assigned to it and found few foes to fight, it looked for tasks to occupy it. It found them in disaster relief in hurricane-prone areas, a worthy endeavor, but one that already engaged the attentions of FEMA in the Department of Homeland Security. In a similar manner, the FBI continues to wage turf battles with the Bureau of Alcohol, Tobacco, Firearms, and Explosives, even though the Bureau was moved from the Department of the Treasury to the Department of Justice after 9/11 to facilitate operations.[5]

Similarly, notwithstanding the rhetorical commitment to maximize efficiency, the post-9/11 innovations were often structured to make that impossible. Thus, the Department of Homeland Security was created by amalgamating both freestanding agencies and organizations drawn from many cabinet-level departments, with the result that the DHS was left with a heterogeneous collection of components with widely varying organizational cultures. The result was low morale that has characterized the department due to the need to transform the separate cultures of these so-called legacy agencies into a single culture that must eventually prevail in the DHS as a whole—a slow and painful process in an organization with 230,000 employees. The spectacular growth of the DHS was paralleled by the post-9/11 expansion of related agencies. As a *Washington Post* investigation revealed, over 1,200 government agencies now deal with terrorism, homeland security, and intelligence, with 17,000,000 square feet of space built in the greater Washington area for related work since 9/11. The result has been both redundancy and the generation of far more data and analysis than can be meaningfully utilized.[6]

A different kind of efficiency problem resulted from the Intelligence Reform and Terrorism Prevention Act of 2004,[7] legislation that sought to give effect to recommendations made by the 9/11 Commission in the report it issued six months earlier. The purpose of the recommendations was to integrate information and promote cooperation within the intelligence community, so that agencies that once would not deign to communicate with one another would now habitually exchange information. The problem in 2001 was that information existed that might have allowed at least some of the hijackers to be identified, but it was fragmented and jealously held instead of being widely distributed among those who could have used it productively.

The reform legislation appeared to enact the 9/11 Commission's recommendations, creating the National Counterterrorism Center (NCTC) and the post of director of National Intelligence at the pinnacle of the intelligence community, but it gave the latter so few powers that he was little more than a figurehead. In addition, the substantial intelligence apparatus of the Pentagon was left virtually untouched. These weaknesses were made clear on December 25, 2009, when Umar Farouk Abdulmutallab, a Nigerian national, very nearly set off a bomb on a Northwest Airlines plane in American airspace, even though significant information of his possible jihadist activities was in the possession of various parts of the U.S. government. Thus, the creation of neither the NCTC nor the DNI could prevent a repetition of a situation very like that before 9/11, where information existed but was unusable.

On the attitudinal side, there was, as earlier chapters have made clear, an overriding fear that terrorists would employ weapons of mass destruction; that is, biological, chemical, radiological, or nuclear weapons—despite case after case in which terrorists employed conventional weapons, often bombs, and often of crude design and construction. Cases in point included not only the Northwest Airlines incident referred to above but also the failed Times Square bombing on May 1, 2010, by Faisal Shahzad.

The Times Square bombing attempt was one among several incidents that raised the question of whether American Muslims had now become radicalized in the manner of coreligionists in some European countries. Faisal Shahzad, a naturalized citizen of Pakistani extraction, said he had engaged in the bombing attempt at the behest of the Pakistani Taliban. Before that, numerous young men of Somalian descent, living in the Minneapolis–St. Paul area, had surreptitiously gone to Somalia to join a jihadist group, although not with the intention of attacking American targets. Of the 131 Americans charged with serious terrorism-related crimes since 9/11, over one-third have been American-born, and several have been converts to Islam. Nonetheless, there does not appear to be the same level of alienation among Muslims in America as exists, for example, in Britain. However, a dramatic case such as Shahzad's can easily convince the public that it is the entering wedge of a large-scale phenomenon, even though there may be relatively little supporting data. If that is then followed by repressive measures by law enforcement, folk belief about the spread of jihadist ideology can readily turn into a self-fulfilling prophecy. Although the Obama administration's National Security Strategy document mentions homegrown cases, that is counterbalanced by a commitment to engage local Muslim communities.[8]

The WMD fixation may be explained in one of two ways: as preparation for a worst-case situation, so that it may be seen as an exercise in prudence; or as the projection on the enemy of our own fears. Although there have been numerous reports of al-Qaeda's attempts to secure nuclear weapons, virtually all of these reports are unsubstantiated, and many appear to be scarcely above the level of rumors.[9] Occasional claims by al-Qaeda itself to have such weapons and the fact that they have not been used further suggests the organization does not possess them. It is equally clear, however, that all WMD have the capacity to deeply frighten Western targets, evident in both the rhetoric Western governments use and the funds expended on detection and defense. The argument that has been offered here is that much of this fear results from the invisibility of toxins, microbes, and radiation, as well as the potentially undetectable terrorists who might employ them.

What therefore appears to be a rational policymaking process has a nonrational substratum. The crisis period after the September 11th attacks was characterized by high anxiety, including the widely held belief that there were already al-Qaeda sleeper cells in the United States programmed to carry out subsequent attacks; again, the motif of the invisible enemy. When the enemy and its weapons are deemed to be invisible, that set of beliefs constitutes a "canvas" upon which the putative victim can paint whatever picture he or she wishes, including a picture of an incipient WMD disaster.

One way to assert control—or at least to be seen as taking control—in such a situation is by taking large measures and foreswearing incremental change. That is precisely what happened. And so came the litany of post-9/11 transformations—the creation of the DHS and NORTHCOM, the intelligence reform legislation, and so on. They were all actions that were large and dramatic, in order to give the impression that the phantom enemy was being kept at bay. In that sense, it may be said that the attitudinal factors at least partially begot the organizational transformations.

Those transformations have turned out to be long-lived. What might have appeared to be improvisatory in 2001 or 2002 has now frozen into institutional form. Organizations that might once have appeared temporary have become vested interests, competing for influence and funds. Those established by legislation, such as the DHS and the NCTC, are unlikely to be significantly altered. Even the Guantanamo system, a product of executive decisions made in the first months after the Afghanistan invasion, has proven extraordinarily difficult to dismantle. Thus decisions made in the heat of crisis are decisions we still live with and are likely to live with for some time, even though they can now be seen to have significant flaws. The organizations involved, even though they were brought into being within a very short period of time—essentially from 2001 to 2004—were created piecemeal, in the sense that no one sat down and asked how all the pieces fitted together. Ironically, although the individual parts were supposed to make what was once an uncoordinated counterterrorism machinery flow more smoothly, the new whole turns out to be almost as uncoordinated as what preceded it. There are still turf wars and budget battles. Information still gets lost or fails to be connected. It is merely that the identities of some of the players on the board have changed.

What Is Now Possible?

The entities that were created between 2001 and 2004 were conceived as resources in the struggle against terrorism, but they can also be seen as constraints. Their size and scope make them claimants for resources, and together they constitute a terrorism "establishment" that suggests that the issue of terrorism should be a continuing matter of the highest policy importance for the foreseeable future. This might well turn out to be the case, but, alternatively, terrorism might decline, leaving the panoply of organizations deprived of their raison d'être. Yet, as has already been observed, the organizations have taken a form that makes it exceedingly unlikely that they will disappear. Concepts of defense and security were reoriented after September 11th, and the new organizations gave shape to the reorientation, such that policymakers could think of little else but terrorism and ways to fight it. Given the new organizational matrix that has taken shape, therefore, the issue is: How much flexibility remains for new policy directions?

Secretary of Homeland Security Janet Napolitano has taken her department in some directions different from those of her predecessor, Michael Chertoff. She has effectively scrapped or significantly delayed two of Chertoff's most cherished initiatives, the U.S.-Mexican border barrier and the

REAL ID driver's license program. She has also expanded her discretionary authority by leveraging the department's all-hazards mandate. Where Chertoff seems never to have understood the relationship between the all-hazards requirement and the demand to fight terrorism, Napolitano has seen in the all-hazards mantra a way of expanding her department's reach into new areas. Thus the DHS became the lead agency in fighting the H1N1 flu pandemic, although the Department of Health and Human Services had superior substantive knowledge. The change, however, is not systemic; rather, it is in leadership styles, and there is no way to predict what the department might do under Napolitano's successors.

The issue of systemic change involves not only flexibility—that is, the range of available choices—but also the significance of terrorism as a policy issue. For the psychological shock of September 11th, its character as a national trauma not only for the citizenry but also for decision-makers, meant that it trumped all other foreign policy issues. Indeed, to the extent that homeland security overlapped the foreign and domestic spheres, terrorism from the fall of 2001 onward became the single most important issue for both foreign and domestic policy. Clearly, however, it could not retain that primacy indefinitely. A sense of proportion that reduced the salience of terrorism as an issue was partially restored.

Two factors caused that reduction. One was inevitable. It was simply the passage of time, reinforced by the absence of an attack upon U.S. territory. As Chapter 8 makes clear, public anxiety declined more rapidly than the anxiety of policymakers. Not until the Northwest Airlines incident in 2009 was there an attempted attack upon U.S. territory. As the horrendous events of September 11th receded in memory, so, too, did the concern that the United States would continue to be targeted by external groups.

The second factor could not have been predicted. It was the world financial collapse that began in 2007. It had, of course, nothing to do with terrorism, but it had everything to do with the relative power and prosperity of the United States. The immediate effect of the economic convulsion was to reduce terrorism to the status of a second-order problem, not only because of the consequences for Americans in their personal lives, but also because of the implications for America's place in the world. Quite unintentionally, the economic crisis makes it far easier to see problems of terrorism clearly. It does so by returning a sense of proportion. There are factors in both world and domestic politics more important than terrorism, in the sense that they may have more consequential and lasting effects for national power and well-being. This return to clarity may also help reduce the fixation on weapons of mass destruction.

Colin Gray, in a brilliant essay written only months after the September 11th attacks, made the nonobvious comment that the effect of a terrorist attack depends upon the victim's behavior: "[T]he terrorist (as an asymmetric opponent) can succeed only with our assistance. He lacks the resources himself to inflict significant direct damage upon us." Even a WMD attack by a terrorist, Gray argued, would fail to do so. Conflict, particularly between such unequal adversaries, is a form of interaction, and the stronger party, even if it is the victim of a surprise attack, has the ability to determine the magnitude of the attack by the manner in which it reacts. The danger is always overreaction. "The temptation to do something, for the sake of being seen to do something—even something strategically stupid—can be politically irresistible."[10]

A great deal was done after September 11th. It could not have been otherwise. What was strategically wise and what was strategically stupid lies outside the boundaries of this discussion. However, it is safe to say that too much was done. Government fastened upon this issue as though there was no other, magnifying an already immense attack until it took on the character of a nation-transforming event. As was so often said at the time, and so often believed, "Nothing will ever be the same." It is now clear, however, that much remained the same. The task now is to work our way back to a proportional conception of terrorism and homeland security.

A Proportional Policy

Casting one's mind back to the months immediately following the World Trade Center and Pentagon attacks brings back a landscape of fear unlike anything in the recent American past. The expectation that a second wave of attacks would follow took many months to gradually disappear. The fear that one cataclysm would beget others was reinforced by the anthrax letters episode, even though the notes that accompanied the virus, which sought to link it with al-Qaeda, were recognized by many as crude fabrications. The FBI did not close the anthrax letters case until February 2010, when it announced with finality that the letters had been sent by Bruce E. Ivins, a scientist at the United States Medical Research Institute of Infectious Diseases, who by that time had taken his own life.[11] The pervasive anxiety was also, paradoxically, reinforced by some of the very measures adopted to increase security and public confidence, such as uniformed and armed military personnel at airports. In this charged atmosphere, terrorism blotted out every other policy concern: Iran, the rise of China, energy, the environment, international economic stability, and so on. For both the public and policymakers, there was one and only one issue: terrorism and its correlative, homeland security.

Although these issues dominated perceptions and consumed attentions, none of the other issues went away. The world did not stand still. The eruption of the global financial meltdown in 2007, along with the escalation of the Iranian nuclear program, tension on the Korean peninsula, and a number of other issues, provides ample demonstration. Some contrarian commentators suggested as much at the time. Thus Joseph Ellis observed that the 9/11 attacks, horrendous though they were, did not constitute an event that placed the survival of the republic in jeopardy in the manner of the Revolutionary War, the burning of the Capitol during the War of 1812, the Civil War, World War II, or the Cuban Missile Crisis during the Cold War.[12]

A proportioned conception of terrorism and homeland security will require casting off some of the psychic baggage that has been acquired, notably the obsessive fear of a WMD attack. Some of that process has already been accomplished by the absence of such an attack, the passage of time, and the blunting force of such other problems as the world economic meltdown. The difficulty in establishing proportionality, it will be remembered, is tied to the fear of the invisible, for what is not visible may be given whatever proportions the mind desires, and where what is not visible is also feared and where information is fragmentary, those proportions are, almost invariably, deemed to be immense. Thus, even though there are factors that have reduced the salience of terrorism and the fixation upon weapons of mass destruction, some conscious effort must still be put forth to prevent WMD from becoming the central issue.

It goes without saying that all reasonable efforts should be made to keep chemical, biological, radiological, and nuclear weapons out of the hands of terrorists. For that matter, they should be kept beyond the grasp of any nonstate group. Indeed, the thrust of international action has been to try to pry them from so-called rogue states, as well as to establish regimes to limit or prohibit their possession by any state, a process that has gone farthest with chemical weapons and somewhat less far with biological weapons.

What we know about such weapons, however, suggests that they are difficult to acquire and, once acquired, are exceedingly difficult to maintain and use. The one clear case of a group that did so and might be termed a terrorist organization—the Japanese sect Aum Shinrikyo—enjoyed the luxury of money, laboratory facilities, trained scientists, and relative freedom from official interference, but it never acquired nuclear or radiological weapons, it abandoned its biological weapons program, and it inflicted only a few fatalities with chemical weapons. It is scarcely surprising, therefore, that terrorists almost always fall back upon those conventional means that can be readily secured and can be used with at least a fair chance of success.

While it is obviously prudent to keep exotic weapons out of malefactors' hands, it does not make sense to build policy around our own fears. That is to do terrorists' work for them, since the business of terrorists is, among other things, to terrorize. Policies that reflect a condition of being terrorized validates the terrorists' success. It also draws resources away from other areas that may be more significant for the medium- and long-term strategic position of a state. It is well to remember that there is truth to the cliché that "terrorism is the weapon of the weak." Since forces also exist that are strong, policies must deal with them, too, and these must have adequate resources to implement them. It makes little sense to channel immense resources to protect against a weak adversary, although it is understandable that there may be short-run pressures to do so if the tactics weak enemies use are especially dramatic, as they were on 9/11. Homeland security policy must be in proportion to real threats, not to imagined threats. It must reflect the most accurate knowledge that can be acquired about the external world, not a reflection of inner landscapes of fear, in which the features of the outside world assume an exaggerated and distorted form.

The principle of proportionality generates an important corollary, and it is this: Now that the institutional apparatus of homeland security is in place and unlikely to be disturbed in the foreseeable future, the all-hazards concept needs to be transformed into a consistent operational policy. In the early years of homeland security, the all-hazards idea was championed rhetorically, but at the operational level, it was understood that the only threat that really mattered was terrorism. This schizoid mentality was ultimately responsible for the Hurricane Katrina fiasco, a story told in Chapter 4. As long as the all-hazards approach was unaccompanied by actions, the result was confusion, for policy declarations and mission statements were often contradicted by resource allocations and behavior, both of which reflected a single-minded commitment to the struggle against terrorism. Yet subsequent events—among them the economic crisis and the Gulf oil spill of 2010—have had a chastening effect, for they demonstrated that threats to security could come from manifold causes besides terrorism and that, indeed, these other threats might be far more serious.

As has already been noted, the transformations of 2001–04 that have given us the homeland security framework are unlikely to be undone. Notwithstanding homeland security's imperfections, it is the new status quo. Since that is the case, weaning it away from its original mission, a single-minded concentration on terrorism, and directing it toward a wider range of threats can give it the greater coherence that it so badly needs. Doing so will not be easy, not only because of organizational inertia, but also because translating all-hazards into actions needs to be done with care. If it is not, too many situations will be unnecessarily transformed into "emergencies," with all the risks for civil liberties, local autonomy, and ordinary routines that this implies. We will need once again to pay heed to the warning Edward Corwin made more than sixty-five years ago.

NOTES

Preface

1 *World at Risk*, xv.
2 Tuan, *Landscapes of Fear*.

Chapter One

1 Wolff, *Sociology of Georg Simmel*, 307–76.
2 Bok, *Secrets*.
3 Hobsbawm, *Primitive Rebels*, 50–60.
4 Reader, "Imagined Persecution," 158, 161.
5 LaValley, *Invasion of the Body Snatchers*, 169–71, 182–83.
6 Davis, "Some Themes of Counter-Subversion."
7 Hobsbawm, *Primitive Rebels*; Billington, *Fire in the Minds of Men*.
8 Morin and Deane, "Half of Residents in Fear, Post Poll Finds."
9 Thomas, *Religion and the Decline of Magic*.
10 Weber, "Science as a Vocation," 139.
11 Ibid., 155.
12 Ibid., 58.
13 Partridge, *Re-Enchantment of the West*.
14 Ibid., 44.
15 Ibid., 70.
16 Ibid., 32–33.
17 Ibid., 53.
18 Lara, "In and Out of Terror."
19 Saniotis, "Re-Enchanting Terrorism."

20 Ibid., 538.

21 Ibid., 539.

22 Juergensmeyer, *Terror in the Mind of God*, 126.

23 Ibid., 126–27.

24 Mueller, *Overblown*, 157–59.

Chapter Two

1   Barton, *Communities in Disaster*, 38.

2   Barkun, "Disaster in History."

3   Hewitt and Burton, *Hazardousness of a Place*, 76.

4   Barkun, "Disaster in History."

5   Hewitt and Burton, *Hazardousness of a Place*, 76.

6   Garrett, *Respectable Folly*, 226.

7   Hilhorst and Bankoff, "Introduction," 2.

8   Ibid.

9   Bankoff, "Historical Geography of Disaster," 29.

10 Ibid., 38.

11 Lavell, "Lower Lempa River Valley," 71.

12 Kasperson quoted in Rosa, "Logical Structure."

13 Hewitt and Burton, *Hazardousness of a Place*, 16.

14 Oliver-Smith, "Theorizing Vulnerability," 17.

15 Rosa, "Logical Structure."

16 Cardona, "Need for Rethinking the Concepts of Vulnerability and Risk," 47.

17 Lavell, "Lower Lempa River Valley," 71.

18 Wisner, "Assessment of Capability and Vulnerability," 183.

19 Rosa, "Logical Structure."

20 Cardona, "Need for Rethinking the Concepts of Vulnerability and Risk," 38.

21 Lavell, "Lower Lempa River Valley," 71."

22 Cardona, "Need for Rethinking the Concepts of Vulnerability and Risk," 37.

23 Mitchell, "Urban Vulnerability," 17.

24 Beck, *Risk Society*.

25 Ibid., 21 (emphasis in original).

26 Ibid., 27 (emphasis in original).

27 Posner, *Catastrophe*, 171–72.

28 Pidgeon, Kasperson, and Slovic, "Introduction."

29 Kasperson et al., "Social Amplification of Risk."

30 Slovic, "Terrorism as Hazard."

31 Frewer, "Truth, Transparency, and Social Context."

32 Murdock, Petts, and Horlick-Jones, "After Amplification."

33 Wiedeman, Clauberg, and Schutz, "Understanding Amplification."

34 Boyer, *When Time Shall Be No More*.

35 Barkun, "Divided Apocalypse."

36 Lindsey, *Late Great Planet Earth*.

37 Commoner, *Closing Circle*; Meadows et al., *Limits to Growth*; Heilbroner, *Inquiry Into the Human Prospect*.

38 Solzhenitsyn, "World Split Apart."

39 Larabee, *Decade of Disaster*.

40 Oliver-Smith, "Theorizing Vulnerability," 17.

41 Sontag, "Imagination of Disaster."

42 Mitchell, "Urban Vulnerability," 23.

43 Tuan, *Landscapes of Fear*.

Chapter Three

1 Gray, "Thinking Asymmetrically in Times of Terror."

2 "Testimony of Secretary Michael Chertoff."

3 "DHS Proposes Biometric Airport and Seaport Exit Procedures."

4 Nakashima, "Terror Suspect List Yields Few Arrests."

5 Nakashima, "Lockheed Secures Contract to Expand Biometric Database"; "FBI Announces Contract Award."

6 Bowcott, "FBI Wants Instant Access to British Identity Data."

7 *Protecting Individual Privacy*, 252–58.

8 Ibid., 82–83, 250–62.

9 Brower, "Terrorist Threat and Its Implications."

10 *First Responders' Ability to Detect and Model Hazardous Releases*, 4.

11 Dye, "Sensors for Screening and Surveillance."

12 Demirev, Feldman, and Lin, "Chemical and Biological Weapons," 323.

13 Hsu, "New York Presses to Deploy More Bioweapons Sensors."

14 "Testimony of Dr. Kimothy Smith."

15 *State of Homeland Security 2007*, 52.

16 *First Responders' Ability to Detect and Model Hazardous Releases*, 5.

17 "DHS' Domestic Nuclear Detection Office Progress"; *State of Homeland Security 2007*, 58.

18 "DHS' Domestic Nuclear Detection Office Progress."

19 "Testimony of Secretary Michael Chertoff."

20 "DHS' Domestic Nuclear Detection Office Progress," 30–31; *State of Homeland Security 2007*, 58; Hsu, "Securing the Cities No Easy Task."

21 "U.S. Department of Homeland Security Awards New York City."

22 Dye, "Sensors for Screening and Surveillance," 5.

23 "Testimony of Secretary Michael Chertoff."

24 Taarnby, "Profiling Islamic Suicide Terrorists"; Schbley, "Defining Religious Terrorism"; "Characteristics of Suicide Terrorists."

25 Whitlock, "Terrorists Proving Harder to Profile."

26 Sageman, *Understanding Terror Networks*.

27 "DHS Releases REAL ID Regulation."

28 "REAL ID Final Rule."

29 "Remarks by Homeland Security Secretary Michael Chertoff at a Press Conference on REAL ID."

30 Ibid.

31 Fussey, "Observing Potentiality in the Global City"; "Video Surveillance."

32 Fussey, "Observing Potentiality in the Global City"; Coaffee, "Rings of Steel."

33 Coaffee, "Rings of Steel."

34 Fussey, "Observing Potentiality in the Global City."

35 "MPD Deploys Additional CCTV Cameras in Northwest DC."

36 Office of Emergency Management and Communications, City of Chicago.

37 *Who's Watching?*, 2.

38 Neuman, "More Delays for Cameras in Subways."

39 Coaffee, "Rings of Steel."

40 Gorman, "CCTV Facial Recognition Analysis."

41 "Q&A on Face-Recognition."

42 "Airports Trial Facial Recognition."

43 Slack, "Minority Report Comes to Britain."

44 Erikson, *Wayward Puritans*, 150–52.

45 Loevinger, "Facts, Evidence, and Legal Proof."

46 Greenberg and Dratel, *Torture Papers*, 27.

47 Ibid., 172.

48 *Special Review, Counterterrorism Detention and Interrogation Activities*, 89.

49 Warrick and Eggen, "Hill Briefed on Waterboarding in 2002."

50 Senate Armed Services Committee Inquiry; Mayer, "Experiment"; *Special Review, Counterterrorism Detention and Interrogation Activities*, 13.

51 Mayer, "Experiment."

52 Biderman, "Communist Attempts to Elicit False Confessions"; Hinkle and Wolff, "Methods of Interrogation."

53 Connor, "Manufacture of Deviance."

54 Jane Mayer, "Secret History."

55 *Special Review, Counterterrorism Detention and Interrogation Activities*, 83, 105.

56 Jensen, "International Campaign against Anarchist Terrorism," 100–101, 106–7.

57 Roberts, *Blacked Out*, 20–21.

58 Ibid., 14–15.

59 Johannesburg Principles.

60 Roberts, *Blacked Out*, 20–22.

61 Urban, *Secrets of the Kingdom*, 62–66.

62 Bok, *Secrets*, 180.

63 Ibid.

64 "Remarks by Homeland Security Secretary Michael Chertoff at a Press Conference on REAL ID."

65 "Remarks and Q&A by the Principal Deputy Director of National Intelligence Dr. Donald Kerr."

66 Warren and Brandeis, "Right to Privacy."

67 Sennett, *Fall of Public Man*, 16.

68 *Protecting Individual Privacy*, 292–93, 301.

69 Ibid., 304.

Chapter Four

1 "Brown Says He's Been Made Katrina Scapegoat."

2 Hurricane Katrina video conference transcript, August 28, 2005; Hurricane Katrina video conference transcript, August 29, 2005.

3 *National Response Plan*, iii.

4 Ibid., i.

5 Ibid., v–viii.

6 Lee Clarke, *Mission Improbable*, 16.

7 *National Response Plan*, CAT-1.

8 Ibid.

9 Ibid., CAT-3.

10 "Hurricane Katrina."

11 *National Response Plan*, CAT-4.

12 Ibid., 33–34.

13 "DHS Secretary Michael Chertoff Testimony before House Select Committee."

14 Ibid.

15 Ibid.

16 "Homeland Security Presidential Directive / HSPD-5."

17 *National Response Plan* (2004), i.

18 "Homeland Security Presidential Directive / HSPD-5."

19 "Homeland Security Presidential Directive / HSPD-8."

20 Waugh, "Terrorism and the All-Hazards Model."

21 Eksborg, "Swedish Emergency Management Agency."

22 Eksborg, "Emergency Management Agency"; Eksborg, "Swedish Emergency Management Agency."

23 Lee Clarke, *Mission Improbable*, 93–94, 123–24.

24 "Securing Our Homeland."

25 *National Strategy for Homeland Security*, July 2002.

26 Ibid.

27 Ibid.

28 Ibid., 3.

29 Ibid., 42.

30 Ibid., 38.

31 Ibid., 9.

32 *National Strategy for Homeland Security*, October 2007.

33 Ibid., 1.

34 Ibid., 3.

35 Ibid., 50.

36 *National Response Framework*, 1.

37 Ibid., 2.

38 Ibid., 25, 55.

39 Ibid., 42.

40 Ibid., 66.

41 Ibid., INC-i, ⟨http://www.fema.gov/emergency/nrf/incidentannexes.htm⟩.

Chapter Five

1 Tuan, *Landscapes of Fear*.

2 Cantril, *Invasion from Mars*, 159–60.

3 Brenzican, "New 'War of the Worlds' Recalls 9/11 Images."

4 Page, *City's End*, 84–85, 219.

5 Hagee, *Attack on America*, 4–5.

6 Lincoln, *Holy Terrors*, 104–7.

7 Page, *City's End*, 118–21.

8 Stephens, "Report from Suzanne Stephens to Jim Stonebraker."

9 Allison, "9/11 Wicked but a Work of Art."

10 Wilton and Barringer, *American Sublime*, 105.

11 Barkun, *Culture of Conspiracy*, 161–66.

12 *Journal of 9/11 Studies*; Scholars for 9/11 Truth; Scholars for 9/11 Truth and Justice.

13 Barkun, *Culture of Conspiracy*, 160.

14 "Hollywood 'Inspired US Attacks.'"

15 Page, *City's End*, 202–3.

16 Lane, "This Is Not a Movie."

17 Page, *City's End*, 24.

18 Sontag, "Imagination of Disaster," 43.

19 Wilton and Barringer, *American Sublime*, 105–7.

20 Ibid., 97.

21 Page, *City's End*, 67.

22 Ades et al., *Jose Clemente Orozco*, 255–56.

23 Steiner, "City Under Attack."

24 Page, *City's End*, 199.

25 Sontag, "Imagination of Disaster," 46.

26 Frayling, *Mad, Bad and Dangerous?*, 41–42.

27 Epstein, "Fictoid #3."

28 Escobar, "Roving Eye."

29 Epstein, "Fictoid #3."

30 Lifton, *Destroying the World to Save It*, 256–59.

31 Hardacre, "Aum Shinrikyo and the Japanese Media."

32 Foden, "War of the Worlds."

33 Page, *City's End*, 123–24.

34 Ibid., 136.

35 Ibid., 189–97.

36 Ibid., 4.

Chapter Six

1 "Remarks by Homeland Security Secretary Michael Chertoff at Roundtable with Bloggers."

2 Tomes, "Making of a Germ Panic," 194.

3 Bennett, *Party of Fear*.

4 "Defending Immigrants," 40; Beirich, "Teflon Nativists," 40.

5 "Defending Immigrants," 45.

6 "Year in Hate," 48–49.

7 "Blood on the Border," 6–15.

8 Buchanan and Holthouse, "Little Prince," 23; Buchanan and Kim, "Nativists," 33.

9 "Statement of Secretary Michael Chertoff Regarding Exercise of Waiver Authority."

10 Ibid.

11 Wald, "Communicable Americanism," 662.

12 Kraut, *Silent Travelers*, 2–3.

13 Tomes, "Making of a Germ Panic."

14 Kraut, *Silent Travelers*, 1–3, 277.

15 Tomes, "Making of a Germ Panic."

16 Wald, "Communicable Americanism," 680.

17 Tomes, "Making of a Germ Panic," 194.

18 Humphreys, "No Safe Place," 846.

19 Tomes, "Making of a Germ Panic," 191.

20 "Opinion Polls/Surveys, Jan. 2003–Jan. 16, 2009."

21 King, "Influence of Anxiety," 435.

22 Rapoport, "Terrorism and Weapons of the Apocalypse."

23 Erikson, *New Species of Trouble*, 150.

24 Humphreys, "No Safe Place," 847.

25 Douglas, *Purity and Danger*, 44.

26 Tomes, "Making of a Germ Panic."

27 Kraut, *Silent Travelers*, 5.

28 "Remarks by Homeland Security Secretary Michael Chertoff at the Stanford Constitutional Law Center's Germ Warfare, Contagious Disease and the Constitution Conference."

29 Erikson, *Wayward Puritans*.

30 Mueller, *Overblown*, 157–59.

Chapter Seven

1 Cohen, *Folk Devils and Moral Panics.*

2 Frankfurter, *Evil Incarnate.*

3 Cohen, *Folk Devils and Moral Panics*, 155–58.

4 Ibid., 1.

5 Ibid., xxvi–xxvii.

6 Ibid., viii.

7 Ibid., xxii.

8 Ibid., viii–xxi.

9 Introvigne, "Moral Panics and Anti-Cult Terrorism."

10 Ungar, "Moral Panics versus the Risk Society."

11 Beck, *Risk Society.*

12 Cohen, *Folk Devils and Moral Panics*, xxv.

13 Ibid., xxvi.

14 Beck, *Risk Society*, 75.

15 Frankfurter, *Evil Incarnate*, 9.

16 Ibid., 32.

17 Ibid., 187.

18 Juergensmeyer, *Terror in the Mind of God*, 148–66.

19 Ibid., 126.

20 Sunstein, *Laws of Fear*, 94–98.

21 Houts, Cleary, and Hu, *Three-Mile Island Crisis*, 13.

22 Sunstein, *Laws of Fear*, 91.

23 Mueller, *Overblown*, 40.

24 Ibid., 41.

25 Ibid., 41–43.

26 Sunstein, *Worst-Case Scenarios*, 26–27.

27 *Toward a National Strategy for Combating Terrorism*, v–vi.

28 *Roadmap for National Security*, 14–18.

29 "Strategic Plan—Securing Our Homeland."

30 "Homeland Security Presidential Directive / HSPD-3."

31 "Remarks by Governor Ridge at Announcement of Homeland Security Advisory System."

32 "Chronology of Changes to the Homeland Security Advisory System."

33 "Homeland Security Presidential Directive / HSPD-3."

34 "Remarks for Secretary Chertoff."

35 "Homeland Security Advisory System."

36 Erikson, *Everything in Its Path*, 234.

37 "After 9/11: Stress and Coping Across America."

38 Greenberg and Parker, *Kennedy Assassination and the American Public.*

39 Richard A. Clarke, "Memorandum for Condoleezza Rice."

40 "Eco-Terrorist Convicted."

41 "Eco-Terrorist Given Nearly Twenty Years in Prison."

42 "Eco-Terrorist Convicted."

43 "The Eric McDavid Story."

44 "Smith County Man Admits Possessing Chemical Weapons."

45 Reynolds, "Homegrown Terror"; Wright, "Tyler Man, Companion Plead Guilty in Fed Court."

46 Reynolds, "Homegrown Terror."

47 "New Details in Cyanide Bomb Investigation."

48 "US Terrorism Plot That the Media Ignores."

49 Reynolds, "Homegrown Terror."

50 "American Morning."

51 "Man Who Built Arsenal Gets Prison Term."

52 Krugman, "Noonday in the Shade."

53 Reynolds, "Homegrown Terror."

54 Posner, *Catastrophe*, 120–22.

Chapter Eight

1 Bankoff, "Historical Geography of Disaster," 32.

2 Wiedeman, Clauberg, and Schutz, "Understanding Amplification of Complex Risk Issues," 286–89.

3 Ibid., 290–93.

4 Ibid., 293.

5 Beck, *Risk Society*, 22.

6 Posner, *Catastrophe*, 171.

7 "Poll: Terrorism Fears Are Fading."

8 Nacos, Bloch-Elkon, and Shapiro, "Prevention of Terrorism in Post-9/11 America," 11.

9 "Poll: Concerns about Terrorist Attacks at Lowest Level since 9/11."

10 "Problems and Priorities."

11 "Domestic Concerns Will Vie with Terrorism in Fall."

12 "Economy and Anti-Terrorism Top Public's Policy Agenda."

13 "Declining Public Support for Global Engagement."

14 "American Attitudes Hold Steady in Face of Foreign Crises."

15 Sageman, *Leaderless Jihad*, 90.

16 Abbott, "Narrative and Emergent Behavior."

17 Ibid., 230–31.

18 Ibid., 228.

19 Arquilla and Ronfeldt, *Swarming and the Future of Conflict*.

20 Barkun, *Culture of Conspiracy*, 3–4.

21 National Intelligence Council, National Intelligence Estimate: "Terrorist Threat to the U.S. Homeland."

22 Ibid.

23 McConnell, "Annual Threat Assessment of the Director of National Intelligence."
24 "Director's Remarks at the Los Angeles World Affairs Council."
25 Sageman, *Leaderless Jihad.*
26 Sageman, *Understanding Terror Networks.*
27 Ibid., 71.
28 Ibid., 138.
29 Ibid., 141.
30 "Guide to the Ulius L. Amoss Papers, 1941–1963."
31 Beam, "Leaderless Resistance."
32 Barkun, *Religion and the Racist Right*, 267, 275, 280.
33 Kaplan, "'Leaderless Resistance,'" 80.
34 Sageman, *Leaderless Jihad*, vii.
35 Ibid., 127.
36 Ibid., 126.
37 Hoffman, "Myth of Grass-Roots Terrorism," 134.
38 Ibid., 134.
39 Hoffman, "Hoffman Replies."
40 Corman, "Hatfields and McCoys of Counterterrorism."
41 Williams, "In Cold Blood."
42 Jackson, "Groups, Networks, or Movements."
43 A strikingly similar analysis of the Sageman-Hoffman conflict appears in Croft and Moore, "Evolution of Threat Narratives," 825–27, which I came upon only after the present work was in an advanced draft.
44 "Fact Sheet: U.S. Department of Homeland Security Five-Year Anniversary Progress and Priorities."
45 Sageman, *Leaderless Jihad*, 90.
46 Weinberg and Eubank, "Backlash."
47 Mueller, *Overblown*, 4, 48.
48 Carr, *Twenty Years' Crisis, 1919–1939*, 157.

Epilogue

 1 "Secretary Napolitano Announces 60-Day Review of Homeland SecurityAdvisory System."
 2 "Secretary Napolitano Announces New National Terrorism Advisory System."
 3 Unclassified Report on the President's Surveillance Program, 31–36.
 4 Corwin, *Total War and the Constitution*, vii–viii.
 5 Markon, "FBI-ATF Turf Battle Hurts Bomb Probes, Official Says."
 6 "Top Secret America."
 7 Intelligence Reform and Terrorism Prevention Act of 2004.
 8 National Security Strategy, 19.
 9 Mowatt-Larssen, "Al Qaeda Weapons of Mass Destruction Threat: Hype or Reality?"

10 Gray, "Thinking Asymmetrically in Times of Terror."

11 Amerithrax Investigative Summary. The FBI's conclusion has not gone entirely unchallenged, for reasons too complex to go into here.

12 Ellis, "Finding a Place for 9/11 in American History." The essay originally appeared in the New York Times, January 28, 2006.

BIBLIOGRAPHY

Abbott, H. Porter. "Narrative and Emergent Behavior." *Poetics Today* 29 (Summer 2008): 227–44.

Ades, Dawn, et al. *Jose Clemente Orozco in the United States, 1927–1934*. New York: Norton, 2002.

"After 9/11: Stress and Coping Across America." RAND Health. ⟨http://www.rand.org/pubs/research_briefs/RB4546/index1.html⟩. August 31, 2010.

"Airports Trial Facial Recognition." BBC News, ⟨http://newsvote.bbc.co.uk/mpapps/pagetools/print/news.bbc.co.uk/2/hi/uk_new/7366694.s⟩. April 25, 2008.

Allison, Rebecca. "9/11 Wicked but a Work of Art, Says Damien Hirst." *The Guardian*. September 11, 2002, ⟨http://www.guardian.co.uk/arts/news/story/0.11711,790058,00.html⟩. March 4, 2005.

"American Attitudes Hold Steady in Face of Foreign Crises." August 17, 2006, ⟨http://people-press.org/report285/american-attitudes-hold-steady-in-face-of-crises⟩. January 26, 2009.

"American Morning, Domestic Terrorism." December 30, 2003. ⟨http://archives.cnn.com/TRANSCRIPTS/0312/30/1tm.09.html⟩. September 1, 2010.

Amerithrax Investigative Summary. Department of Justice. February 19, 2010, ⟨http://www.justice.gov/amerithrax/docs/amx-investigative-summary.pdf⟩. June 29, 2010.

Arquilla, John, and David Ronfeldt. *Swarming and the Future of Conflict*. Santa Monica, Calif.: Rand, n.d.

Bankoff, Greg. "The Historical Geography of Disaster: 'Vulnerability' and 'Local Knowledge.'" In *Mapping Vulnerability: Disaster, Development and People*, edited by Greg Bankoff, Georg Frerks, and Dorothea Hilhorst, 25–36. London: Earthscan, 2004.

Barkun, Michael. *A Culture of Conspiracy: Apocalyptic Visions in Contemporary America*. Berkeley: University of California Press, 2003.

———. "Disaster in History." *Mass Emergencies* 2 (December 1977): 219–32.

———. "Divided Apocalypse: Thinking About the End in Contemporary America." *Soundings: An Interdisciplinary Journal* 66 (Fall 1983): 257–80.

———. "Terrorism and the'Invisible.'" *Perspectives on Terrorism* 1, no. 6 (2007). ⟨http://www.terrorismanalysts.com/pt/index⟩. January 4, 2008.

———. *Religion and the Racist Right: The Origins of the Christian Identity Movement.* Chapel Hill: University of North Carolina Press, 1997.

Barton, Allen H. *Communities in Disaster: A Sociological Analysis of Collective Stress Situations.* Garden City, N.Y.: Doubleday, 1969.

Beam, Louis. "Leaderless Resistance." *The Seditionist*, no. 12 (February 1992), n.p., ⟨http://www.louisbeam.com/leaderless.htm⟩. March 23, 2009.

Beck, Ulrich. *Risk Society: Towards a New Modernity.* London: Sage, 1992.

Beirich, Heidi. "The Teflon Nativists." *Intelligence Report.* The Southern Poverty Law Center. Issue 128 (Winter 2007): 40–45.

Bennett, David H. *The Party of Fear: The American Far Right from Nativism to the Militia Movement.* New York: Vintage, 1995.

Biderman, Albert D. "Communist Attempts to Elicit False Confessions from Air Force Prisoners of War." *Bulletin of the New York Academy of Medicine* 33 (September 1957): 616–25.

Billington, James H. *Fire in the Minds of Men: The Origins of the Revolutionary Faith.* New York: Basic Books, 1980.

"Blood on the Border." *Intelligence Report.* The Southern Poverty Law Center. Issue 101 (Spring 2001): 6–18.

Bok, Sisela. *Secrets: On the Ethics of Concealment and Revelation.* New York: Vintage, 1989.

Bowcott, Owen. "FBI Wants Instant Access to British Identity Data." *The Guardian.* January 15, 2008, ⟨http://www.guardian.co.uk/print/0,,332065468-105744,00.html⟩. January 15, 2008.

Boyer, Paul. *When Time Shall Be No More: Prophecy Belief in Modern American Culture.* Cambridge: Harvard University Press, 1992.

Brenzican, Anthony. "New 'War of the Worlds' Recalls 9/11 Images." *USA Today,* June 30, 2005, ⟨http://usatoday.printthis.clickability.com/pt/cpt?action=cpt&title=USATODAY.com⟩. July 14, 2005.

Brower, Jennifer L. "The Terrorist Threat and Its Implications for Sensor Technologies." 2005, ⟨http://nato-asi.org/sensors2005/papers/brower.pdf⟩. December 7, 2007.

"Brown Says He's Been Made Katrina Scapegoat." CNN, February 13, 2006, ⟨http://www.cnn.com/2006/POLITICS/02/10/katrina.brown⟩. August 31, 2010.

Buchanan, Susy, and David Holthouse. "The Little Prince." *Intelligence Report.* The Southern Poverty Law Center. Issue 120 (Winter 2005): 20–24.

Buchanan, Susy, and Tom Kim. "The Nativists." *Intelligence Report.* The Southern Poverty Law Center. Issue 120 (Winter 2005): 25–42.

Cantril, Hadley. *The Invasion from Mars: A Study in the Psychology of Panic.* Princeton: Princeton University Press, 1940.

Cardona, Omar P. "The Need for Rethinking the Concepts of Vulnerability and Risk from a Holistic Perspective: A Necessary Review and Criticism for Effective Risk Management." In *Mapping Vulnerability: Disasters, Development and People*, edited by Greg Bankoff, Georg Frerks, and Dorothea Hilhorst, 37–51. London: Earthscan, 2004.

Carr, Edward Hallett. *The Twenty Years' Crisis, 1919–1939: An Introduction to the Study of International Relations*. New York: Harper & Row, 1964.

"The Characteristics of Suicide Terrorists: An Empirical Analysis of Palestinian Terrorism in Israel," ⟨http://nssc.haifa.ac.il/Terror/articles/profile.html⟩. March 21, 2007.

"Chronology of Changes to the Homeland Security Advisory System." Department of Homeland Security, ⟨http://www.DHS.gov/xabout/history/editorial_0844.shtm⟩. March 18, 2008.

Clarke, Lee. *Mission Improbable: Using Fantasy Documents to Tame Disaster*. Chicago: University of Chicago Press, 1999.

Clarke, Richard A. "Memorandum for Condoleezza Rice." January 25, 2001, ⟨http://www.gwu.edu/~nsarchiv/NSAEBB/NSAEBB147/clarke%memo.pdf⟩. April 15, 2008.

Coaffee, Jon. "Rings of Steel, Rings of Concrete and Rings of Confidence: Designing out Terrorism in Central London pre and post September 11th." *International Journal of Urban and Regional Research* 28 (March 2004): 201–11.

Cohen, Stanley. *Folk Devils and Moral Panics: The Creation of the Mods and Rockers*. London: Routledge, 2002.

Commoner, Barry. *The Closing Circle: Nature, Man, and Technology*. New York: Knopf, 1971.

Connor, Walter D. "The Manufacture of Deviance: The Case of the Soviet Purge, 1936–1938." *American Sociological Review* 37 (August 1972): 403–13.

Corman, Steven R. "The Hatfields and McCoys of Counterterrorism." *COMOPS Journal*, ⟨http://comops.org/journal/2008/06/09/the-hatfields-and-mccoys-of-counterterrorism/⟩. July 23, 2008.

Corwin, Edward S. *Total War and the Constitution*. New York: Knopf, 1947.

Croft, Stuart, and Cerwyn Moore. "The Evolution of Threat Narratives in the Age of Terror: Understanding Terrorist Threats in Britain." *International Affairs* 86 (2010): 821–35.

Davis, David Brion. "Some Themes of Counter-Subversion: An Analysis of Anti-Masonic, Anti-Catholic, and Anti-Mormon Literature." *Mississippi Valley Historical Review* 47 (September 1960): 205–24.

"Declining Public Support for Global Engagement." September 24, 2008, ⟨http://people-press.org/report/pageid=1386⟩. January 26, 2009.

"Defending Immigrants." *Intelligence Report*. The Southern Poverty Law Center. Issue 106 (Summer 2002): 39–43.

Demirev, Plamen A., Andrew B. Feldman, and Jeffrey S. Lin. "Chemical and Biological Weapons: Current Concepts for Future Defenses." *Johns Hopkins APL Technical Digest* 26 (2005): 321–33.

"DHS' Domestic Nuclear Detection Office Progress in Integrating Detection Capabilities and Response Protocols." Office of Inspector General. Department of Homeland Security. December 2007.

"DHS Proposes Biometric Airport and Seaport Exit Procedures." April 22, 2008, ⟨http://www.DHS.gov/xnews/releases/pr_1208186058701.shtm⟩. April 23, 2008.

"DHS Releases REAL ID Regulation." January 11, 2008, ⟨http://www.dhs.gov/xnews/releases/pr_1200065427422.shtm⟩. January 14, 2008.

"DHS Secretary Michael Chertoff Testimony before House Select Committee on Hurricane Katrina Preparation and Response." October 19, 2005, ⟨http://www.semp.us/publications/biot_printview.php?BiotID=287>. October 4, 2007.

"Director's Remarks at the Los Angeles World Affairs Council." Remarks by Central Intelligence Director Michael Hayden. September 16, 2008, ⟨http://www.cia.gov/news-information/speeches-testimony/directors-remarks-at-lawac-html⟩. September 17, 2008.

"Domestic Concerns Will Vie with Terrorism in Fall." June 27, 2002, ⟨http://people-press.org/report/157/domestic-concerns-will-vie-with-terrorism-in-fall⟩. January 26, 2009.

Douglas, Mary. *Purity and Danger: An Analysis of Concept of Pollution and Taboo.* London: Routledge, 1966.

Dye, David H. "Sensors for Screening and Surveillance." Conference on Technology for Preventing Terrorism. March 12–13, 2002, ⟨http://media.hoover.org/documents/dye_TechConf.pdf⟩. December 7, 2007.

"Economy and Anti-Terrorism Top Public's Policy Agenda." January 15, 2004, ⟨http://people-press.org/report/?pageid=778⟩. January 26, 2009.

"Eco-Terrorist Convicted: Sacramento Federal Jury Convicts Eric McDavid with Conspiracy to Commit Domestic Terrorism." News Release. United States Attorney. Eastern District of California. September 27, 2007, ⟨http://www.docstoc.com/docs/708953/McGregor-W-Scott-United-States-Attorney-Eastern-District⟩. March 23, 2009.

"Eco-Terrorist Given Nearly Twenty Years in Prison." Department of Justice. United States Attorney. Eastern District of California. May 8, 2008, ⟨http://sacramento.fbi.gov/dojpressrel/pressrel108/sco050808.pdf⟩. March 23, 2009.

Eksborg, Ann-Louise. "An Emergency Management Agency—Why?" Speech Delivered at the Solbacka Course on August 20, 2002.

———. "The Swedish Emergency Management Agency: Experience and Conclusions after Two Years." Swedish Emergency Management Agency. September 2004, ⟨http://www.krisberedskapsmyndigheten.se/templates/Archive_8950.aspx⟩. March 20, 2009.

Ellis, Joseph J. "Finding a Place for 9/11 in American History," ⟨http://www.mtholyoke.edu/news/stories/4038605⟩. March 23, 2009.

Epstein, Edward Jay. "Fictoid #3: The Lair of Bin Laden," ⟨http://www.edwardjayepstein.com/nether_fictoid3.htm⟩. January 17, 2007.

"The Eric McDavid Story." *Earth First! Journal*, ⟨http://www.earthfirstjournal.org/ article.php?id=326⟩. May 12, 2008.

Erikson, Kai T. *Everything in Its Path: Destruction of Community in the Buffalo Creek Flood*. New York: Simon & Schuster, 1976.

———. *A New Species of Trouble: The Human Experience of Modern Disasters*. New York: Norton, 1994.

———. *Wayward Puritans: A Study in the Sociology of Deviance*. New York: Wiley, 1966.

Escobar, Pepe. "The Roving Eye: Showdown on the Roof of the World." *Asia Times*. October 4, 2001, ⟨http://www.atimes.com/c-asia/CJ04Ag01.html⟩. March 21, 2005.

"Fact Sheet: U.S. Department of Homeland Security Five-Year Anniversary Progress and Priorities." March 6, 2008, ⟨http://www.dhs.gov/xnews/releases/ pr_1204819171793.shtm⟩. March 20, 2008.

"FBI Announces Contract Award for Next Generation Identification System." Press Release. February 12, 2008, ⟨http://www.fbi.gov/pressrel/pressrel08/ ngicontract021208.htm⟩. February 13, 2008.

First Responders' Ability to Detect and Model Hazardous Releases in Urban Areas Is Significantly Limited. Washington: Government Accountability Office, June 2008.

"Five Years Later . . . Diminished Public Appetite for Military Force and Mideast Oil." Washington: The Pew Research Center for the People and the Press, 2006.

Foden, Giles. "War of the Worlds." *The Guardian*. August 24, 2002, ⟨http://books .guardian.co.uk/review/story/0,12084,779530,00.html⟩. March 4, 2005.

Foertsch, Jacqueline. *Enemies Within: The Cold War and the AIDS Crisis in Literature, Film, and Culture*. Urbana: University of Illinois Press, 2001.

Frankfurter, David. *Evil Incarnate: Rumors of Demonic Conspiracy and Satanic Abuse in History*. Princeton: Princeton University Press, 2006.

Frayling, Christopher. *Mad, Bad and Dangerous? The Scientist and Cinema*. London: Routledge, 2005.

Frewer, Lynn J. "Truth, Transparency, and Social Context: Implications for Social Amplification of Risk." In *The Social Amplification of Risk*, edited by Nick Pidgeon, Roger E. Kasperson, and Paul Slovic, 123–37. Cambridge: Cambridge University Press, 2003.

Fussey, Pete. "Observing Potentiality in the Global City: Surveillance and Counter-terrorism in London." *International Criminal Justice Review* 17 (September 2007): 171–92.

Garrett, Clarke. *Respectable Folly: Millenarians and the French Revolution in France and England*. Baltimore: Johns Hopkins University Press, 1975.

Gorman, Alexander. "CCTV Facial Recognition Analysis," ⟨http://www.cse.osu.edu/ ~jholliday/COEN150spo3projects/AlexGormanCOENProject.pdf⟩. December 14, 2007.

Gray, Colin S. "Thinking Asymmetrically in Times of Terror." *Parameters: US Army War College Quarterly* (Spring 2002): 5–14.

Greenberg, Bradley S., and Edwin B. Parker, eds. *The Kennedy Assassination and the American Public: Social Communication in Crisis*. Stanford: Stanford University Press, 1965.

Greenberg, Karen J., and Joshua L. Dratel, eds. *The Torture Papers: The Road to Abu Ghraib*. New York: Cambridge University Press, 2005.

"Guide to the Ulius L. Amoss Papers, 1941–1963." ⟨http://nwda-db.wsulibs.wsu.edu/findaid/ark:/80444/xv35579⟩. March 23, 2009.

Hagee, John. *Attack on America: New York, Jerusalem, and the Role of Terrorism in the Last Days*. Nashville: Thomas Nelson, 2001.

Hardacre, Helen. "Aum Shinrikyo and the Japanese Media." JPRI Working Paper No. 19. April 1996, ⟨http://www.jpri.org/publications/workingpapers/wp19.html⟩. March 4, 2005.

Hayden, Michael. "Director's Remarks at the Los Angeles World Affairs Council." September 16, 2008, ⟨http://www.cia.gov/news-information/speeches-testimony/directors-remarks-at-lawac.html>. September 17, 2008.

Heilbroner, Robert L. *An Inquiry into the Human Prospect*. New York: Norton, 1974.

Hewitt, Kenneth, and Ian Burton. *The Hazardousness of a Place: A Regional Ecology of Damaging Events*. Toronto: University of Toronto Press, 1971.

Hilhorst, Dorothea, and Greg Bankoff. "Introduction: Mapping Vulnerability." In *Mapping Vulnerability: Disasters, Development and People*, edited by Greg Bankoff, George Frerks, and Dorothea Hilhorst, 1–9. London: Earthscan, 2004.

Hinkle, Lawrence E., Jr., and Harold G. Wolff. "The Methods of Interrogation and Indoctrination Used by the Communist State Police." *Bulletin of the New York Academy of Medicine* 33 (September 1957): 600–615.

Hobsbawm, E. J. *Primitive Rebels: Studies in Archaic Forms of Social Movement in the 19th and 20th Centuries*. New York: Norton, 1959.

Hoffman, Bruce. "Hoffman Replies." *Foreign Affairs* 87 (July–August 2008): 165–66.

———. "The Myth of Grass-Roots Terrorism: Why Osama bin Laden Still Matters." *Foreign Affairs* 87 (May–June 2008): 133–38.

"Hollywood 'Inspired US Attacks'." BBC News. October 17, 2001, ⟨http://news.bbc.co.uk/2/hi/entertainment/1604151.stm⟩. March 21, 2005.

"Homeland Security Advisory System." Department of Homeland Security, ⟨http://www.dhs.gov/xinfoshare/programs/Copy_of_press_release_0046.shtm⟩. March 18, 2008.

"Homeland Security Presidential Directive / HSPD-3." March 11, 2002, ⟨http://www.fas.org/irp/offdocs/nspd/hspd-3.html⟩. July 25, 2007.

"Homeland Security Presidential Directive / HSPD-5." February 28, 2003, ⟨http://www.fas.org/irp/offdocs/nspd/hspd-5.html⟩. July 25, 2007.

"Homeland Security Presidential Directive / HSDP-8." December 17, 2003, ⟨http://www.fas.org/irp/offdocs/nspd/hspd-8.html⟩. July 25, 2007.

Houts, Peters, Paul D. Cleary, and The-Wei Hu. *The Three-Mile Island Crisis: Psychological, Social, and Economic Impacts on the Surrounding Population*. University Park: Pennsylvania State University Press, 1988.

Hsu, Spencer S. "New York Presses to Deploy More Bioweapons Sensors." *Washington Post*, January 9, 2008, ⟨http://www.washingtonpost.com/wp-dyn/content/article/2008/01/08/AR2008010803892_pf⟩. January 9, 2008.

———. "Securing the Cities No Easy Task." *Washington Post*, February 3, 2008, ⟨http://www.washingtonpost.com/wp-dyn/content/article/2008/02/02/AR2008020202220_pf⟩. February 5, 2008.

Humphreys, Margaret. "No Safe Place: Disease and Panic in American History." *American Literary History* 14 (Winter 2002): 845–57.

"Hurricane Katrina: A Nation Still Unprepared. Executive Summary." Report of the Senate Committee on Homeland Security and Governmental Affairs. May 2006, ⟨http://hsgac.senate.gov/_files/Katrina/FullReport.pdf> October 15, 2008.

Hurricane Katrina video conference transcript. August 28, 2005, ⟨http://www.cbsnews.com/htdocs/pdf/transcript_82805.pdf⟩. April 14, 2009.

Hurricane Katrina video conference transcript. August 29, 2005, ⟨http://www.usatoday.com/news/katrinatranscript-0829.pdf⟩. April 14, 2009.

Intelligence Reform and Terrorism Prevention Act of 2004. Public Law 108-458. December 17, 2004.

Introvigne, Massimo. "Moral Panics and Anti-Cult Terrorism in Western Europe." *Terrorism and Political Violence* 12 (Spring 2000): 47–59.

Jackson, Brian A. "Groups, Networks, or Movements: A Command-and-Control Approach to Classifying Terrorist Organizations and Its Applications to Al Qaeda." *Studies in Conflict and Terrorism* 29 (2006): 241–62.

Jensen, Richard Bach. "The International Campaign against Anarchist Terrorism, 1880–1930s." *Terrorism and Political Violence* 21 (January–March 2009): 89–109.

The Johannesburg Principles on National Security, Freedom of Expression, and Access to Information. 1996, ⟨http://www1.umn.edu/humanrts/instree/johannesburg.html⟩. April 2, 2009.

Journal of 9/11 Studies, ⟨http://www.journalof911studies.com⟩. March 6, 2009.

Juergensmeyer, Mark. *Terror in the Mind of God: The Global Rise of Religious Violence*. Berkeley: The University of California Press, 2003.

Kaplan, Jeffrey. "'Leaderless Resistance.'" *Terrorism and Political Violence* 9 (Autumn 1997): 80–95.

Kasperson, Jeanne X., Roger E. Kasperson, Nick Pidgeon, and Paul Slovic. "The Social Amplification of Risk: Assessing Fifteen Years of Research and Theory." In *The Social Amplification of Risk*, edited by Nick Pidgeon, Roger E. Kasperson, and Paul Slovic, 13–46. Cambridge: Cambridge University Press, 2003.

King, Nicholas B. "The Influence of Anxiety: September 11, Bioterrorism, and American Public Health." *Journal of the History of Medicine and Allied Sciences* 58 (2003): 433–41.

Kraut, Alan M. *Silent Travelers: Germs, Genes, and the "Immigrant Menace."* New York: Basic Books, 1994.

Krugman, Paul. "Noonday in the Shade." *New York Times*, June 22, 2004, ⟨http://www.nytimes.com/2004/06/22/opinion/noonday-in-the-shade.html⟩. March 23, 2009.

Lane, Anthony. "This Is Not a Movie." *The New Yorker*, September 24, 2001, ⟨http://www.newyorker.com/archive/2001/09/24/010924crci_cinema?printable=true⟩. November 6, 2008.

Lara, Maria Pia. "In and Out of Terror: The Vertigo of Secularization." *Hypatia* 18 (Winter 2003): 183–96.

Larabee, Ann. *Decade of Disaster*. Urbana: University of Illinois Press, 2000.

LaValley, Al, ed. *Invasion of the Body Snatchers, Don Siegel, Director*. New Brunswick, N.J.: Rutgers University Press, 1989.

Lavell, Allan. "The Lower Lempa River Valley, El Salvador: Risk Reduction and Development Project." In *Mapping Vulnerability: Disaster, Development and People*, edited by Greg Bankoff, Georg Frerks, and Dorothea Hilhorst, 67–82. London: Earthscan, 2004.

Lifton, Robert Jay. *Destroying the World to Save It: Aum Shinrikyo, Apocalyptic Violence, and the New Global Terrorism*. New York: Metropolitan Books, 1999.

Lincoln, Bruce. *Holy Terrors: Thinking about Religion after September 11*. Chicago: University of Chicago Press, 2003.

Lindsey, Hal, with C.C. Carlson. *The Late Great Planet Earth*. New York: Bantam, 1973.

Loevinger, Lee. "Facts, Evidence, and Legal Proof." *Western Reserve Law Review* 9 (March 1958): 154–87.

"Man Who Built Arsenal Gets Prison Term." May 5, 2004. ⟨http://lubbockonline.com/stories/050504/sta_050504055.shtml⟩. September 1, 2010.

Markon, Jerry. "FBI-ATF Turf Battle Hurts Bomb Probes, Official Says." *Washington Post*, August 27, 2010. ⟨http://www.washingtonpost.com/wp-dyn/content/asrticle/2010/08/26/AR010082606631.html⟩. August 27, 2010.

Mayer, Jane. "The Experiment." *The New Yorker*, July 11, 2005, ⟨http://www.newyorker.com/archive/2005/07/11/050711fa_fact4?printable=true⟩. June 19, 2009.

———. "The Secret History." *The New Yorker*, 22 June 2009, ⟨http://www.newyorker.com/reporting/2009/06/22/090622fa_fact_mayer?printable=true⟩. June 15, 2009.

"McCain's Negatives Mostly Political, Obama's More Person." May 29, 2008, ⟨http://people-press.org/report/?pageid=1317⟩. January 26, 2009.

McConnell, J. Michael. "Annual Threat Assessment of the Director of National Intelligence for the Senate Select Committee on Intelligence." February 5, 2008, ⟨http://www.fbiic.gov/public/2008/feb/Annual_threat_assessment.pdf⟩. March 19, 2009.

Meadows, Donella H., et al. *The Limits to Growth: A Report for the Club of Rome's Project on the Predicament of Mankind*. New York: Universe Books, 1972.

Mitchell, James K. "Urban Vulnerability to Terrorism as Hazard." In *The Geographical Dimensions of Terrorism*, edited by Susan L. Cutter, Douglas B. Richardson, and Thomas J. Wilbanks, 17–26. New York: Routledge, 2003.

"More Americans Question Religion's Role in Politics." August 21, 2008, ⟨http://people-press.org/report/?pageid=1364⟩. January 26, 2009.

Morin, Richard, and Claudia Deane. "Half of Residents in Fear, Post Poll Finds." *Washington Post*, October 23, 2002, A01.

Mowatt-Larssen, Rolf. "Al Qaeda Weapons of Mass Destruction Threat: Hype or Reality?" Belfer Center for Science and International Affairs, Kennedy School. January 2010, ⟨http://belfercenter.ksg.harvard.edu/files/al-qaeda-wmd-threat.pdf⟩. February 1, 2010.

"MPD Deploys Additional CCTV Cameras in Northwest DC." October 9, 2007, ⟨http://newsroom.dc.gov/show.aspx/agency/mpdc/section/2/release/11960/year/2007⟩. January 3, 2007.

Mueller, John. *Overblown: How Politicians and the Terrorism Industry Inflate National Security Threats and Why We Believe Them*. New York: Free Press, 2006.

Murdock, Graham, Judith Petts, and Tom Horlick-Jones. "After Amplification: Rethinking the Role of the Media in Risk Communication." In *The Social Amplification of Risk*, edited by Nick Pidgeon, Roger E. Kasperson, and Paul Slovic, 156–78. Cambridge: Cambridge University Press, 2003.

Nacos, Brigitte L., Yaeli Bloch-Elkon, and Robert Y. Shapiro. "Prevention of Terrorism in Post-9/11 America: News Coverage, Public Perceptions, and the Politics of Homeland Security." *Terrorism and Political Violence* 20 (January–March 2008): 1–25.

Nakashima, Ellen. "Lockheed Secures Contract to Expand Biometric Database." *Washington Post*, February 13, 2008, ⟨http://www.washingtonpost.com/wp-dyn/content/article/2008/02/12/AR2008021202777_pf.htm⟩. February 13, 2008.

———. "Terror Suspect List Yields Few Arrests." *Washington Post*, August 25, 2007, ⟨http://www.washingtonpost.com/wp-dyn/content/article/2007/08/24/AR2007082402256_pf.htm⟩. February 18, 2009.

National Intelligence Council. National Intelligence Estimate: "The Terrorist Threat to the US Homeland." July 2007.

National Response Framework. U.S. Department of Homeland Security. January 2008, ⟨http://www.fema.gov/pdf/emergency/nrf/nrf-core.pdf⟩ and ⟨http://www.fema.gov/pdf/emergency/nrf/nrf-annexes-all.pdf⟩. March 1, 2009.

National Response Plan. December 2004, ⟨http://www.au.af.mil/au/awc/awcgate/nrp/nrp.pdf⟩. March 1, 2009.

National Response Plan. Support Annexes. December 2004, ⟨http://www.learning services.us/pdf/emergency/nrf/nrp_catastrophicincidentannex.pdf⟩. April 12, 2008.

National Security Strategy. May 2010, ⟨http://www.whitehouse.gov/sites/default/files/rss_viewer/national_security_strategy.pdf⟩. June 28, 2010.

National Strategy for Combating Terrorism. (September 2006). ⟨http://www.white-house.gov/nsc/nsct/2006/nsct2006.pdf⟩.

National Strategy for Homeland Security. Homeland Security Council. July 2002, ⟨http://www.dhs.gov/xlibrary/assets/nat_strat_his.pdf⟩. March 20, 2009.

National Strategy for Homeland Security. Homeland Security Council. October 2007, ⟨http://www.dhs.gov/xlibrary/asswets/nat_strat_homelandsecurity_2007.pdf⟩. June 7, 2008.

Neuman, William. "More Delays for Cameras in Subways." *The New York Times*, June 26, 2008, B1–B6.

"New Details in Cyanide Bomb Investigation." KLTV. December 12, 2003, ⟨http://www.thememoryhole.org/terror/tyler-terror.htm⟩. May 12, 2008.

Office of Emergency Management and Communications. City of Chicago, ⟨http://egov.cityofchicago.org/city/webportal/portalContentItemAction.do?BV⟩. January 3, 2008.

Oliver-Smith, Anthony. "Theorizing Vulnerability in a Globalized World: A Political Ecological Perspective." In *Mapping Vulnerability: Disaster, Development and People,* edited by Greg Bankoff, Georg Frerks, and Dorothea Hilhorst, 10–24. London: Earthscan, 2004.

"Opinion Polls/Surveys, Jan. 2003–Jan. 16, 2009. ⟨http://usiraq.procon.org/view.resource.php?resourceID=000673⟩. August 31, 2010.

Page, Max. *The City's End: Two Centuries of Fantasies, Fears, and Premonitions of New York's Destruction.* New Haven: Yale University Press, 2008.

Partridge, Christopher. *The Re-Enchantment of the West.* 2 vols. London: T&T Clark, 2004–5.

Pidgeon, Nick, Roger E. Kasperson, and Paul Slovic. "Introduction." In *The Social Amplification of Risk,* edited by Nick Pidgeon, Roger E. Kasperson, and Paul Slovic, 1–12. Cambridge: Cambridge University Press, 2003.

"Poll: Concerns about Terrorist Attacks at Lowest Level since 9/11." CNN, September 11, 2008, ⟨http://articles.cnn.com/2008-09-11/politics/terrorism.poll_1_iraq-war-john-mccain-americans?_s=PM:POLITICS⟩. September 11, 2008.

"Poll: Terrorism Fears Are Fading," ⟨http://cnn.site.printthis.clickability.com/pt/cpt?action=cpt&title=Poll%3A+Terrorism+fears⟩. July 8, 2008.

Posner, Richard. *Catastrophe: Risk and Response.* New York: Oxford University Press, 2004.

"Problems and Priorities," ⟨http://www.pollingreport.com/prioriti.htm⟩. November 20, 2008.

Protecting Individual Privacy in the Struggle against Terrorists: A Framework for Program Assessment. Washington: National Academies Press, 2008.

"Q&A on Face-Recognition." American Civil Liberties Union, ⟨http://www.aclu.org/privacy/spying/14875res20030902.html⟩. December 17, 2007.

Rapoport, David C. "Terrorism and Weapons of the Apocalypse." *National Security Studies Quarterly* (Summer 1999): 49–67.

Reader, Ian. "Imagined Persecution: Aum Shinrikyo, Millennialism, and the Legitimation of Violence." In *Millennialism, Persecution, and Violence: Historical Cases,* edited by Catherine Wessinger, 158–84. Syracuse: Syracuse University Press, 2000.

"REAL ID Final Rule: Questions & Answers," ⟨http://www.dhs.gov/xprevprot/programs/gc_1172767635686.shtm⟩. January 14, 2008.

"Remarks and Q&A by the Principal Deputy Director of National Intelligence

Dr. Donald Kerr." 2007 GEOINT Symposium. October 23, 2007, ⟨http://www.dni
.gov/speeches/20071023_speech.pdf⟩. April 2, 2009.

"Remarks by Governor Ridge at Announcement of Homeland Security Advisory
System." March 12, 2002, ⟨http://www.whitehouse.gov/news/releases/2002/03/
20020312-11.html⟩. March 13, 2008.

"Remarks by Homeland Security Secretary Michael Chertoff at a Press Conference
on REAL ID." January 11, 2008, ⟨http://www.dhs.gov/xnews/speeches/
sp_1200320940276.shtm⟩. January 15, 2008.

"Remarks by Homeland Security Secretary Michael Chertoff at Roundtable with
Bloggers." March 3, 2008, ⟨http://www.dhs.gov/xnews/releases/pr_1204587093735
.shtm⟩. March 20, 2008.

"Remarks by Homeland Security Secretary Michael Chertoff at the Stanford Constitutional Law Center's Germ Warfare, Contagious Disease and the Constitution
Conference." April 11, 2008, ⟨http://www.dhs.gov/xnews/testimony/testimony_
1208193768327.shtm⟩. April 15, 2008.

"Remarks by Homeland Security Secretary Michael Chertoff on 2007 Achievements
and 2008 Priorities." December 12, 2007, ⟨http://www.dhs.gov/xnews/speeches/
sp_1197513975365.shtm⟩. December 13, 2007.

"Remarks for Secretary Michael Chertoff, U.S. Department of Homeland Security,
George Washington University Homeland Security Policy Institute." March 16,
2005. ⟨http://www.dhs.gov/dhspublic/display?theme=42&content=4392&print=
true⟩. February 14, 2006.

Reynolds, Michael. "Homegrown Terror." *Bulletin of the Atomic Scientists* 60
(2004), ⟨http://vnweb.hwwilsonweb.com/hww/results/results_single_ftPES.jhtml⟩.
May 13, 2008.

Roadmap for National Security: Imperative for Change. U.S. Commission on National
Security/21st Century. February 15, 2000, ⟨http://govinfo.library.unt.edu/nssg/
PhaseIIIFR.pdf⟩.

Roberts, Alasdair. *Blacked Out: Government Secrecy in the Information Age.* New York:
Cambridge University Press, 2006.

Rosa, Eugene. "The Logical Structure of the Social Amplification of Risk Framework
(SARF): Metatheoretical Foundations and Policy Implications." In *The Social
Amplification of Risk*, edited by Nick Pidgeon, Roger E. Kasperson, and Paul Slovic,
47–79. Cambridge: Cambridge University Press, 2003.

Sageman, Marc. *Leaderless Jihad: Terror Networks in the Twenty-first Century.*
Philadelphia: University of Pennsylvania Press, 2008.

———. "The Reality of Grass-Roots Terrorism." *Foreign Affairs* 87 (July–August 2008):
163–65.

———. *Understanding Terror Networks.* Philadelphia: University of Pennsylvania
Press, 2004.

Saniotis, Arthur. "Re-Enchanting Terrorism: Jihadists as 'Liminal Beings.'" *Studies in
Conflict and Terrorism* 28 (November 2005): 533–45.

Schbley, Ayla. "Defining Religious Terrorism: A Causal and Anthropological Profile." *Studies in Conflict & Terrorism* 26 (2003): 105–34.

Scholars for 9/11 Truth, ⟨http://911scholars.org⟩. March 6, 2009.

Scholars for 9/11 Truth and Justice, ⟨http://stj911.org⟩. March 6, 2009.

"Secretary Napolitano Announces New National Terrorism Advisory System to More Effectively Communicate Information about Terrorist Threats to the American Public." Department of Homeland Security. January 27, 2011, ⟨http://www.dhs .gov/ynews/releases/pr_1296158119383.shtm⟩. January 27, 2011.

"Secretary Napolitano Announces 60-Day Review of Homeland Security Advisory System." Department of Homeland Security. July 14, 2009, ⟨http://www.dhs.gov/ ynews/releases/pr_124786668272.shtm>. July 15, 2009.

"Securing Our Homeland: U.S. Department of Homeland Security Strategic Plan." February 24, 2004. ⟨*http://homelandsecurity.tamu.edu/framework/dhls/dhsoverview website/securing-our-homeland-u-s-department-of-homeland-security-strategic-plan*⟩. August 31, 2010.

Senate Armed Services Committee Inquiry into the Treatment of Detainees in U.S. Custody. ⟨http://levin.senate.gov/newsroom/supporting/2008/Detainees.121108 .pdf⟩. June 19, 2009.

Sennett, Richard. *The Fall of Public Man*. New York: Knopf, 1977.

Slack, James. "Minority Report Comes to Britain: The CCTV that Spots Crimes BEFORE They Happen." *Mail Online*. November 28, 2008, ⟨http://www.dailymail.co.uk/ sciencetech/article-1089966/Minority-Report-comes-Britain⟩. December 3, 2008.

Slovic, Paul. "Terrorism as Hazard: A New Species of Trouble." *Risk Analysis* 22 (2002): 425–26.

"Smith County Man Admits Possessing Chemical Weapons." Department of Justice. United States Attorney's Office. Eastern District of Texas. November 13, 2003, ⟨http://www.fbi.gov/dojpressrel/pressrel103/texas111303.htm⟩. August 29, 2005.

Solzhenitsyn, Alexander. "A World Split Apart." In *Solzhenitsyn at Harvard*, edited by Ronald Berman. Washington: Ethics and Public Policy Center, 1980.

Sontag, Susan. "The Imagination of Disaster." *Commentary* (October 1965): 42–48.

Special Review. Counterterrorism Detention and Interrogation Activities (September 2001–October 2003). Office of Inspector General. Central Intelligence Agency. May 7, 2004.

"Statement of Secretary Michael Chertoff Regarding Exercise of Waiver Authority." Department of Homeland Security. April 1, 2008, ⟨http://www.dhs.gov/xnews/ releases/pr_1207083685391.shtm⟩. April 2, 2008.

The State of Homeland Security 2007: An Annual Report Card on the Department of Homeland Security. Majority Staff of the Committee on Homeland Security, U.S. House of Representatives, 2007.

Steiner, George. "The City Under Attack." *Salmagundi* 24 (1973): 3–18.

Stephens, Suzanne. "Report from Suzanne Stephens to Jim Stonebraker from the Stockhausen Home Page, September 29, 2001," ⟨http://www.stockhausen.org/ eyewitness.html⟩. March 4, 2005.

"Strategic Plan—Securing Our Homeland." Department of Homeland Security. October 31, 2007, ⟨http://www.dhs.gov/xabout/strategicplan/index.shtm⟩. March 18, 2008.

Sunstein, Cass R. *Laws of Fear: Beyond the Precautionary Principle*. Cambridge, UK: Cambridge University Press, 2005.

———. *Worst-Case Scenarios*. Cambridge: Harvard University Press, 2007.

Sylves, Richard, and William R. Cumming. "FEMA's Path to Homeland Security: 1979–2003." *Journal of Homeland Security and Emergency Management* 1 (2003): article 11.

Taarnby, Michael. "Profiling Islamic Suicide Terrorists." A Research Report for the Danish Ministry of Justice. November 2003, ⟨http://64.233.167.104/search?q=cache:2TkYJ11V1xEJ:www.jm.dk/image.asp%3Fpage%3⟩. March 21, 2007.

"Testimony of Dr. Kimothy Smith, Acting Director of the National Biosurveillance Center before the Senate Homeland Security and Governmental Affairs Committee, Subcommittee on Oversight of Governmental Management, the Federal Workforce, and the District of Columbia." October 4, 2007, ⟨http://www.dhs.gov/xnews/testimony/testimony_1191608625983.shtm⟩. March 27, 2008.

"Testimony of Secretary Michael Chertoff before the Senate Committee on Homeland Security 'Confronting the Terrorist Threat to the Homeland: Six Years After 9/11.'" September 10, 2007, ⟨http://www.dhs.gov/xnews/testimony/testimony_1189515509899.shtm⟩. March 27, 2008.

Thomas, Keith. *Religion and the Decline of Magic: Studies in Popular Beliefs in Sixteenth and Seventeenth Century England*. London: Weidenfeld, 1971.

Tomes, Nancy. "The Making of a Germ Panic, Then and Now." *American Journal of Public Health* 90 (February 2000): 191–98.

"Top Secret America, A Washington Post Investigation." ⟨http://projects.washingtonpost.com/top-secret-america/articles⟩. July 19, 2010.

Toward a National Strategy for Combating Terrorism. Advisory Panel to Assess Domestic Response Capabilities Involving Weapons of Mass Destruction. December 15, 2000, ⟨http://www.twotigers.com/Resources/terror2.pdf⟩.

Tuan, Yi-Fu. *Landscapes of Fear*. Minneapolis: University of Minnesota Press, 1979.

Unclassified Report on the President's Surveillance Program. July 10, 2009, ⟨http://www.fas.org/irp/eprint/psp.pdf⟩. July 12, 2009.

Ungar, Sheldon. "Moral Panics versus the Risk Society: The Implications of the Changing Sites of Social Anxiety." *British Journal of Sociology* 52 (June 2001): 271–91.

Urban, Hugh B. *The Secrets of the Kingdom: Religion and Concealment in the Bush Administration*. Lanham, Md.: Rowman & Littlefield, 2007.

"U.S. Department of Homeland Security Awards New York City $29 Million under the Securing the Cities Initiative." September 16, 2008, ⟨http://www.dhs.gov/xnews/releases/pr_1221602938361.shtm⟩. September 17, 2008.

"The US Terrorism Plot That the Media Ignores," ⟨http://www.thememoryhole.org/terror/tyler-terror.htm⟩. May 12, 2008.

"Video Surveillance," ⟨http://epic.org/privacy/suveillance⟩. January 3, 2008.

Wald, Priscilla. "Communicable Americanism: Contagion, Geographic Fictions, and the Sociological Legacy of Robert E. Park." *American Literary History* 14 (2002): 653–85.

Warren, Samuel D., and Louis D. Brandeis. "The Right to Privacy." *Harvard Law Review* 4 (December 1890): 193–220.

Warrick, Joby, and Dan Eggen. "Hill Briefed on Waterboarding in 2002." *Washington Post*, 9 December 2007, ⟨http://www.washingtonpost.com/wp=dyn/content/article/2007/12/08/AR2007120801664_pf⟩. December 10, 2007.

Waugh, William L., Jr. "Terrorism and the All-Hazards Model. 2004, ⟨http://www.training.fema.gov/EMIWeb/downloads/Waugh%20Terrorism%20and%20 Planning.doc⟩. November 9, 2006.

Weber, Max. "Politics as a Vocation." In *From Max Weber: Essays in Sociology*, edited by H. H. Gerth and C. Wright Mills, 77–128. New York: Oxford University Press, 1958.

Weinberg, Leonard, and William Eubank. "Backlash: Reactions against Terrorism Studies." Paper presented at a conference in honor of Prof. David C. Rapoport, UCLA, June 21–22, 2008.

Whitlock, Craig. "Terrorists Proving Harder to Profile." *Washington Post*, March 12, 2007, ⟨http://www.washingtonpost.com/wp-dyn/content/article/2007/03/11/AR2007031101618_p⟩. March 13, 2007.

Who's Watching? Video Camera Surveillance in New York City and the Need for Public Oversight. New York: New York Civil Liberties Union, 2006.

Wiedeman, Peter M., Martin Clauberg, and Holger Schutz. "Understanding Amplification of Complex Risk Issues: The Risk Story Model Applied to the EMF Case." In *The Social Amplification of Risk*, edited by Nick Pidgeon, Roger E. Kasperson, and Paul Slovic, 286–304. Cambridge: Cambridge University Press, 2003.

Williams, Phil. "In Cold Blood: The Madrid Bombings." *Perspectives on Terrorism* 2 (2008). ⟨http://www.terrorismanalysts.com/pt/index.php?option=_rokzine&view=article&id=57⟩. August 25, 2008.

Wilton, Andrew, and Tim Barringer. *American Sublime: Landscape Painting in the United States 1820–1880*. Princeton: Princeton University Press, 2000.

Wisner, Ben. "Assessment of Capability and Vulnerability." In *Mapping Vulnerability: Disaster, Development and People*, edited by Greg Bankoff, Georg Frerks, and Dorothea Hilhorst, 183–93. London: Earthscan, 2004.

Wolff, Kurt H., ed. *The Sociology of Georg Simmel*. New York: Free Press, 1950.

World at Risk: The Report of the Commission on the Prevention of WMD Proliferation and Terrorism. New York: Vintage Books, 2008.

Wright, Anne. "Tyler Man, Companion Plead Guilty in Fed Court." November 13, 2003, ⟨http://www.thememoryhole.org/terror/tyler-terror.htm⟩. May 12, 2008.

"The Year in Hate." *Intelligence Report*. The Southern Poverty Law Center. Issue 125 (Summer 2007): 48–70.

INDEX